Kevin Mitchell

Kevin Mitchell writes for the *Observer* and the *Guardian* as boxing and tennis correspondent. He has been Sports Journalist of the Year and Sports Feature Writer of the Year. *War, Baby: The Glamour of Violence* was shortlisted for the William Hill Sports Book of the Year.

Break Point

The Inside Story of Modern Tennis

KEVIN MITCHELL

JOHN MURRAY

First published in Great Britain in 2014 by John Murray (Publishers)
An Hachette UK Company

First published in paperback in 2015

I

© Kevin Mitchell 2014, 2015

A CIP catalogue record for this title is
available from the British Library

ISBN 978-1-84854-929-6
Ebook ISBN 978-1-84854-931-9

Typeset in Bembo MT Pro by Palimpsest Book Production Limited,
Falkirk, Stirlingshire

Printed and bound by Clays Ltd, St Ives plc

John Murray policy is to use papers that are natural, renewable and
recyclable products and made from wood grown in sustainable
forests. The logging and manufacturing processes are expected to
conform to the environmental regulations of the country of origin.

John Murray (Publishers)
Carmelite House
50 Victoria Embankment
London EC4Y 0DZ

www.johnmurray.co.uk

For Marie, Ed and Matt

Contents

Introduction

Of the many images that illuminated men's tennis around the world in 2013, Andy Murray bathed in the glow of high summer on Centre Court at Wimbledon, champion at last, will live most vividly for British fans. It was also impossible to ignore Rafael Nadal, who conjured up the most extraordinary comeback from an injury that threatened to end his career. After winning the Australian Open at the start of the year, Novak Djokovic dreamed of doing the Grand Slam but Nadal stopped him in Paris and New York, and Murray destroyed him at Wimbledon, revenge for defeat in Melbourne. There is, of course, one name missing from these struggles. Since he won the first of his seventeen Majors a decade earlier at Wimbledon, Roger Federer had come to be regarded as the greatest player of all time. But 2013 was his worst season by a distance. And, while the citadel of the Big Four, as they have come to be known, was not in immediate danger of collapse, there were rumblings over the hill. As Harold Macmillan famously said of the most obvious determining factor in history: 'Events, dear boy, events.'

There were two events more than any other that changed the tone and direction of the story. The first was the unexpected rebirth of Nadal after an injury that seriously jeopardised the Spaniard's future in the game at just twenty-seven years of age. The second was the possibly terminal but more predictable decline of Federer at thirty-two. The flip in circumstances of the two best players of the modern era significantly altered the tennis landscape. Nadal's was the story that captured the upbeat headlines, almost by the week, as he defied even his own expectations to win ten titles, two of them Majors, and finished his finest campaign in twelve years as a Tour professional by returning to number 1 in the world for the third time. He did it all on legs as reliable as butter. It was a Lazarusian comeback, one to match Andre Agassi's recovery from the party-driven complications that had plagued the American a dozen or so years earlier.

Alongside Nadal's heroic efforts, Federer's slide was alarming and depressing. After jousting with Nadal for the world number 1 ranking to the exclusion of every other player on the Tour between 2005 and 2010, Federer might have imagined he would have an easier run to re-establish his supremacy in 2013. But as the Swiss tumbled down the slopes of the rankings towards the lower reaches of the top ten, his fans grew disconsolate in the face of the unthinkable prospect of not having him in their lives, or, at the very least, not having him contest the final of a major title again. It was inconceivable that he should be touched by ignominy, or even minor embarrassment. A classicist from the archives who floats above the battlefield, Federer had arrived before all the others, in 2003, when he succeeded Pete Sampras, the last of the great serve-and-volley traditionalists who himself had begun to suffer at the hands of the young baseline thumpers before manufacturing a farewell that might have been scripted in Hollywood. It seemed only natural that Federer would fade before the others, but a late-season revival gave him hope and, before retreating to his winter lair to recuperate, he promised he would return refreshed. He reckoned he had at least another eighteen months of top-quality tennis left in him. Retired tennis dogs, from Boris Becker to John McEnroe to Ilie Năstase, agreed. Năstase was cheeky enough to say, 'Federer can play to sixty if he wants to.' Sampras admired the fact he could travel the world with two young children (with a third expected in 2014). But none of them would say with any confidence that Federer would win an eighteenth Major.

Federer, eloquent in five languages and able to smile on cue, was always going to be the antidote to the new brutality engulfing the game, invented partly by Pistol Pete. The Swiss not only had an intellect that was almost audible, sweat-free poise and the appearance of defying gravity when necessary, but a single-handed backhand that made him beautiful to behold yet vulnerable, especially on clay. It was a weapon as lethal as it was lovely. And he would need it time and again to keep in touch with Nadal, then Djokovic and Murray. His dilemma was doubly perplexing: not only was he desperate to stay in the picture, but he also had to find a way to leave gracefully. Sampras departed after beating Andre Agassi to win the US Open in 2002, aged thirty-two. Federer turned thirty-two in 2013. Could he somehow write an exit line to match that of the man whose records he had tracked and surpassed throughout his career? It looked unlikely, but he would not die wondering.

Embroidering the script, there was Murray's breakthrough at the All England Club, a British high point that let the ghost of Fred Perry merge with all the others of the game, and ended the torture of a nation that had waited – famously, boringly, interminably it seemed – seventy-seven years for another Wimbledon champion. It had been an almost ludicrous *longueur anglais*. It was also one that caused as much agonising over Britishness as the other two staples in the nursery of organised sport, football and cricket. Once Tim Henman had given his all and fallen short early in the millennium, the widely held view was that British tennis was a lost cause, part of the summer season sold to tourists, our gift to the sport and the tourism industry. Wimbledon was, in short, an annual invitation to foreign players to come to London and avail themselves of the wonderful facilities of the All England Club and take home the oldest trophy in tennis. Then along came the obdurate, mercurial Scot.

He had collapsed tearfully on the clay of Rome and opted to miss the French Open, a shrewd move that allowed him to gather his resources and beat Djokovic in a brutal final at Wimbledon. The remainder of Murray's season, however, was one of anticlimax, frustration, disappointment and anxiety as a chronic back problem that had locked him in its grip for nearly two years worsened to the point of crisis. Hampered by an increasingly stiff and sore back, Murray under-performed in Canada, Cincinnati and, most importantly, at Flushing Meadows, where he was unable to hang on to his US title. If that were not enough for a TV mini-series in itself, Murray then risked aggravating his injury so he could help Great Britain win the Davis Cup tie against Croatia, a victory that returned them to the main competition for the first time since 2008. He said later he played partly because he did not want to appear 'unpatriotic'. This was not a man insensitive to public opinion, whatever his protestations to the contrary.

Then Murray took the more critical decision to have a disc operation that put him out of tennis for four months. It was a gamble that could have gone horribly wrong, but it did not (although tweeting 'I can't feel my legs' after his first proper hit on court in late November was not one of his best practical jokes). He came through it, just as Nadal had done when he rolled the dice to leave the Tour for seven months to mend his knees. Federer, too, had faltered, taking a seven-week break after exacerbating chronic back problems on the hard courts of Indian Wells. Thereafter, he managed rather than conquered his problem. But would Murray be able to return to the game, as his Spanish friend has done? It would prove to be the next big challenge of his career which we would discover when they returned to Melbourne in January 2014, bruised but still standing.

As a counterpoint to the mayhem of the 2013 season, there was the continued although not entirely smooth progress of Djokovic, who lost his world number 1 ranking to Nadal in the closing weeks of the season, yet found the energy to win the ATP World Tour Finals in London in November, even though he later revealed he was 'exhausted'. It was not so much a revelation as a confirmation of the obvious. Within a week, Djokovic, his tank pretty much empty, beat Tomáš Berdych and levelled the Davis Cup final against the Czech Republic at 2–2 in his home town of Belgrade on the final afternoon of the season, although he could not get himself to the line in the earlier doubles, which the Czechs won. He said he did not have the energy to play in both matches, and that probably cost Serbia the trophy – although he might have lost to Berdych had he played in the doubles. Djokovic has often said that helping Serbia win their first Davis Cup in 2010 changed his life and his career, and there ought to be no questioning that declaration, given that he went on to win forty-three matches in a row the following year to place himself not just alongside Nadal and Federer but ahead of them, and everyone else. So it was no surprise that Djokovic was devastated when his young compatriot Dušan Lajović collapsed in front of the experienced Czech Radek Štěpánek in the deciding rubber of the 2013 final. Whatever the wealth and the glamour, the richest players care as much as the poorest, not just about winning but also about staying true to what inspired them to play tennis in the first place.

Elite sport was once a cavalier indulgence for gifted athletes who could afford the time and money to travel the world with a smile and minimal resources. That was a long time ago. Now it makes extreme physical demands on its champions, and tennis, for all that it is beautiful, is no different. The exhaustion that even the elastic Djokovic was moved to identify has become the default condition of the game's best players, the ones who consistently reach the final weekend of tournaments. They are red-lining not only in the fortnight slog of the four Majors but also in the shorter Masters 1000 events that sustain their rankings. And they are required to perform for their countries in the Davis Cup; such an effort by Murray for Great Britain against Croatia was his last appearance of 2013 before light work-outs after Christmas in preparation for the 2014 Australian Open. Murray discovered that the only haven away from the grind of work was an operating table – with no guarantee that he would play again – a sobering reminder not only of his treadmill schedule but of the consequences of that commitment. Players are all so encumbered. When they are not playing, they are practising to play, pushing their bodies to previously unknown limits. They cannot do so indefinitely. The fascination remains fixed on the Big Four, however fragile. No quartet in the history of the game has ruled in the way Federer, Nadal, Djokovic and Murray do. None. Not even in more than a century of what we might regard as proper international competition.

For several years now, in this weirdly one-dimensional age of excellence, there has been no room for anyone less than a supernova. The others are as attendants to the needs and whims of the tennis gods. Never have so few players dominated so many for so long. In the modern era, Connors, McEnroe, Borg, Lendl, Agassi and Sampras prevailed in interrupted stretches of excellence. Before them, Rod Laver was considered the greatest player of his time – probably of all time, until that point – while, in distant memory, tennis had many fine champions who played a different game to that of their contemporaries, among them Tilden, Budge, Vines and Perry. But none of these players, ancient or modern, experienced the intense, prolonged rivalry with their peers that has been set in concrete between Djokovic, Federer, Nadal and, finally, Murray.

At the start of the 2013 season these four gifted but very different individuals were playing tennis as it had never been played before – and where they or their successors would take it, nobody was sure. It was just about the perfect sporting scenario, pregnant with possibilities. Who, among the contenders, would deliver the most telling punch? Perhaps there would be nothing but air swings, threats with no clout. Maybe there was nobody who could land the killer blow.

It is tempting to imagine that, had any three of the four not been playing contemporaneously, the remaining member of the quartet would have been a colossus beyond challenge – much as Tiger Woods once was in golf – but that would be to ignore the chemistry between them. This is the secret of sport's great rivalries. Each had contributed to the legacy of the others. Without Nadal, would Federer have reached such heights? Possibly, but it was the Spaniard who pushed him up that Everest – and vice versa. Yet it is not outrageous to speculate that but for the presence of Nadal, Federer, for instance, might have won another six Majors, putting him even further beyond the reach of those around him. Nadal, his nearest challenger for most titles, could have had sixteen already – had Federer and Djokovic not been rivals. So many ifs. Djokovic, who had six Major titles at the start of the season, might have had another four, perhaps, without the interruption of Federer, Nadal and Murray. Ah, poor Andy. Would he not have been spared the serial lament that he spent his best years under the gilded heel of the Invincibles? He has never seen it that way, which is just as well. He has always welcomed the tests the others put to him, insisting those experiences have made him a better player. How right he is. It did not happen overnight for him.

The reason these four players have prevailed more often and more spectacularly than any other quartet in the history of tennis, in the record books and in the public imagination is simple: when they hit a pitch of aggression and commitment in important matches, nobody else can stay with them. They have had no equals, except each other. Also, while Federer and Nadal had already established their stellar credentials, Djokovic and Murray were still building theirs, and it is this interlocking of age, form and fitness, as the punishing schedule of the Tour takes its toll on all four, that makes the story compelling.

In varying combinations – Federer–Nadal, Nadal–Djokovic, Djokovic–Murray – the Big Four have ruled with intertwined rivalries that exclude the challenge of nearly every other player. This makes them special in many ways, not least in terms of the nature of their relationships, which are as fascinating as are their confrontations on court. They are not especially close. At best, they are what Murray said of Djokovic before beating him at Wimbledon: 'professional friends'. But I would discover that this was not the whole story.

While writing this book, I asked several players and experts in and around the sport not only what they thought about the Big Four but where they thought tennis was going. How fit can the players get? How long can they run? How hard can they hit? Will someone we have yet to applaud come from nowhere with a game to shock his contemporaries? The gap between the game most of us grew up with – either playing or watching – and the scarily physical wars that rage every week over eleven months on the different surfaces of the courts of more than sixty tournaments of the ATP World Tour has expanded almost beyond comprehension. It is not remotely the same sport. And tennis at its highest level is so far removed from where it was even twenty years ago that nobody can be sure where it is going next. Will the next evolution take it to unthinkable levels of physicality? Or will someone find a way to guide it back to its essential artistry, using the weapons that still can kill a point and thrill a crowd, when Federer wraps his right hand around his racquet and stirs hearts everywhere?

Into this equation come drugs, the scourge of the phenomenon that is the international sports entertainment business. Tennis was the first sport to introduce testing, in 1985, yet it stands accused nearly thirty years later of complacency and lack of rigour. As prize money grows, so does temptation. Players who might once have settled for an undemanding if low-key existence outside the top 100 now could be tempted to take risks in order to get among the big money that has finally filtered down the food chain. To mix in better and more lucrative company, however, they will need more than banned stimulants. They will need expensive back-up teams and winter training blocks. They will need what the rich players already have, and they will have to back themselves with investment. If they do not, then they have little or no chance. Long gone are the times when players could rely on pure talent. There are no shortcuts in this jungle, but there is plenty of quicksand, and there is genuine concern that a spate of drugs busts will do considerable damage to a sport that has largely avoided the opprobrium heaped on cycling, athletics and, lately, boxing. Automatically that makes demands on the candour and openness of the game's administrators, and that could not always be taken for granted in 2013.

Some say tennis is boxing with a net. To an extent it is. Murray has drawn the comparison of two combatants facing each other in a defined rectangle, propelling bad intentions towards each other, looking for openings and choosing the optimum moment to deliver the final blow. Each is a form of physical chess, demanding split-second analysis of all the many options in every exchange. In this regard, tennis is very much like boxing. And the ambitious participants of both sports are coming under increasing pressure to push themselves beyond previously recog-nised limits in order to compete for the biggest honours and biggest cheques. One of Murray's best friends is the former world heavyweight champion David Haye, with whom he has spoken often about conditioning and nutrition. The two trained together when they were in Florida at the same time, and in the Middle East. Pointedly, Haye's body finally broke under the pressure of his sport late in 2013. A few days after Murray had landed in Miami to start hitting the ball again, Haye announced he was leaving the sport, perhaps permanently, and cancelled a pay-per-view fight against the unbeaten Mancunian Tyson Fury that would have netted him well over £5 million. A surgeon in Germany took five hours to rebuild Haye's right shoulder, the one that had powered many of his twenty-four knockouts, and which had finally given up on him. After surveying the state of the fighter's ruptured subscapularis and biceps tendon attachments, the specialist suggested Haye 'seriously consider' quitting boxing, at thirty-three. If his friend's probable retirement had any effect on Murray, it might have been to concentrate his mind. At twenty-six, Murray knew he had to make the most of the years left to him. He had just fixed his suspect back, which for at least two years had prevented him from playing his shots freely, although in which time he had won two Majors and an Olympic gold medal. That is the measure of the sacrifice athletes make.

The tennis season stretches from January to November, with a month or so off before Christmas . . . so the players can get fit enough to return in the new year and do it all again. There is no sport in the world with such a demanding calendar, and these resilient athletes can never enjoy the freedom or joy available to previous generations of players. They are handsomely compensated, of course. But it is doubtful that they envisaged their lives would be so remorselessly intense when they started hitting a tennis ball. While they are competing, they have little time to fully appreciate what they are doing. We do, though. And we should enjoy them for as long as they remain standing.

They are wealthy, fit athletes – except when they fall. Then they bleed like the rest of us. They have all given more than we could properly expect in delivering us the sort of entertainment that has come to be regarded as the norm. I saw at first-hand how Murray pushed himself through weeks of pain to prepare for a season, and I can safely say that, in so many ways, there is little that is normal about what these champions do for a living.

I

The Tempest

New York, 8 September 2012

Word spreads almost as quickly as the approaching tornado: evacuate. With high winds roaring into the region from the Atlantic, players, journalists and spectators scurry from the upper reaches of the National Tennis Center at Flushing Meadows with a good deal more calm than those giving the instructions. Those in the top levels of the media building – mainly television and radio journalists, as well as a host of former players working as expert commentators – congregate on the ground floor, leaving behind their microphones and various gadgets. In the locker room, Novak Djokovic and David Ferrer, waiting to play their semi-final, gather up their racquets, bags and sponsored accoutrements. Bemused more than concerned, they are also herded from the scene. Once it is safe to do so, they are ferried back to their respective hotels. When they return the following day to play their match, it is the Serb, desperate to keep his title, who has more storm in his eyes. But there is a Scottish wind on the way.

~

This, in small part, is the story of the relationship between a knot of travelling journalists and one tennis player, Andy Murray. He has been for several years and, with any luck, will continue to be for some time to come, the focus of our attention. It is about our collective worries and hopes about the future of the sport in this country, and it is set in the context of what is regarded as a period of unprecedented and prolonged excellence. This era is different to those that have gone before. It is relentlessly brutal. Soldiers now are cut down not only by each other's bullets but also by lactic acid, muscle fatigue, back spasms, rolled ankles, boredom, frustration, expectations, self-doubt and the debilitating mental demands of a sport that girdles the planet nearly the whole year, addling the brain in a succession of queues at airports from Heathrow to Shanghai and all points in between. And we would not have it any other way . . .

As far as Murray was concerned, the story of 2013 began that previous September, on a storm-threatened Monday night in Flushing Meadows, across the Hudson River from Manhattan. Again the US Open arrived at its conclusion a day later than scheduled, as it had done in the previous four Septembers. It seemed the only people unaware that this was the month in which the hurricane season raked the eastern seaboard were the tournament's owners and organisers, the United States Tennis Association, their broadcast partners, CBS, and possibly a few guys nursing bottles of gut-rock on the darker pavements of Hell's Kitchen. However, none of them could lay the blame for this fifth straight fixtures cock-up entirely in the lap of the gods. Even as exasperated administrators of the USTA again looked balefully to the skies, they must have known it was also their own intransigence that annually brought their tournament to a delayed climax and, again in 2012, hurled the final between Murray and Djokovic into miserable Monday.

For as long as anyone could remember, the USTA had been relaxed to the point of indifference about the inclemency that had drenched the east coast. If it wasn't a hurricane, it was a tropical storm or a plain old New York downpour; in 2011 the rumbling edge of an earthquake from the south even disturbed Flushing, causing Murray to stop in mid-practice and wonder if his time had come. Yet the USTA and CBS were deaf to pleas for change as the wet and windy filth screamed up from the Caribbean and darted in from the Atlantic to tear down power lines and swamp whole suburbs and towns. That ugliest of autumns, bad weather brought New York to the edge of breakdown as the still dangerous remnants of Hurricane Sandy seeped into the lower reaches of Manhattan, forcing the evacuation of 300,000 people. But it was not as if there was no precedent. Since 1954, hurricanes Carol, Donna, Agnes, Belle, Gloria and Bob had dumped their junk on New York at about this time of the year (equalling the number of hurricanes in the previous one hundred years). These storms returned every September like drenched homing pigeons. A multicoloured map of the eighty-four recorded tropical and subtropical cyclones that have crashed into this stretch of the continent since the seventeenth century would make a very agreeable tapestry. In between the post-war hurricanes, there have been several other less vicious but no less unwelcome visitors, all of them bedevilling the witless efforts of the USTA to hold their tournament in peace. If we were looking for metaphors for change, we needed only to look to the skies.

In 2013, with memories of Hurricane Sandy not yet faded, there would be, curiously, no urgency to get as much tennis as possible on court before the almost certain arrival of the rain, and a point-blank refusal to cover the courts – on 'aesthetic grounds', believe it or not. The argument was that ugly tarpaulins, while protecting the courts and keeping them in good order for the players, would ruin the look of the tournament. There could be no arguing with such cock-eyed logic.

Persisting in the maddening habit of delaying the entry of the main players until the first Wednesday contributed significantly to the log-jam. This was designed to create ratings-driven excitement on the final weekend of the final Slam of the year, no matter the threat from the skies. By back-end loading the fortnight, they ensured it started like a tortoise and finished like, well, a hurricane.

They scheduled both men's semi-finals for what they sold as Super Saturday, with the final to be played just twenty-four hours later, heaping absurd expectations on players whose physical renown the game had increasingly come to take for granted, and infuriating fans who year after year scrambled for a ticket for the men's final in the expectation it would be held on the day promised.

Soon enough, CBS would deal their way out of their association with the event, handing the responsibility over to ESPN. At roughly the same time, the USTA, after years of procrastination, approved plans to put a roof on the Arthur Ashe Stadium, which presented engineering challenges (not to mention the possibility of an expanding budget), but which would bring the US Open into line with the other Slams: Wimbledon, the Australian – where paranoia about sun cancer is matched only by illogical suspicion that it will rain at any moment – and even the French, who had finally been forced to acknowledge that, in the sports entertainment industry, rain can be more than a passing get-wet experience.

Sanity beckoned at last. And although the big fish would still lurk unemployed in the wings for the first three days while the minnows swam, the final would, from 2013 onwards, actually be scheduled for the Monday rather than be plonked there by accident – and there would at least be a humane pause after the semi-finals. If the weather and the schedule couldn't guarantee a decent break between the semi-finals and the final, the ATP players' council, who used their considerable clout in negotiations, eventually could. The US Open was growing up. Not everyone was thrilled. There were some who hankered for a little confusion and uncertainty, to surrender to the skies occasionally and deal with them the best they could. But, increasingly, there was reduced space for such romance in the sport – in sport generally. It took the Americans a little while to cut the last links to an ad hoc past, even though laissez-faire sport and best business principles had long been out of sync.

Eighty years after Sidney Wood shocked Fred Perry at Forest Hills, the 2012 US Open was still full of surprises. It was so New York. It was a hailed cab that flew past in the night. It was a half-cooked burger from a street-side vendor. It was that look-twice dinner check, with its hidden extras and no apology. And it was, for many of us, the perfectly insane summit of the Grand Slam season, the last old-fashioned tennis tournament, with unrestrained noise and thunder and lightning, on and off the court. Flushing, parked under the flight path of nearby LaGuardia Airport and filled for two weeks by the most boisterous fans in tennis, had always provided a very American counterpoint to the Old World settings that preceded it. There were points to be collected or wasted still in Asia and Europe and the gathering of the eight best players in the world at the ATP World Tour Finals at the O2 Arena in Greenwich, but the US Open was the sport's September pinnacle, a roaring lion of a finale, in the game's most authentic coliseum. Coming a few months after the altogether more genteel tennis on the decorous lawns of Wimbledon, the US championships struck like a left hook after an exploratory jab. The American tournament, born in 1881 and only four years younger than Wimbledon, had long shed its country club origins, and presents still the cheeky, chocolate-smeared face of modern times, irreverent and loud.

If tennis tournaments were Shakespearean plays, the US Open surely could be regarded as *The Tempest*. Its most memorable passage (from act 4 scene 1) might aptly adorn the entrance to the USTA Billie Jean King National Tennis Center at Flushing Meadows.

> Our revels now are ended. These our actors,
> As I foretold you, were all spirits and
> Are melted into air, into thin air:
> And, like the baseless fabric of this vision,
> The cloud-capp'd towers, the gorgeous palaces,
> The solemn temples, the great globe itself,
> Yea, all which it inherit, shall dissolve
> And, like this insubstantial pageant faded,
> Leave not a rack behind. We are such stuff
> As dreams are made on, and our little life
> Is rounded with a sleep.

Dreams abound. Sleep is more hard-won. Play starts early and finishes when it pleases. The journey, by bus, car or subway, back to Manhattan for those of us annually stationed there is invariably closer to breakfast the following day than to dinner that evening. Nobody complains. Well, not a lot. New York, built with optimism on a grid but driven by the unpredictable fires of capitalism and with a healthy disdain for convention or order, was always a place to make a buck and move on, and the fifth weather-delayed final on the spin that cool Monday night of 10 September 2012 clicked nicely with the anarchic mood of a vibrant city.

For now, we were stuck in the immediate past – and the future, as it happened, because the inheritor of the Perry spirit, a raw-boned Scot with a game born in Dunblane, nurtured in Spain and given full expression in New York, finally pulled alongside his peers by beating Novak Djokovic to win the title. It was Murray's first Major, and would not be his last.

Of wider, historical significance, he simultaneously buried seventy-six years of suffering for British fans who had been waiting with British patience for a Grand Slam champion to join the sainted Perry in the history books. Hallelujah! History placated, the immediate focus in that tense and draining final was on the man who did the deed, not a dead man remembered among the current generation for his shirts rather than his shots (and long forgotten for that third-round failure against Wood). Change rode on that crisp night air, and, at long bloody last, we could leave the past where it belonged.

Murray was New York's perfect hero, appropriately windswept, someone to capture the magic of the chaos, to engage with rather than fight the elements and produce a quite stunning denouement. Since he was crowned the boys' champion here in 2004, aged seventeen, Flushing Meadows had been his favourite place to play tennis, New York his favourite city to wander alone (although he would find that more difficult soon enough). Here, five thousand miles from home on a rapid court that suited his quirkiness of shot and speed of mind, he felt unencumbered and comfortable. He felt at home, the past very much another country.

Without arrogance, Murray always reckoned he was the equal of the game's trinity: Federer, Nadal and Djokovic. He wanted a bit more than that, though. For his own peace of mind, he needed to match their proven pedigree and beat them when it mattered, and he wanted to do it every time he stepped on to a court with any of them, on hard, grass or clay. A few optimists reckoned his first title might inspire him to take one or two more Major trophies. Federer, a little loftily, allowed that Murray 'could win another one'. When Murray beat world number 1 Djokovic to win the 2013 Wimbledon title – eleven days after the Swiss had been eliminated in the second round from a tournament he had won seven times – more detached observers reckoned not only that they were witnessing a generational power shift, but that a player whose burning competitive spirit had at last drowned out his natural diffidence had the ability to win more than just 'another one'.

Among Murray's admirers were four of the game's greatest players: Pete Sampras, Jimmy Connors, John McEnroe and Ivan Lendl, who between them had won thirty-seven Grand

Slam titles. Their predictions for the number of Slam trophies they thought Murray might eventually win ranged from some to several, the numbers shifting like the Jersey wind of September 2012. McEnroe had long been a believer. The two men had much in common: a deft touch with the racquet, a shakier hold on the volatility of their emotions, and a penchant for candour. The one-time Brat saw much of himself in the player once known as 'The Sulk'. From about 2010, the year Murray lost here to Federer in his first Slam final, McEnroe sympathised, empathised and spoke with growing confidence about Murray and his chances of winning in New York.

Once a loud presence on court, McEnroe was now a paid expert, and an excellent one – some say the best – the volume turned down only to accommodate the demands of the many microphones he addressed throughout the year. 'I worried too much about the bad things that could happen as opposed to just knowing how good I was and sort of trusting myself,' McEnroe said when we spoke in Paris a little while back about the perceived similarities between himself and Murray. 'I would sort of think about what could go wrong. I had the same problem [of expectations].' McEnroe seemed to enjoy these pre-tournament chats with a few British tennis writers. It was a change of pace for him and he felt comfortable talking at length on just about anything to do with tennis, past or present. And Murray engaged him more than most.

But he also saw a change in Murray not long before he made his breakthrough. And it had nothing to do with tennis. He looked happier, McEnroe said, more relaxed. And he figured a lot of that must have sprung from Murray's relationship with Lendl, McEnroe's old enemy from his own playing days.

McEnroe reflected on those high-pressure times. 'I didn't enjoy it enough. I wish I had enjoyed it more. I enjoy it more now, but so what? I remember [Jimmy] Connors one year I lost at Wimbledon. He was supposedly going through a separation and he looked more fierce than ever! I fell apart if my girlfriend rang me and got pissed off. I was not able to brush it off.'

He was no mere cheer leader, however. Although he always said Flushing would be where Murray would break through, he looked at the 2012 field and he paused. 'Murray has made huge headway since the Olympics [where he won gold a couple of months earlier by beating Federer in a glorious, emotional final],' McEnroe confided one morning as the players assembled at Flushing Meadows, 'but, when Djokovic is playing his A-game, he still has a little edge on him. Whether or not that changes remains to be seen but Novak's got a little more to offer at this stage. It's going to be interesting how it develops and I also think someone else is going to make a breakthrough, too. Someone's going to come out and do something big besides those guys.'

It was a persuasive view, and not many argued with it at the time. Djokovic, it has to be said, had more of a commanding air about him. He was the favourite. Nadal, injured, was absent. Federer was very much there, but not in his customary upbeat and relaxed mood. He'd beaten Murray in the Wimbledon final after trailing, making the most of going under the Centre Court roof with a comeback of stunning virtuosity. It all but wrecked Murray. And now Federer, to the dismay of the millions who adored him, looked vulnerable again. The Wimbledon victory had been his first Slam success in two and a half years. Questions were being asked, and he bridled. He was thirty-one, he said, not a hundred and one. But he was thirty-one, the age at which Sampras left here with a win, bowing to time with a wonderful farewell flurry. The others – Nadal, Djokovic and Murray – were five and six years younger than the Swiss heir to Sampras's King of Tennis crown, and tennis had become a battlefield where strength and youth prevailed more often than not.

Federer needed to find more talent than had ever been demanded of him; he had to flat-pedal just to make the quarter/

semi-finals, where in the past he had been able to cruise into the latter stages of a two-week tournament. Of course, he never took such progress for granted; he remained dedicated, committed and utterly in love with the game. But some things were beyond even his control. The languid game was still in place. He refused to compromise on the purity of his tennis, going for his shots in the belief that enough of them would land legally to bring him victory, but the decline was so minute that even he struggled to see it. Certainly the rest of us were not as well placed. What we might have detected – or said we did – was the smallest increments of reflex degradation, the barely visible slowing of those balletic, floating movements. But what was impossible to miss was the scoreboard. And, in an increasing number of tournaments now, it did not hail the great man.

Ultimately, Lendl's opinion proved more relevant than McEnroe's that September. It was his appointment as Murray's coach at the start of 2012 that triggered a noticeable change in the player's attitude, to both himself and his sport. The Czech, a long-time American citizen and a partly forgotten relic of his sport, had dragged himself away from his favourite golf courses after eighteen years out of the mainstream to help Murray fulfil his destiny. Although it remains a point of contention about who approached whom, Lendl was happy to be the expert hired help rather than the boss. He was as shrewd an operator as there was in tennis and he had watched Murray from a distance, judging that, for all his on-court nerves, he had inner strength and knew his own mind. Theirs was a partnership that made sense. Lendl steadfastly stuck to the view that the only title that counted was the next one; the numbers would take care of themselves. He was determined to free Murray from the weight of history, and this was part of the reason Murray hired him; he knew Lendl's history as well as Lendl knew that of Murray and every other failed

British tennis player for the previous seven decades and more. Lendl did not win the first of his eight Slam titles until the fifth attempt, having failed at Roland Garros in 1981, Flushing Meadows in '82, Melbourne in '83 and again in New York that year. Then he broke through in France in '84. That is the very acme of persistence. The Lendl magic worked beautifully almost from the start. We subsequently discovered it would keep working. They were, beyond debate, the most successful partnership of recent years, and neither wanted it to end.

Since Murray's first appearance in a Slam final – at the same venue four years earlier, when he lost to Federer – he had tried and failed twice to crack the dominance of the three players widely and correctly regarded as his betters, although he had regularly been a threat to all of them in big tournaments. He lost to Federer a second time in a Slam final, in Melbourne in 2011, and again in the Australian title decider the following year, to Djokovic. Each of those heartbreak finals had lasted just three sets. Some people made the most hurtful accusation in sport: Murray was a choker. He might even have flirted with the notion himself that there was something fundamental missing in his make-up, something that prevented him from expressing himself on the big stage, even though he had done it many times elsewhere against the same players.

'Andy is good enough to win Grand Slams but the way he plays in finals won't win him trophies,' said John Newcombe, who had himself been good enough to win seven of them in Slam tournaments. 'He plays not to lose instead of to win, which is why he hasn't won a set in his two Australian Open finals and at the US Open final a few years ago.'

Rod Laver, the only man to sweep all four Slams in a season twice, agreed. 'Andy has got to be more aggressive and dictate play, although the expectations in Britain don't help because they haven't had a Grand Slam champion for so long.'

These former greats from Australia were painting a gloomy picture for the Scot's prospects of ever joining them in the sport's most elite club. But he had changed. Maybe they didn't notice. At his fourth attempt to win a Major, he had come achingly close but had been powerless to resist Federer at Wimbledon. There was nothing to be ashamed of this time, though. He did not capitulate, he just lost to a great player on one of his great days. The tennis Federer played in the closing stages of that match was irresistible and would have proved too much for either Nadal or Djokovic. It was a defeat from which Murray took heart, and the evidence was quickly seen. A month later, in beating Federer to win the Olympic gold, Murray had not only soundly defeated the former world number 1 with two sets to spare in a five-set final (one Lendl regarded as being on a par with the Slams); his self-esteem rocketed. There was a light in his eye. Despite his aching back, he was moving near to maximum efficiency. He was, at last, dangerous for a whole match rather than in bursts. But, as he and his new coach knew, he still had to deliver in a Slam. Beat Djokovic this wild Monday night to win the US Open and his life would change more than he might ever have dreamed.

The Olympics win was important because Murray at that time was still perceived as the most fragile of the quartet, even though several times he equalled or bettered them on his day. He did not want to be one of those 'on his day' players, though. There were plenty of them on the Tour, seriously talented under-achievers, and Murray knew them well – none better than Richard Gasquet, a close contemporary and once regarded as the best teenager in the world. But, at the highest level, tennis was not a teenage pursuit. It was a down-to-the-bone business, and it was getting tougher by the year. Gasquet, among several, could not keep up.

On the eve of the 2012 US Open, however, Murray had yet to leave behind his childish ways. While Lendl encouraged him to believe that winning Olympic gold was as good as winning a Major, he was not convinced. Years of disappointment proved hard to ignore. He wanted to prove that he was not a shooting star. He wanted to show his peers that his talent would carry him to the top of the mountain, despite the popular perception that his nerves would always get the better of him. It was the talking point of the sport. The player himself did not fully understand why his best tennis deserted him when he reached the final of a Slam. It confused him to the point of depression, and his lifetime love of tennis was severely tested. After each big loss came an equally significant funk and a lousy run of form against players who would not reach the final of a Grand Slam tournament if everyone else was blindfolded.

It seemed to some that the Scot was good but not good enough. The other three, after all, had won a total of thirty-five Slam titles. He had none. Between them, they had been ranked 507 times as number 1 in the world. He had risen to number 2 and no further. New York was Murray's *Tempest*, a new dawn for him and the game, and it was not an illusion. The Serb was the world number 2 at the time, fully fit and coming off a convincing semi-final win over David Ferrer, ranked number 5, so there could be no argument about Murray's standing if he managed to finally beat Djokovic when it mattered. If the experts still had doubts, Djokovic knew this was a different Murray. He knew it would be a struggle from start to finish, and he wasn't altogether sure he would be the conqueror again.

Sportswriters are privileged to witness countless memorable events if they hang around press boxes and venues long enough. For all that journalists strive for impartiality, there can be no denying the power of spectacle to draw us into its vortex. Those who claim detachment not only are deluding themselves but missing out on the full impact of what we are paid to witness. Sport is pointless without the humanity that gives it a meaning beyond mere games. And so it has been with Andy Murray, almost from day one.

There was a time when the world moved a little less frantically, when reflection was something other than what we saw in a mirror. When Cardigan plunged the doomed Light Brigade into the Valley of Death at Balaclava in 1854, it took William Howard Russell, the only independent witness, three weeks to get his report of the carnage into the pages of *The Times*. Three weeks after that, Tennyson wrote a poem that glorified the military disaster – which says much about the parallel thirst for sentiment and fact in Victorian times.

However, when Murray performed his heroics in New York in 2012, time not only refused to stand still; it sprinted away from us like Mo Farah. As Djokovic feathered a weary riposte over the baseline to surrender his US Open title after 4 hours and 54 minutes of truly compelling tennis, a good number of Her Majesty's Press were buried in the bowels of the media centre, fingers poised over laptops as we prepared to record a slice of sporting history. As the Scot drank in the significance of what he had just done in his own way – scrambling around in his bag for his sponsor's watch even as the crowd rose to acclaim him – our prized objectivity was as shredded as Djokovic's resolve surely had been in the gladiatorial pit from which we had just scampered. When Murray became the first British player to win a men's Grand Slam since Perry did it in the same town in 1936 by beating Budge, a cocktail of two drugs engulfed us. It was not a response wholly predicated by a desire to wash away a nation's shared pain of the past as quickly as possible, it has to be said, because we had more immediate tasks to perform. First we punched the air. Then we punched the send button. Any temptation to linger over the celebrations quickly gave way to the professional obligation to file with haste. And so the magic moment passed almost before we had realised it. We live, after all, in a world where the Vatican is on Twitter.

Earlier, it seemed that witnessing Murray's victory might never end, as one thumping rally followed another. This is the curiosity of the business: hours of struggle getting to a single second of execution, the guillotine hovering with intent then slamming into the neck of a tired loser. Tennis is beautifully suited to such an extension of drama before the inevitable drop of the blade. The points ebb and flow, contained in the exquisite format of the game's structure, from deuce to advantage to deuce to break point to dismay. Or ecstasy. Time is frozen, then stretched, before being ultimately contracted into a single, air-slicing moment. The crescendo fades and it is done.

For most of that windy evening, we had huddled together maybe 15 feet from the action, just behind the umpire's chair on the centre court named after Arthur Ashe, as close to the grand stage of sporting theatre as is possible outside a ringside seat at a boxing match. We heard the thud of every cannonball strike, the gasps of relief and satisfaction from each player, the grunt of the ball-kids, even the occasional exasperation of the chair umpire. Without the luxury of time afforded either Russell or Tennyson, we filed in haste and, hopefully, without the blight of error or poor judgment. As Murray dragged himself to the service line for the final kill at 5–2 in the fifth set, those of us on tight deadlines scurried away from the final shots of the battle, up the steps of the stadium, down emptied stairs at the back and into the cranking, coffee-fuelled buzz of the media room, where we switched our attention to the TV monitors. There was just enough time to feel happy for the quiet and complex man from Scotland.

My memories of the match I will trust to my contemporary scribblings, because those expressed at the time usually go more quickly to the heart of the matter. So indulge me for a piece published in the *Guardian* the following morning, on Tuesday, 11 September, after the tropical storm had ripped through New York and Murray had done a similarly spirit-wrecking job on Djokovic.

This fairytale of New York written by Andy Murray was more than just an achievement to savour for itself. Few sporting voyages have carried such baggage, and Murray's alone has resembled a flea carrying a piano up a mountain. In a single win, wind ruffling his Scottish locks, Murray put a deal of pain to rest.

It is unlikely he will ever win any of these big matches easily and Monday's for the US Open and his first Slam title was straight from the Murray blueprint of struggle. Yet there was an underlying conviction, even in some of his mistakes. There was cool to go with the heat. When he went two sets up, he knew he had to just hold his nerve and the prize was his.

There have been few doubts about his talent, some about his temperament, hardly any about his commitment. But everyone's got a take on Murray; the most pertinent and relevant belong to those closest to him, of course, nobody so ever-present in that regard than his mother, Judy.

A decent player herself (and a better coach, subsequently), she has accompanied him on this journey since he first swung a racquet with his bony arm as a ten-year-old around the cold halls and council courts of Scotland. She was here, naturally, as emotional as when he made her cry at Wimbledon after losing to Roger Federer – then beating the great Swiss at the Olympics. She had Sir Alex Ferguson for company in Andy's box, after he turned up an hour late; a little further away, Sir Sean Connery, her other New York drinking partner this weekend, bristled silently. The clans had gathered.

Those Wimbledon matches were seen as defining contests in Murray's often turbulent career. It turned out they were. They coincided with the growing confidence the player has in his coach Ivan Lendl, a court-side fixture these past nine months whose mien might frighten the ball-kids but encourages the Scot to reach for his full potential as he sheds, almost by the week, some of that psychic collateral.

The sulking has all but gone. The forehand now flows with muscled freedom. His second serve is improving, to go with the potency of the first. And, crucially, Murray's reluctance to attack, borne of his noted ability to defend, has been recalculated.

He remains a sometimes enigmatic individual, but so what? He will forever have the tics and the squirms of memory-built repetition. And he will go again in quiet moments to sit alone in an empty Wimbledon, as he did many times this summer before cracking the secrets of that cathedral for a gold medal.

Murray might not get lost on the Paris Metro again, but he will surely walk the streets of Manhattan by himself, tweet when he is happy, but not when he's not, and he can cry if he wants to.

Mark Petchey, his first coach when he went on the Tour, said during the media agonising a year ago over who should guide the player's career after another minor upheaval in his team: 'Everyone sees Andy on the court and they see this volatile, stroppy kid but I can assure you, you can't get more of a 360 away from the court. As much as the toughness is there, and it seems to be there on the court, away from it things affect him much more than people realise. This spotlight on him is difficult to deal with because he's the only one who is actually doing something in British tennis and yet here we are, having this major discussion about what is wrong with Andy. Hang on a minute – there's a whole lot wrong with what's behind him.'

And, of course, Murray picked Lendl. They started working together just before the Australian Open. Murray reached the semi-finals, where he gave Djokovic 4 hours and 50 minutes of hell. He could have won, but he didn't. Critics who don't understand tennis jumped on him. The fact is, that match could have gone either way. It was without a doubt one of the best performances of Murray's career, better than a lot of his wins.

Lendl was proud but did not show it. He looks hard, and he is hard. It is one of the reasons Murray employs him, although the genesis of their contact has never been made clear. It suits both of them to leave it vague, [but] I suspect it was Lendl who made the first approach. It hardly matters. There have been few partnerships in tennis that have clicked so pleasingly in such a short space of time.

Lendl has settled Murray's mind. When he arrived, older hacks remembered him from his playing days, and he remembered them. An initial wariness gave way to calculated warmth. There is something that binds him to Murray: defeat – each lost their first four Slam finals.

Lendl does not talk much – to the media or, as it happens, at length to Murray, but they did celebrate his Olympic gold. He told him he won because he'd lost.

'I said to him, "A loss is a loss; and a loss is not a loss. You learn from certain losses and become depressed from other ones. When you have losses, when you put it all out there and go hard, you can be proud of yourself. And you can learn from it, and that is really important."'

It might have been the best talking-to anyone has ever given him.

Most of our celebration that night was reserved for Murray. A little of it, probably, was in empathy with the nation and, if I'm honest, some of it was for us. We were, it was and remains blindingly obvious, in the Murray business. As long as he kept winning, we kept writing. Without Murray, there would be precious little tennis in the sports pages, save wondering if the next best man – James Ward, mostly – would get back into the top 100 in the world, hoping that Kyle Edmund would grow into a tough professional with the poise and maturity he carried as a promising teenager, or pondering if the fragile genius of Dan Evans would ever conquer his waywardness. The following summer, and a month after Evans excited expectations again with eye-catching performances for Great Britain in a Davis Cup tie against Russia in Coventry, he was losing in straight sets in the quarter-finals of a Futures event in Newcastle to fellow Brit Ashley Hewitt, ranked 652 in the world. Such is the British tennis roundabout outside the world of Andy Murray. But we had not heard the last of Dangerous Dan, and we shall return to Birmingham's favourite rascal later.

Certainly, that September, there were the heroics of Laura Robson, who had roused the nation from its tennis slumber as a fourteen-year-old when winning Junior Wimbledon and was now moving nicely if nervously through the top fifty, gathering notable scalps in between lapses that grew further apart as she found consistency in her shots and a little more movement in her teenaged feet. And her rival Heather Watson, whose win in the Japan Open made her the first British woman to win a singles title on the WTA Tour since Sara Gomer in 1988, provided a reason to celebrate as well as wonder. But they were not Virginia Wade. Not yet, anyway. We would, in the main, be more concerned about young Andy.

Fans of the gentle game (as was) are not so tribal as those in other sports, so, as much as the vast majority of Murray's compatriots wanted him to do well, a significant number reserved their affection for Federer or Nadal, some also for Djokovic. This was one of those rare occasions when sports writers and an athlete they are paid to both criticise and praise when required could find common ground. We were genuinely glad for him. And just about as relieved.

After I had filed, I went out into the midnight air, which earlier had carried the menace of havoc but was now less heavy with possibilities. Standing, beaming, in the grounds was Steve Busfield, the *Guardian*'s New York sports editor. We hugged and smiled, mouthing stuff like, 'How about that, then?' It was a stupidly emotional and nice moment. Very *Guardian*. I don't know that the guys from the *Sun* and the *Mirror* were hugging in the dark, but they probably were just as thrilled. Then Steve and I went to my favourite bar in Manhattan, Jimmy's Corner on West 44th Street, run by a venerable old boxing trainer, Jimmy Glenn, whose wisdom reaches back almost to Fred Perry's time. The bar is not on a corner, but no matter. The corner refers to that in a boxing ring. A competent amateur, ordinary pro, much better cornerman and excellent host, Jimmy, in the space of three decades, has turned his eponymous Corner into the best-value drinking establishment in New York, bang in the middle of Manhattan, which is a bit like putting a whelk stall in Harrod's and outselling the smoked salmon counter. All around Jimmy is wealth. It is his crowning achievement to stay in business. 'I survive,' he said, 'because I'm cheap.' His signature drink, as they say in the trade, is Jimmy's Hurricane, a knock-your-toupé-off mix of amaretto, spiced rum and other juices, but most of his clientele drink good, cold beer at $4 a bottle.

I shared a few of those with Malcolm Folley of the *Mail on Sunday* (Steve supped on a lemonade) as we marvelled at Murray's achievement, dissected the match and wondered if he could ever do it again. From memory, the consensus was that he could, but it would be no easier than this time, we reckoned. Indeed, we probably agreed, every final he reached would be a fight. He surely could not get the job done in straight sets, could he? No, we reckoned, it would never be that easy.

The core members of Murray's entourage, meanwhile, led by his mother Judy, had gone on ahead to his favourite New York restaurant, Hakkasan, on West 43rd Street, around the corner from where we were celebrating and, being wise, there they tucked into the champagne and fancy cocktails, rattling up a tab a good deal heftier than the one in Jimmy's. By the time Murray appeared, a couple of hours into the celebrations, the party was swinging like the ball had been in the post-cyclonic wind on Centre Court a few hours earlier. 'The problem was,' Murray said later, 'when I arrived, everyone was so drunk already it would have taken a while to catch up, so I didn't bother having a drink. Not one.' He did actually. He had a lemon soda, which cost $6. The bill came to $6,448. Murray paid – and left a tip of $1,289.

The check at Hakkasan was closed at 2.03 p.m. Steve, Malcolm and I soldiered on in Jimmy's. On a cool night, there was a glow emanating from the departing winning party, most noticeably around the beaming young champion who had not had what some would call a 'proper drink' since he was a teenager at his first training academy in Spain.

When Murray got back to his hotel room from the Japanese restaurant, buzzing on no more than a carbonated soft drink and adrenaline, he sat on his bed and stared at the wall. The scene reminds me of Jonny Wilkinson, the England fly half who, after kicking England to victory over Australia in Sydney in 2003 to secure rugby's World Cup, detached himself from the hysteria. His captain, Martin Johnson, wondered where Jonny was as the rest of the team soaked up the applause, and he reckoned he knew where to find him. As he opened the door to the England dressing room, there was his quiet string-puller and king of the boot, sitting by himself, eyes fixed on nothing in particular, mind clear and a quiet smile playing on his lips. 'Just wanted to grab this moment for ever,' he said to Johnson, who patted him on the shoulder and returned to the celebrations continuing on the pitch. They are similar, Wilkinson and Murray, very British heroes.

After the buzz of the Flushing triumph and a few hours' sleep, we met up the following morning at the palatial 3rd Avenue penthouse of Danny Lopez, Britain's consul general in New York. Murray sipped on an Irn-Bru and talked quietly about those precious moments alone when he contemplated the significance of what he had just done.

We probably got back to the hotel about 3 a.m. I didn't get to sleep until about 5 a.m. and was up at 6.30. Wasn't sleeping long enough to have any dreams about it. I was in shock, disbelief . . . whatever it was. All of that will probably hit me when I get back. It's something that will take a bit of getting used to. It's not something that I've always been that comfortable with; you guys have seen that over the years. It might take a bit of time to get used to it. I spoke to Ivan [Lendl, his coach] a couple of times during the year and he said, 'What worries you?' I said to him at the French Open this year, 'I worry what might happen if I win a Major, how my life might change, because I want it to be the same.' I didn't really want it to change. He said, 'I thought the same thing, but all that happens is you get more people congratulating you. You get nicer tables in restaurants. You get to go on all the good golf courses for free.' And that was basically what he said. But he also said, 'It doesn't change much. You can keep your life exactly the same as you want.' I'm pretty sure it won't change too much . . . I will try to keep things pretty much the same as they are.

He has not changed – a triumph in itself. But our perceptions of him have. The once diffident kid walks taller now. He has engaged the British public in a different way. We are more sure of him, just as he is more sure of us. There is trust and mutual affection. He relies on us to help him win, where once he was not sure of our support. What was once a respectful cathedral at Wimbledon has become a cauldron not unlike Twickenham a few miles away. As for we cynical hacks, there will always be a place reserved for criticism when it is warranted, because no athlete is perfect. But there is a growing sense among even the most sceptical that Murray has grown into an enduring and unreservedly likeable champion, a tennis player to bring pride to his sport and his country.

It does not happen often in sports-writing, this symbiosis. Look at the strained relationship between footballers, their managers and the writers who follow them. There is little empathy. They are set against each other through mutual suspicion, serially unfaithful to each other as confidences are turned into headlines, followed by denials and divorce. The cloying presence of sponsors and the demands of branding have reduced contact between footballers and writers to one of meaningless soundbites, except in those circumstances where controversy boils over into front-page drama. It is all a long way from the days when journalists and players drank in the same pubs, laughed at the same jokes, backed the same horses and, in some cases, romanced the same women.

That is not to say that tennis is an open book. There are still barriers. The formal routine of communication is more like that which exists in golf than in football, and regulated, formulaic press conferences can be drowned in sycophancy. The repetition is deadening. There are endless questions about the speed of the court, the balls, the weather, the wind, the sun. None of them adds much to the sum of our understanding of what we might have just witnessed, except perhaps that tennis encourages the most grovelling of enquiries by writers too keen to please and rarely prepared to cause a fuss. However, as Murray is our single object of interest, in the narrowest parochial sense, we have regular access to him after all the other sportswriters from Europe, America and beyond have packed up and gone. It is in these sessions where he opens up a little, feels more relaxed with people he has come to know. He reserves a few doubts about us, possibly, but he is painstakingly polite and unendingly co-operative. Occasionally, he will mix socially with us. Occasionally, he enjoys it. On balance, we are probably luckier to have him than he is to have us.

Over the next twelve months, he would reveal more about himself than he ever had done before.

2

Man or Superman?

Melbourne, 22 January 2013

Novak Djokovic cannot contain his joy. He has not only just beaten Tomáš Berdych in four sets to reach the semi-finals of the Australian Open, the first Slam tournament of the year, he has emphatically refuted the whispers that have lingered since he quit mid-match here against Andy Roddick four years earlier while defending the title. That retirement, one of several early in his career, had him marked as a quitter. It took a couple of epic efforts in Melbourne in 2012 – against Andy Murray then Rafael Nadal – to stop the talk. This year, he has done it again, beating the re-born Stanislas Wawrinka in five of the toughest sets of his life to come through the fourth round. Now he has seen off Berdych. Soon he will have to do the same against David Ferrer in the semi-finals. There is only one way Djokovic can kill the rumours. He is condemned – or blessed, perhaps – to win again and again in long, brutal matches for the rest of his career . . .

~

'You will believe a man can fly.' That was the tag line for the 1978 movie *Superman*, and it was not long before it was appropriated to describe the mesmerising basketball star Michael Jordan. For years, 'Air Jordan' suspended belief whenever he glided towards the backboard for the Chicago Bulls, selling the myth that he could, indeed, defy gravity; simultaneously, he convinced millions of teenagers around the world (or their parents) to buy his eponymous shoes.

The notion that Jordan was capable of human flight was, of course, a marketing construct. Probably, it was the bastard child of a long lunch. And it was no closer to reality than were the screen heroics that the writer Mario Puzo created for an alien orphan with a kiss-curl, a day-job on the *Daily Planet* and a girl-friend who didn't know he was two people. While comic-book kryptonite was Superman's scourge, what it did for Jordan was age and ego. It was written that he would deliver fantasy for mass consumption, and, for as long as his body allowed, he fulfilled his destiny with distinction. Inevitably, after two comebacks (and a dabble in baseball), Jordan, at forty years of age, had to put away his cape and underpants.

This is the ineluctable magic of sport. It hypnotises and it defies logic, yet it makes some sort of sense, because we all want to believe, and, more often than not, it does not lie. There have always been supreme athletes – Muhammad Ali, Tiger Woods, George Best, Donald Bradman – capable of creating the illusion of miracles and letting us share in peripatetic pleasures far removed from the relative dullness of our existence. Sport at the highest level is not about the mundane. It is about reaching for the impossible. If we can't do it, somebody else will do it for us. And even when these miracle-sellers fall to earth, stripped of their powers – when we realise they are, ultimately, not so different from the rest of us – we are left with the memories only they could create. You can see Jordan flying now, can you not, just like Ali, floating and stinging across the canvas in the jungle night in the company of George Foreman, capturing time and stretching it to suit his needs. Ali believed. There is a well-worn and let-it-be-true tale about this charismatic, complex individual, refusing to buckle up when flying from Washington DC to New York at the height of his celebrity. 'Superman don't need no seat belt,' he told the flight attendant. 'Superman didn't need no airplane, either,' she reminded him. And ultimately the boxer, too, grew old and grey, noble in his palsied state but reduced and muted as he edged closer to death than to life, which he always had lived so loudly. Nobody escapes.

Tennis, a once decorous pastime in long trousers, is now a bare-fanged conflict with players wielding weapons like lightsabers from *Star Wars*. In many respects, it is pugilism with racquets. Over the first dozen years of the new millennium, the conviction that extraordinary feats would be the norm became embedded in the expectations of fans, commentators and even the players themselves. We are living in an era of super-tennis, it is said; and indeed the game is now perceived to be considerably detached from its past. Ivan Lendl, Andy Murray's coach, has observed, shortly after taking up the job: 'The fitness, the training, the preparation and the understanding of the game have all changed since I played twenty years ago. These guys are more complete players. There are few or no weaknesses in their games today. Now you have to be strong, agile, quick, and be able to last longer than the opponent if it comes down to it.'

Paradoxically, Lendl was among the first players of his era to fall in love with the gym. But his is not a view embraced without reservation by some of his contemporaries. Boris Becker, John McEnroe and Mats Wilander, fierce rivals around Lendl's time, will not concede that their tennis was much behind that of Djokovic, Nadal, Federer and Murray – in terms of stamina, at least – and they reckon that they, too, could survive the marathon matches of today's blitzkrieg tennis.

'Are you suggesting that we were not fit, that the players in the seventies and eighties didn't go to the edge?' Becker asks in mock-horror over some calorie-rich and fabulous Indian delicacies in a restaurant in London's West End. Maybe, Boris. Maybe. Great players never shake their past, they just loosen their belts, although Becker is in good shape at forty-five, forever that exuberant freckle-faced teenager who lit up Wimbledon before he could vote, then just kept going. Some champions are capable of viewing history with detachment, and Becker is one of those.

'But yes, you're right . . . in a way. With the style of play – the majority of players are playing at the baseline, the counter-punchers – there is a different physicality needed now than there was ten years ago. Having said that, [Björn] Borg and [Guillermo] Vilas, [Jimmy] Connors and Lendl and these guys also played from the baseline and they had four- and five-hour matches as well. I think it's just the nature of the beast, being a top professional tennis player: you have to be extremely fit, otherwise your opponent runs you off the court.'

I would hear counter-arguments from players of the current era. They spoke of being left behind by players who could afford to spend weeks in training camps, who did more work off the court than on it, and who had turned the game into a test of strength rather than wit.

Late in 2013, another redhead (albeit clinging to the strands with less confidence) is thousands of miles away in Melbourne, accepting the honour of being the Australian Open's first global ambassador. Revered in the sixties as the finest player of all time (and lauded still by those inclined to look further back than last week), Rod Laver, at seventy-five, is the only player to complete the grand slam of his sport twice, in 1962 and 1969, yet he says he rarely played long rallies and, if he could not kill the point early, he doubted he would be able to match his modern counterparts for strength and staying power. Even unreliable memory suggests this might be falsely modest; Laver was a sublime talent playing in an era of many similarly gifted opponents, and Becker agrees he would have won several Majors, whatever the time, place or opposition. But Laver – unfailingly polite, candid and, in sum, a treasure – would rather celebrate the present than glorify the past. Becker moves on: was Laver better than Federer? Who was the greatest? Could players then compete now?

'Roger is certainly the most successful,' he says of the man who owns more Majors than anyone else. 'Greatest is a word that's not [easily] defined. You speak about Laver: two Grand Slams in his career – and with wooden racquets! For some, that's the greatest achievement in sport. Sampras: there are the accomplishments he achieved in a very competitive era, one with many other superstars. Talk about Borg: in a short career, six French and five Wimbledons back to back – impossible, you might think. So the greatest? I have a hard time saying who is the greatest.'

McEnroe, who had several bruising battles with Borg, and Wilander, who could grind with the best of them (most enthusiastically when facing Lendl), agrees with Becker that players from their period could cope today. 'I don't remember Borg ever being unable to play those long matches,' he said with whimsy when asked to compare eras. 'He was as fit as anybody today . . . OK, I didn't spend a lot of time in the gym, but I could hang in there. So could Jimmy and Lendl. Wilander too.' Something else McEnroe recognises that is common to all eras is ego. While the best players are single-minded in their desire to win, they have pride in their art, in their ability to do things on a court that others cannot do. In short, in a sport where artistic expression is often smothered by expediency, some players love to show the world what they can do. 'In some ways,' said McEnroe, 'you want to show off and say you are not a one-trick pony.' But they are professionals. In the amateur era players enjoyed playing their shots more; they liked to go through their repertoire in order to impress, because they were performing in public and the consequences of getting it wrong did not seem so horrible. There was more slack in the game previously. It was easier to come back from a cock-up. Not any more. Modern tennis demands one hundred per cent concentration, with no room for fancy tennis. I asked Murray once if he ever took simple pleasure in the hitting of a tennis ball, something he must have done a million times and more since he was three years old. He looked slightly puzzled. 'The purpose of hitting the ball,' he said, 'is to win the point. That gives me a lot of pleasure.'

'Sometimes,' McEnroe said, 'you have to put aside how you look and be more worried about whether you want to win or not. It's a tough line to find yourself in.' And it pays extremely well.

What all these players agree on is that modern tennis, with its patience-bending baseline exchanges on slower courts, with space-age rocket launchers for tennis racquets, requires more than just purpose and guile. It demands unfailing strength and flexibility to hit power shot after power shot from deeper behind the baseline than ever before, or on the run, and to be ready to cover acres of court, much of it side to side, but going backwards and forwards too (the drop-shot and lob are still weapons of confusion, the hand-grenades to augment the cannons). It demands that a championship player approach his sport like a championship fighter: to win, he has to put the work in beforehand. He cannot afford to fade in the late stages of a match, and that bank of energy can only be filled in the off-season, with relentless gym and track work.

It was not always like this. Once players got fit by playing. They also got better at tennis. There is an argument that maybe this is a way back from the brutalism of the modern game, to pour more energy into developing skills, strategy, on-court smarts. There is a uniformity about the Tour that is striking if you watch tennis day in, day out, over the course of the year. Many players are indistinguishable from each other in style and method, their body types even conforming to the accepted norm of tall, lean and powerful, which leads them to play a certain way, with power and precision from deep and not a lot of time spent at the net. When Rod Laver says he could not compete in the modern way, he looks at the quandary from a vantage point some way under the nose of 6-foot-10-inch John Isner.

Check out the 2013 end-of-year top ten: Nadal is 6 foot 1 inch;

Djokovic, 6 foot 2 inches; Ferrer, 5 foot 9 inches; Murray, 6 foot 3 inches; del Potro, 6 foot 6 inches; Federer, 6 foot 1 inch; Berdych, 6 foot 5 inches; Wawrinka, 6 foot; Gasquet, 6 foot 1 inch; Tsonga, 6 foot 2 inches.

And the inaugural top ten when the ATP rankings began in 1973: Năstase was 6 foot; Orantes, 5 foot 10 inches; Smith, 6 foot 4 inches; Ashe, 6 foot 1 inch; Laver, 5 foot 8 inches; Rosewall, 5 foot 9 inches; Newcombe, 6 foot; Panatta, 6 foot; Okker, 5 foot 10 inches; Connors, 5 foot 10 inches.

So, there is just one player under 6 foot in today's top ten: Ferrer; in 1973 there were five. Four of the latter were Slam winners, with Tom Okker a finalist at Flushing Meadows in 1968. At the US Open in 1975, Manuel Orantes came back from 0–5 in the fourth set to beat Guillermo Vilas in a semi-final that finished just before midnight; the following day the Spaniard beat Jimmy Connors in three sets to win the title. Stamina is not a twenty-first-century phenomenon.

Further inspection of the stats confirms the fact that the best players forty years ago generally hit the accepted norm of the time, 6 foot or under. Jan Kodeš and Paolo Bertolucci were 5 foot 9 inches. Björn Borg, lurking inside the top thirty in those days, was 5 foot 11 inches. Today? Milos Raonic, at 6 foot 5 inches, and Kevin Anderson and the rising young Polish star Jerzy Janowicz, both 6 foot 8 inches, look to be giants from central casting. Each owns a booming serve delivered from a height probably in line with the top of the umpire's chair on Centre Court at Wimbledon.

There are many players shorter than that, of course, and they have regular success, but diet and science cannot be denied. Guys are getting bigger, and some of the biggest reckon they can be pretty good tennis players.

Whatever the era, the size, the conditions or the equipment, tennis players have always needed the following: intelligence to know where to go; fitness to get there; balance and co-ordination when there so as to best hit the ball; guile to know where to hit it; composure to complete the stroke; resilience to reply; and commitment to do it all again for as long as it takes to get the job done. The difference, said Jim Courier, once a world number 1 and now a smooth TV face, is the quality of the defence.

> These top players are so good offensively and defensively that they can get by in a bad game with just defence alone. In past years, players like Becker and Sampras, if they had an off-day offensively, they could be vulnerable. That's just not the case with these guys. They are so well rounded and just so physically strong and, for the most part, durable when it comes to the best of five sets, as the records clearly show.

Great player though he was, Sampras was beatable when repeatedly asked to retrieve; he relied on the extraordinary power of his attack, behind an imposing serve and withering volleys, which garnered him fourteen Slam titles. Pistol Pete ruled because he converted power into titles, crushing opponents with the uncomplicated force of his racquet so completely and consistently that he was number 1 in the world for 286 weeks, while Andre Agassi, born with more innate talent but less discipline, was king for 101 weeks. Sampras beat Agassi twenty times in thirty-four matches – memorably, in his last competitive match, to win and retire with the US Open title. 'That's Hollywood,' Becker chuckles. 'That's not sport. He announced it was going to be his last one, and he had Agassi in a five-setter. I was in the stadium, and you don't write a script like that, because nobody will believe it. He's the only one who's done it. I don't think Roger can do it, but I think we should respect him and give him the time that he needs to finish his career on his own terms. He's too smart to keep playing and losing in the second round and saying he's happy with that. That won't happen.'

We will know in good time. But the Sampras–Agassi rivalry provides an interesting parallel with that of Nadal and Federer, both statistically and stylistically. The latter's fans can be divided into those who appreciate the Spaniard's animal-raw aggression and lovers of the rapier touch of the Swiss, who slices rather than bludgeons and whose very name sounds like 'featherer'.

Wilander's take on the progression from the guile and power of the Sampras–Agassi era on faster courts to the attrition of today on slowed-down surfaces is nuanced. He would like to see players take more chances, either at the net or in their ground-strokes, because he leans towards a cerebral game. Maybe then, he says, they could make a dent in the tank driven by the Big Four. He does not particularly enjoy the waiting game at the back of the court, even though he was pretty good at it himself.

Surviving is one thing; thriving is another. As I write, the touch players still have not broken through to join Federer along-side the muscle of Nadal, Djokovic and Murray. A few are shining intermittently: the seasoned nearly men – Berdych, Tsonga, Ferrer, Wawrinka, del Potro and Gasquet among them – along with the skittish contributions of Gulbis, Tomic and Dimitrov. There is plenty of clever and pretty tennis out there. It doesn't all have to be played on the red line.

Wilander agrees that super-tennis is partly a result of tech-nology, partly a redefined court strategy and outlook – one that has a stranglehold on the imagination – and possibly is the result of younger players not being brave or confident enough to depart from the orthodoxy and try instead a little of what Haas, Youzhny and the French serve-and-volley maestro Michaël Llodra regard as their obligation to tennis. Using super-zinging strings stretched across a bigger sweet spot to impart more topspin and bring down hard-hit shots inside the box on dull-paced courts, most of the younger players have been sucked into a vortex of struggle in which they wait for the other man to drop from exhaustion or just get plain bored.

As Pat Cash, who rarely bored on court, puts it: 'There's an argument that this generation of men's tennis is boring and I think it's a valid one. It's not boring to see two great players like Rafael Nadal and Novak Djokovic compete in a final. What is getting mundane is watching the same tactic in every single match of every single Grand Slam for the last five or six years. Nowadays they all settle down and say, "OK, this is going to be two hours of baseline rallies." The guy who outlasts the other one wins. It's taken a lot of the skill out of tennis.'

The prince of art over functionality, the epitome of Cash's perfect player, perhaps, is Federer. Yet, in an interview with Sydney's *Sunday Telegraph* shortly before the 2010 Australian Open, Cash attempted to deconstruct the unchallenged Federer myth. As much as he admired Federer's tennis, he sensed he could not sustain it against the relentless physicality of his peers. It was a bold statement. In part, Cash said, 'The next couple of years is the only time he will have been challenged by more than one person. Nadal has a winning edge over him and he has it over him mentally, too. I think del Potro and Andy Murray are really troubling him lately and I just hope we haven't seen Federer peak when there weren't any challenges.'

Although Federer beat Murray in the final, Cash's prognosis stirred a debate hitherto unspoken. Here's Cash again.

It doesn't really make it a fair indication of how good he really is if there hasn't been anyone really to challenge him. It will almost be a false impression of how good he really is. But I think over the next few years we'll see how good he really is. You've got to look at who you play. You can't just put a man in a boys' tournament and say, 'Wow, how good is he?' Because suddenly you drop another man in there and think, 'He's not as good as we thought he was.' And, at the moment for me, that's what is still in question. Federer really was in a league of his own for a while, partially because he's so good. He brought a different aspect to the game, but a lot of players have become accustomed to his style now and they have worked him out. It's going to be not so easy for him any more.

Nor has it been.

McEnroe is more forgiving, of the past and the present. In Paris he commented: 'The players from years ago were probably as good athletes as now, maybe not so physical, but they played more tennis. It's athlete v. player, sometimes. What would be great, and I don't know where this is going to come from, would be some young guys to start playing some of that tennis, to do both, in fact. But who is there out there playing that sort of tennis? Can [John] Isner do that? I don't know. I mean, who is out there? I think Federer can still do it, still win another Slam.' That latter sentiment is widespread among former players, especially those with lots of trophies in the cupboard: they do not feel inclined to disrespect a fellow legend.

If there is disenchantment with style and strategy, however, and disagreement about who is the greatest, what is not disputed is that nobody in tennis has matched the long-term domination that Federer and Nadal, together, have imposed on their peers. There is no mystery about where this high-powered game has come from: it is a dividend of that rivalry, and it has been built on subsequently by the two players seen as their natural successors, thus excluding all the others. Djokovic and Murray intruded on the Federer–Nadal turf and thus a sport within a sport has been formed almost to the point where, in every Grand Slam or Masters 1000 tournament, those are the only players any sensible gambler would consider worthy of an investment.

Becker, like Cash, wonders whether this is because the rest of the field is substandard or because this quartet is so good. I would contend the latter, because there will always be very good players – and, given the rewards, there are probably more of them hanging in there today than in the past. Tennis provides a pretty good living inside the top 100, an exceedingly good one inside the top fifty, and catapults players into serious riches from that stage onwards. Not everyone wants to make the sacrifice to get that far. Those that do pay a price they reckon is worth paying. That is what makes them special – and just a little crazy.

3

Transition

New York, 11 September 2005

Ivan Lendl, whose sense of humour leans heavily on sarcasm, is, for once, getting serious. He is being inducted into the US Court of Champions at Flushing Meadows before the start of the US Open final, and he is asked to name the highlight of his garlanded career. 'Grand Slam for the first time is more special than the others,' he says. 'I'm not going to put the US Open above the Australian, or the French above the US Open. I'm not going to do one or the other. Every time I won a Grand Slam for the first time, it's more special than the others — and the ones behind that were not too shabby either. They were very enjoyable.' Seven years later, he is in the locker room side by side with his player Andy Murray, who has just won his first Grand Slam title. 'It is the one you will remember most,' Lendl tells Murray. 'I think you're right,' Murray replies.

~

There is a view, widely held — by the player himself, as well — that Murray might not have beaten Djokovic in New York had he lost to Federer in the Olympic final in London three months earlier. While it is as difficult to prove as Fermat's Theorem, that is how the story panned out, and, although Murray had a lot going for him that summer in 2012, he still brought with him (less so subsequently) a measurable sense of uncertainty to nearly any court, big or small, against any opponent, good or not so good.

This inbuilt gloom was at the core of Murray's being, sustained by an almost birdlike suspicion of every twitch in his universe, where omens, pre-final dreams, feathers on the ground, midges in the air and the slightest disturbance to his routine could unsettle him. Watching Murray play tennis could be like going to the theatre to see a friend pitched into playing Hamlet and fearing he might not get through the evening if heckled by a drunk in the front row.

A colleague of mine once wrote that a boxer's biggest enemy was self-consciousness, a sweat-inducing concern – like that of an actor – about what people would think and which had the ineffable power to paralyse a performance. Murray, who famously loves boxing, used often to exude that feeling. He boxed worried. He cared – not only about winning the match but about losing even a rally within a game, the mark of a dedicated professional, of course. His worrying went deeper than mere competitiveness, though; it seemed to gnaw at his soul and he transmitted it to those around him. He did not want to disappoint either himself, those who got him ready for battle or the many thousands willing him to win.

It is the way of professional sport that gifted young athletes who grow up without giving a thought to the weight of public performance can freeze when the stage gets bigger than they had ever imagined. Murray says he harboured childhood thoughts of being a Wimbledon champion. But did he seriously imagine when swinging a grown-up's racquet as a rat-thin kid in Dunblane and hoping the shot would clear the net that, one day, he would be so in command of his discipline, so familiar with its demands, that he would be doing the same thing but far more proficiently – and in front of several thousand people on Centre Court at Wimbledon or Flushing Meadows – while knowing there were millions more watching on television who hoped he did not cock it up? Did the dread of performing invade his innocent dreams back then? Unlikely. But, occasionally, the dreams would later turn into nightmares. And here he was, a couple of decades after falling in love with tennis as a small boy, with the requisite physical skills and trained in the ways of his sport, asked to perform and not fluff any of his lines. Not now, Andy. For God's sake, Andy, not now.

That day he walked on to court pigeon-toed and slightly stiff, each leg following the other rather than leading, his back leaning a little forward from the perpendicular, as if pushing against an imaginary storm to come, and then he arranged his paraphernalia beside his courtside seat with a distracted air, and you wondered if he might forget where he'd left his water bottle or towel. He never did, of course; this was the part of the ritual so familiar to him he could have done it in the dark. Yet his nervousness was as palpable as electricity. For those who cared about him winning (and in the press seats we were supposed to remain coolly objective), it was like watching a force field surround him. Then, when he got up to engage his opponent and looked across the battlefield, he often gave the impression this was not going to be a pleasant experience, either for him, the other guy or for any of us. Suffering was imminent. There was a good reason for that: from his ankles to his hips and his back, Murray was a painkiller away from collapse. And he struggled to mask that pain on court.

Students of body language could probably write books on Murray. He will never move with the balletic ease of Federer, nor does he quite have the awesome elasticity of Djokovic (nobody except Spiderman does), but he is wickedly quick and efficient under pressure. That is his core strength: the ability to hunt down the unreachable ball and counter it with interest. But pain and inconvenience were never far away throughout 2012, and it showed on his face and in his between-point shuffle. These were the pauses in the fight, his minute on the stool, when he had to summon up strength to fight another round, or several. It says much for his innate athleticism, contained deep in that pill-fed frame, that he could, after he'd warmed up in the course of a match (sometimes as late as the third or fourth set), start to move like a gazelle – or, at least, a very agile duck. Murray's speed off the mark and over a short distance has put him in the upper reaches of his sport's retrievers. He's not a player to be easily caught out by a drop shot or anything hit wide or over his head. He has a quick-clicking ignition and good gears. And yet I am always nervous watching him. His vulnerability invites concern, and then, in bursts of brilliance, he can obliterate any opponent, as if visited by some outside force. It is an eerie experience to watch these transformations, sometimes in the course of a single point.

I do not mean to say Murray was a jabbering bag of nerves . . . well, I do. Because he was. He has said so himself. But were these spirit strings that connected his brain to his hands and feet any more frazzled than those of his peers, or of players from previous eras? It is impossible to say. No player is totally nerveless; nearly all have quirks and tics born of repetition and, in some cases, superstition. Murray's are not as extreme, say, as those of Nadal, who aggravates opponents with the metronomic tugging of his nose, hair and shorts, and who amuses them with the precise placement of his water bottles. The Scot, like many, is a practised friend of the towel, wiping his brow and his serving hand between nearly every point, from the start of the match until the finish, on cool, sweat-free days as well as hot. It would be fascinating if towels were banned, because a good eighty per cent of players would not know what to do with their hands at the end of each rally.

All sports encourage such innocent foibles, yet in a game as movement-repetitive as tennis these are manifest in conformity, with everyone mimicking everyone else. It can be a joyless spectacle, at odds with the shots players are forced to play when the pre-planned strategy is gradually broken down. The pressure to win in a high-stakes match can paralyse the best attacking instincts, leaving defence-minded players marooned deep in the court, waiting for mistakes on the other side rather than inducing them. As players strive, say, for the £1.6 million on offer for winning Wimbledon and other life-altering sums, they look scarily pre-programmed, like Amazon worker-drones, operating to a timetable.

Once, the game was full of free spirits, few freer than Torben Ulrich, the Dane whose racquet swung to the beat of his mood and for whom defeat or victory were met with the same equanimity. After blowing a lead of 8–7 and 40–love in the deciding set of one match against the Spaniard Manuel Santana, Ulrich observed: 'Manuel is so good under pressure that it is a disadvantage to lead 40–love. You have a better chance leading 30–love, or 30–15. But 40–love is very dangerous.' It is impossible to identify anyone on the Tour now embracing such apparently lunatic thoughts. But Ulrich – the father of Lars Ulrich, the drummer of American heavy metal band Metallica – was never just a tennis player. He wrote, played the clarinet, made films and, when the mood took him, could light up a tennis court.

Another eccentric of the circuit was the engaging and hugely talented American Art Larsen, a left-field left-hander known as Tappy, after his habit of tapping random items, only on certain days and at certain times, for no apparent reason. He also imagined that an eagle was sometimes about to land on his shoulder, and he would swivel about in mid-point to make sure the pesky bird was not about. But he is best remembered for his refusal to be constricted by the conventions of the game, like taking an easy point when it was on offer. Often, Larsen would extend the rally rather than finish it, if he were having fun. He once explained this behaviour to his occasional doubles partner, Gordon Forbes. 'Don't be crazy kid, we have points to spare. There's no fun going about killing balls like a butcher.'

While the likes of Ulrich and Larsen were rare then, they are extinct now. Only Gaël Monfils comes close to such irreverent disregard for convention, sometimes inventing shots on the spur of the moment, then paying the price for his profligacy. Difference now is measured in other ways.

Federer, for instance, likes to give the impression – to his opponent and the world – that he is never truly stretched, that he is in control of not only his own game but of the one unfolding around him, as if he has only to perform like we all know he can and he will surely win – without betraying a bead of sweat or a second of bother. It is an illusion, of course, as anyone who remembers his early, racquet-bashing days will recall. What Federer has done is master that snarling, inner beast better than anyone in the history of the game. Probably. Nadal does not bother with the charade. He is aquiver from start to sweat-drenched finish, twitching and grimacing as if someone has put pepper in his pants and told him defeat will result in his house being burnt down. Djokovic? He is, for the most part, controlled. He is the machine among them, the one who has measured out his lentils by the spoon and extended every sinew so dramatically that he is coiled like a cobra, ready to spit venom for as long as it takes. Yet he has cracked here and there. And, when he collapses, his struggle is to contain the acknowledgment of it. He loathes weakness, in himself and others. There is a louder jungle roar inside Djokovic than in any of the others and, on occasions, it is damn scary.

However, from observing Murray closely, I do think he has had to fight inordinate shyness in tandem with the unwanted curse that springs from wanting to give an honest performance on behalf of others. Sometimes he has been wrapped so fixedly in the gaze of national expectation that he has not been able to play near to his maximum. All he ever wanted was to play freely, without burden, to give himself the best chance of winning. That, surely, would please everyone, wouldn't it? *Just give me the chance*, he would whisper to himself. *Just give me the chance.*

And so, in the summer of 2012 Murray rose up to his full height, flexed his man muscles, trusted his matured talent and won his first Grand Slam title. He outlasted the machine from Serbia, and who would have predicted that? What impressed, too, was his subsequent candour in admitting he almost 'lost it' after letting his tennis grow ragged under the cosh in the fourth set, which he should have won. But he finished like a train. (Or was it a gazelle, at last?) His triumph was not without anxiety; that would have been expecting too much. Yet victory became him. He handled it perfectly, on his own terms, in his own way. He was neither loud nor stupidly over-humble. In a single evening, he grew up.

In January 2012, he took Lendl on as his coach and like-minded muse, and his self-belief climbed by the week – by the tournament. He was not only sick of failing, he now knew how to avoid it. It was as if he had been reborn; that the young, nervous Andy had been banished, and a new one had control of the racquet. There were some technical changes; important ones, too. He lost his trepidation about moving forward, about powering up on his forehand and cutting down on the full-out hitting on his serve in practice. 'Do you want your arm to fall off?' Lendl had asked him after seeing his hour-long serving sessions. So, they fine-tuned a few things. And they talked; quite a lot, especially at the beginning, as they got to know each other and their philosophies on life and on tennis. They were not clones but neither were they polar opposites. Later, Lendl would ring Murray every night before he went to sleep, to leave in his brain something positive to wake up to. It might be a word of encouragement about practice that day, or a final piece of advice about his opponent's vulnerable backhand. The conversations were usually short, and Murray welcomed them. They not only demonstrated his coach's commitment, they nearly always made sense. They were dancing to the same song, and the respect was mutual.

The humour helped. Both men liked practical jokes, some of it cruel. Various members of the team would become the butt of their japes. Lendl liked nothing better than bashing balls at Dani Vallverdu, Murray's long-time friend and hitting partner. Dani learned to laugh at it. There were forfeits and bets and constant ribbing. When Murray's strength and conditioning coach, Jez Green, lost a challenge to Lendl on the dreaded Versaclimber, a machine invented by the devil to test stamina in one-minute bursts, he had to recite a public acknowledgment at Murray's first press conference at the 2013 Australian Open. Unaccustomed to a lot of public speaking, he suffered more in front of the hacks than on that blessed machine, a device that would kill a marine.

But this was still a partnership in progress when Murray began his 2012 campaign. As much as he and Lendl seemed to get on, neither of them could be sure in those early days if the relationship would survive the inevitable crises, whatever the mutual goodwill and the considered belief of Lendl that Murray was good enough to win not just one Grand Slam title but several. However, Lendl recognised in Murray not the child but the man. He saw at first hand the steady physical and mental maturation of a champion. He knew about Murray's foibles, his tics and doubts. He had seen, from a distance, Murray's awkwardness with the media. Murray did not mirror Lendl's own infamous grumpiness when he played, but they were in the same neighbourhood. As we would come to learn, Lendl made the rules with the media and, if we did not like it, so be it. Usually, he was fair and accommodating. But there were moments . . .

In the beginning, there was calm. Lendl saw qualities in Murray that others missed. He recognised his cussed streak, his unwillingness to 'play the game', and he liked Murray's drive and his determination to do things his own way. It did not worry Lendl that Murray had gone through five coaches in his career. If anything, that told him the player had the ruthlessness needed to get to the top, that Murray was a single-minded professional athlete prepared to put his goals before sentiment, to be selfish when he needed to be. Not all players can do this. Those who dream but never wake up are two a penny. Murray, like Lendl, recognised that time could be an enemy or a friend, and, if it was treated lightly, a career could easily drift from promise to mediocrity. There was a timetable from day one, albeit flexible, and both were committed to it.

All of these things were thrashed out when they took up in Australia that January after exploratory talks in Florida, where they both had winter residences. Murray had agonised so long about who would replace the team of Miles Maclagan and Alex Corretja it seemed he could turn up for the Australian Open coachless and clueless. But they had gone about negotiations realistically, and, from the start, it looked like a good fit between two unusual yet similar characters.

The Czech, who grew up poor and appreciated wealth, was not one for platitudes. Neither was he afraid to tell Murray what he thought. While previous coaches were expected to know their place – none was allowed to talk to the media without Murray's say-so, for example – Lendl was an eight-time Slam winner and a former world number 1, and he would talk to us when he chose – after telling Murray, of course. And so he did at Kooyong, the old Australian Open venue, just before the 2012 edition of the championship, renewing handshakes with a few of the veterans in the press corps – Neil Harman of *The Times*, Barry Flatman of the *Sunday Times*, Mike Dickson of the *Daily Mail* – as well as those of us of a more fleeting acquaintance and a couple of clean-skins who'd never met the formidable presence known as Old Stone Face.

'So,' he said, pausing like a good comedian, 'here we are . . .' And a conspiratorial smile, the sort a salesman might wear while offering you the Brooklyn Bridge, etched on to features that had grown craggy and bronze through many hours on the golf course. Except Lendl wasn't selling anything beyond his trust. He would give us his if we reciprocated. If not, end of deal. It was a pleasant exchange of an hour or so, punctuated by a few reminiscences, some lame jokes and a couple of vague thoughts for the future. 'I admire his guts for hiring me,' he said, 'because he had to know it's not going to be a quiet thing.'

What shone through was Lendl's cast-iron commitment to protect his player. 'I don't mean to be evasive,' he said, being evasive. 'There is a relationship between a player and a coach and if that's violated, it's wrong. It's almost like the doctor–patient privilege. Whatever is said between Andy and I will never come from me any time, even after Andy has retired.' But he did say he would talk to us whenever we wanted . . . 'Every day, if you like.' Into that silence a strangled chuckle or two passed.

Significantly, none of Lendl's Majors arrived at Wimbledon, despite his best efforts and dedication to conquering the grass; so, when they embarked on their journey they shared that bond, namely All England Club virginity. The partnership started well and survived the familiar ups and downs before the high-point of the 2012 summer. Murray won in Brisbane, gave Djokovic a fight over 4 hours and 50 minutes in the semi-finals in Melbourne, reached finals in Doha and Miami, and then crashed on the back-wrecking clay of Monte Carlo, Barcelona, Rome and Roland Garros. Just to keep us on our toes, a first-round hiccup at Queen's preceded his best Wimbledon campaign to that point – and the disappointment of surrendering a two-set lead to Federer in the final. Previously, such a crushing defeat would have devastated Murray. This was no picnic, but it was different. This time, Murray handled it without collapsing into a funk of despair.

His demeanour now was more even, his moods more predictable. The sulking gave way to determination and a sense of realism. Where once he had looked for blame in defeat, now he found resolve. Murray might even have beaten Federer in the Wimbledon final in June had the weather not forced them under the roof into a windless haven where the Swiss felt more comfortable than in the swirling breeze, Murray's domain that day and on many other days. Murray is a lot like Michael Schumacher, a conqueror of difficulty. The great Formula One driver told me once when we spent a day together in Barcelona that his favourite surface was the one on which his rivals felt uneasy, such as the treacherous Hungaroring outside Budapest. There, he said, he could leave the stragglers behind. Murray, although he said indoor on hard-court was his best environment (he grew up as a player in a multitude of cold huts in Scotland), also embraced adversity. It suited his nature. Struggle appealed to him to such a degree that, when asked about his form or lack of it, he would rush to explain how horrible everything was – and yet, in defiance of the odds, he managed to triumph more often than not. Yes, Federer got the better of him in the 2012 Wimbledon final, but he was properly pasted in the Olympic gold medal event a month later. And, whatever Murray says about that result being nothing about revenge, nobody believes a word of it. Nor, probably, does he.

After the wildness of New York, then, there was the relative indoor calm of London. At the ATP World Tour Finals, Djokovic beat Federer in the final. It was a good match, taking the Serb 2 hours and 15 minutes to subdue the Swiss, who had reached imperious levels in the week-long tournament, the ATP's show-case finish to the season. He went into the final lifted by a good win over Murray in the semi-finals, but that match was a most curious affair. Federer had the house with him – in the adopted city of a Scot who had just brought the nation together by beating Federer for Olympic gold at Wimbledon. The Swiss won a definite majority share of the applause from the 18,000 fans who packed the arena, and it was an unsettling experience after the hysteria that had greeted Murray at Wimbledon. There, finally, after years of ambivalence, Murray had the crowd with him in a match against Federer, the most popular player of his era. Now he was returned to the status all Federer opponents had become used to: that of dancing partner.

There were various explanations, the most often proffered being that the Olympic audience was not 'hard-core tennis'. That summer's day, Murray had the affection and support of a country besotted by his quest for gold – and not just the trust of tennis fans who wanted him to do well. That day, Federer was Swiss, not their darling Roger. Patriotism kicked in as part of the Team GB energy driving the home Olympics. Other loyalties were put aside.

The crowd's support at the O2 went roughly 60–40 for Federer, I reckoned at the time. Others had it more even. Whatever the explanations or the calculations, there were faint echoes of the 'Anyone but Murray' prejudice that had dogged him since his 'Anyone but England' throw-away remark several years previously. It did not entirely explain the weirdness of the match, but the suspicion was that there was an element of this unfounded prejudice lingering in the Murray saga, and the fear that it might always be there. Combined with the phenomenal power Federer held over his fans, this conundrum went some way to explaining the disjointed atmosphere at Greenwich. What could not be denied was that Federer was the better player on the night. He thoroughly deserved his win. There was life in him yet. Murray, meanwhile, left London determined never to lose to Federer again.

Murray always felt he could match Federer, punch for punch, in the course of any big fight. He also reckoned he knew Federer's game well enough to devise a winning strategy. What he had struggled to do was bring both those elements together at the same time. He did it in the Olympics. Two months after Greenwich, he would do it again in Melbourne. This, by the majority reckoning, was the more significant turning point in their rivalry, not the Olympic final. The gold medal was fine, but it came around only every four years. The lead-up matches were the best of three, so the achievement, in that regard at least, was diluted. It was an elusive prize, a little hit-and-miss. Majors were not. Not for Federer, anyway. He had seventeen of them. They were the benchmarks of the business, not quadrennial gold, of which he had just the one medal, won with Stanislas Wawrinka for Switzerland in the doubles in Beijing in 2008.

Murray, deep down, knew all that, even if no such pondering could leaven his achievement – for his country and for himself. In one wonderful afternoon, kissed by the sun, he had won an Olympic gold medal and the love of a nation. That was some high point. Nevertheless, he reckoned there were prizes to be won on tougher proving grounds.

When they lined up at Greenwich that November in 2012, Murray was still nursing the pain in his lower back that had arrived, coincidentally or not, around the time a groin injury had forced him to quit the ATP World Tour Finals at the O2 Arena in November after winning his first-round match the year before. It was chronic, and it was a worry. It would not go away. There were two solutions: management or some form of surgery. Murray and Lendl decided early in 2013 that he could cope with the inconvenience of the stiffness that accompanied each attack, but he would have to rely heavily on painkillers, several of them, injected before tournaments and during them. It was a tough choice, because it meant the underlying problem would not easily disappear, if at all. Also, he would have to live with the prospect of that debilitating pain returning at any moment – as it had done in the second round of the 2012 French Open against Jarkko Nieminen. This uncertainty played on Murray's mind, not just in mid-shot or during a rally, but before each match. He had to develop the skill of ignoring his predicament. He had to kid himself, and to trust that the drugs in his system would get him through a match that might last an hour and a half or five hours. He was governed by both his body's frailties and the medicine that repaired and soothed his agony. This was professional sport in the raw. It had nothing to do with the celebration of victory, or even sympathy in defeat. It was a long way from the Olympics, too. This was the week in, week out reality of the Tour, a journey of unrelenting sacrifice. But I suspect the cheers of his home crowd for his opponent that night might have hurt as much, even if he has always denied it. That resentment would bubble up soon enough. The following January, in the semi-final of the Australian Open against Federer, the player he unreservedly admired but not so wholeheartedly embraced as a friend, Murray would win. And he would win with a sneer that was not to be forgotten. But let's not get ahead of ourselves . . .

Getting to know Murray has been a fascinating process. He is different from just about any athlete I have had to write about on a regular basis; a complex, intense, honest man with a clear sense of purpose. For the British writers who follow him around the world, Murray is a good deal more productive in terms of positive copy than were the years in which Tim Henman enchanted middle England and his 'soft south' tennis constituency with delightful grass-court skills but without delivering the cherished Grand Slam title. The almost annual frustration Henman unwittingly inflicted on a nation became a masochistic ritual.

In 2009, long after he had retired and as he prepared for his second BBC commentary stint at Wimbledon, Henman spoke candidly about his relationship with the media. His life then revolved around golf at Sunningdale (where today he plays off scratch or thereabouts), horse-riding and holidays with his wife and three daughters. He would admit he started his new career as a pundit with an air as relaxed as his ground-strokes, although he subsequently brought more application to the job and has blossomed into one of the best analysts of his sport. Henman the player, however, had little time for the observations of some of his critics, as he told me that day.

'Dealing with the press,' he reflected, 'it was pretty obvious there was a right answer and there was an honest answer. I think quite a lot of the time I gave the right answer. That was my defence mechanism. It was me trying to deflect extra attention away from myself, because I didn't want distractions; I wanted to concentrate on what I was doing and try to be the best player I could.'

Did the press understand that?

'I think they understood that but . . . it's easy, you know, to label me a boring twat! You know what I mean? For fifteen years I very rarely read anything about myself. No disrespect, but the vast majority of [journalists] had never played the game. They'd never got any experience, they'd never really understood it, so what was I going to achieve by reading someone else's opinions? It's your job, and it's what you're perfectly entitled to give, your opinion. I have no problem with that. I would say, hand on heart, I probably had a very good relationship with the press. The tennis journalists that followed me throughout my career . . . sure, you know, we had a few bumps in the road, if you like, but that's what you're paid to do.'

That is not exactly the way some of the tennis writers saw it. They felt let down by this revelation. Without exception, they had been supportive of Henman, recognising how good a player he really was, constantly watching him on the circuit, talking to him away from press conferences, listening to his explanations and trying to understand how hard it was for him to deliver what everyone (including their sports editors, of course) demanded of him. But Perry's ghost was powerful, whatever Henman said in press conferences. He tried desperately hard to win Wimbledon; it just didn't happen. And when the writers learned, after he had retired, that he had viewed their opinions so lightly, they were offended, and rightly so. The old argument that only those who have played are entitled to pass judgment is contentious, to say the least. There is much to be said for detachment and, using the skills learned over many years in this business, the ability to bring a view more considered and informed than might be provided by even the player himself.

I had missed a lot of that experience, thankfully. Back then, I was a tourist. Now I was one of the troops. And, in the afterglow of Murray's breakthrough at the Olympics and then the US Open, I felt guilty. I had come to the job of tennis correspondent almost by accident, succeeding two excellent and experienced writers in Stephen Bierley and Jon Henderson, and I had been there in New York, then Wimbledon, at the pinnacle of British tennis to see something I felt belonged to them. Like generations of British tennis writers, they had existed on the fumes of hope rather than expectation. Both had slogged around after Henman for a decade and more, living in a state of permanent anxiety, waiting, along with all the other writers and commentators, to chronicle the 'great moment'. Tournament after tournament, disappointment after disillusionment, they had been asked to remind the world that Perry was the last British male to win a Slam but, with a bit of luck and some hearty cheering on Henman Hill, Timbo might deliver too. How he tried, in his quiet way, a little misunderstood, a little underrated, much grittier than he appeared. He reached four Wimbledon semi-finals, and there weren't many players in the history of the game who could say that. There had been Virginia Wade, of course, who won the women's title in 1977, but the men's game had looked to be in a diabolical state for as long as there had been black and white television. How long could we repeat the tired joke that no British player in shorts had ever won Wimbledon? Well, only until older scribes pointed out that Angela Mortimer did so when she beat Christine Truman in the 1961 final. (First prize, a £20 voucher to be spent on a tennis-related item.)

So, like so many before him across the sporting spectrum, from footballers to cricketers and rugby players, Henman was now one of us: an expert. Strictly, he was an expert's expert, another player in the box. And, just as we had only him to talk about in the men's game, he has only Murray. They are friends and Henman is staunch in his support, conceding with admirable grace that Murray is clearly better than he was. In the crossover of their careers, a young Murray won three-setters in Basel, Toronto and Cincinnati before Henman got one back in Bangkok in 2006. But now we had a winner, the story changing on one memorable New York evening. This was a new journey, and I was privileged, and slightly guilty, to be part of it.

I inherited the duty of chronicling the engrossing theatre of British tennis through a shrinking prism. Stephen and Jon both took redundancy at a time of turmoil at our sister newspapers. After twenty years as the *Observer*'s chief sportswriter – having tried to fill the large boots of our trade's most distinguished artist, Hugh McIlvanney – there was a rearrangement of the editorial furniture, and I was asked to do two beats: boxing, which had for a long time been my preferred waterfront, and tennis, a sport I had covered with a wider eye. While I had always liked tennis, I wasn't at that point addicted to the subtle charms of racquets and fluffy balls. But you never know how much kick there will be on the next serve.

I had covered Wimbledon on and off for thirty years, as well as the Australian, French and US Opens sometimes, and reckoned the sport was more interesting now than at any time since John McEnroe simultaneously graced and disgraced it. I was at Wimbledon the day my favourite American unintentionally inspired the Great Brawl between American and British writers during a press conference, and so have always retained a soft spot for one of sport's enigmatic rebels. The fight didn't last long, but the anecdotes did.

Come to think of it, that might have been the perfect blending of two beats: boxing and tennis. So memorable (and shaming) an event was it – the War of Independence II, as it became known – that the thirtieth anniversary of the Big Mac Brawl inspired a welter of reminiscences at Wimbledon in 2011. There wasn't really a winner when the Brits and the Yanks scrapped over a tough question for McEnroe about his on/off girlfriend of the time, Stacy Margolin, but Nigel Clarke, then with the *Daily Mirror*, now with the *Express*, decked Charlie Steiner, who was working for an American radio station and subsequently became a big shot on ESPN. Nigel, like Murray, loves boxing. But he is not too proud to admit he cheated a little in that quick bout: he threw his kayo blow while standing on a chair. It is unlikely there will be any trouble from now on. For a start, the chairs are fixed to the floor. Also, our transatlantic friends are rubbish at tennis and start to lose interest about day three.

But what made me pause ever so briefly when thinking about doing the tennis job full-time was Murray. I had admired his tennis since he arrived at Wimbledon as a pale, monosyllabic teenager, pleading that he tired during matches because he was still growing (a complaint I had no sympathy with at the time), and, in his dealings with the media, seeming to cower a little, confident of his own talent but as unsure of himself in public as any shy young man is entitled to be. I wondered if it was possible for someone who did not shout to make a definitive statement in an environment as unforgiving as modern tennis. Did he have the steel to tough it out against the physical monster that was Nadal, the intellectual fortitude to ward off the frustrations that opponents of the artful Federer found so debilitating? He was closest in every way to Djokovic – born a week earlier and rising alongside him in the juniors since the age of eleven – but the Serb had matured more quickly (and would be first to the big podium in the Majors, the first to torment Nadal and Federer).

All of these questions occurred, and were, in time, dismissed.

I had written a frankly uncharitable piece about the younger Murray a long time before I joined the circus full-time, pointing out that his sulky demeanour betrayed a lack of joy that surely would undermine his hunger when the really big questions were asked, the ones that mattered, the ones that would determine if he were able to ditch that ancient Perry monkey. How wrong I was. The more I saw of him, the more I liked him, the more I believed in him. And what I liked was not necessarily a mellowing but a hardening, a quiet resolve that was difficult to see in the days of his teenage petulance. It became apparent, on closer examination, that such fits of pique were not the manifestation of delayed hormonal overload, but were directed inwards, indicating his dissatisfaction with himself when he played poorly, not because he doubted himself but because he believed. He believed – in fact, was convinced – he could do better and was worth his place in higher company. Frustration translated itself in the early days as self-pity. As his body and spirit grew, however, he opened up his chest and his mouth, although never with vulgarity or malice. He got a little louder, but never vulgar. He spoke more firmly and with more conviction. As his voice deepened, so did his determination. And all the time, he was as polite as a bank clerk. In the years I have been following him, I have never seen Murray properly lose his temper away from the court – although, no doubt his brother, Jamie, mother, Judy, and father, Willie, could offer contradictory testimony.

It is a dangerous game for a journalist to claim incontestable knowledge of any athlete's personality. Nobody that I know has the sort of round-the-clock access needed for such certainty. Even his family sometimes must wonder how well they know Andy. But I can say with some confidence that Murray is not the miserable git of public perception. He is, as he told a few of us in a quiet chat at the Boodle's club one sunny afternoon, 'a very nice person'. He plays wonderful, inventive tennis. He never dodges a question. He is intelligent and funny in that lugubrious Scottish way that has you wondering if he really did just say that. He is a complex, professional athlete aware of the outside world but not always 'of' it. There is an obsession with the trivial which is appealing, that talks to his childlike self and which suggests ordinariness, in the best sense of that word. He did not like bananas, he wrote in his autobiography, because, 'they are bendy with a black bit at the end and don't have any juice in them'. He also hated having a red Ferrari because he was embarrassed driving it. So he sold it. How could you not love a banana-phobic Ferrari-hater?

Nobody works harder at getting ready for his tennis than Murray. It has made the difference between winning and losing. Which brings me to the painful subject of his pre-Christmas training block in Miami just a few weeks after the ATP World Tour Finals. For years, we British tennis writers had asked Murray to show us first-hand how he prepares for the season, and maybe let us experience some of it for ourselves. For years he had decided that it was probably not in our best interests. By the time we finished sharing a day of his pain, most of us came to the conclusion it had been an idiotic suggestion in the first place.

Jez Green, a former martial arts expert, knows Murray's body as well as the player himself does, and as his conditioner, he oversees every second of Murray's preparation on the deceptively welcoming sands of Miami Beach and the more nakedly demanding environment of the nearby gym. Green, an affable soul, viewed our arrival like some gathering of middle-aged holidaymakers about to get sunburnt and sick. He was half right.

This luxuriously heated patch of Florida is as welcome a resting place in the middle of the European winter as a player could wish for – deceptively so. But Murray was not gifted the Christmas bolt hole. He had to work hard to win the money to afford the lifestyle. He has an apartment with fabulous views and courts, a beach and a gym with all the gadgets to use in a swanky building full of corporate types that destroy any notion of relaxation. His regime is extreme by our standards – and even by those of his peers – but he seems to revel in it.

We meet in the lounge of a hotel near his apartment. Murray had just had one of his 'heavier days', more than six hours of solid and varied work. He was glowing with good health, but was clearly tired. Would we mind if he got away quickly after chatting, he asked, because he had to be in bed by 9 p.m. The thought occurred if that a footballer said anything like that before an interview it would be surreal. Murray didn't complain about the Spartan training because he had been doing it for so long. This was his sixth annual torture session in Miami, and he said he had only really begun to see the benefits after three years. Everything he had done there since had built on those gains, in strength, stamina and explosive power. Today he has converted what was a slim, regulation-size tennis body into a near perfect V-shaped frame packed with muscle. It has not been put together randomly; Green and his fellow conditioner, Matt Little, work out a precise programme to target the muscles Murray needs most in the course of a match. Everything is done with a purpose.

The following day, there was the stationary-bike warm-up: two minutes at a low-resistance setting, ratcheted up four times until you would imagine you had inherited every drop of lactic acid in Florida. Then came the balancing on the Swiss balls, a chance to laugh at each other struggling with the simplest tricks. Murray has been doing these exercises since he was a boy and could easily get a job in a circus. There were standing jumps on to a box – which looked straightforward until the point of take-off – and subsequent missed landing. Then came the chin-up bar, a seemingly innocent pole that quickly becomes the enemy. (I will not tell you how the others did, but I confess to just about managing three-quarters of a move.)

The leg-press was almost a relief, although Neil Harman very nearly came to grief when trying to straighten his legs before the safety locks had been put in place. (That was why we had signed those waivers.)

But the chief instrument of torture, surely, was the Versaclimber. This, too, looks friendly enough. You climb on to a pair of steps, grab a pair of handles, and start pumping up and down at an angle of about 80 degrees. The idea is to get your heart rate up to about 170 for a minute, mimicking the sort of demands made on court, rest for a minute, then resume. Murray does thirty of these. I managed one. Just.

By the time we headed for a truncated Bikram yoga session, there were some worried looks in a little group. I had tried this a few times in New York and Melbourne with Simon Briggs of the *Daily Telegraph*, and he had become quite addicted to the discipline: twenty-six moves in 90 minutes in a room heated to 107 degrees Fahrenheit. It does not sound threatening but, until you get used to it, Bikram is a killing exercise. We did just 45 minutes with Jez Green that day and survived well enough.

Murray spoke about how he had changed, not just physically and in the way he played tennis, but in the way he viewed himself. 'I've felt more confident, maybe, as a person,' he said. 'I walk down the street with my head up. Before I was, like, always head down. I never wanted anyone to say anything to me. That's obviously changed since the Olympics. After that, I felt much more comfortable, a bit more accepted. The US Open was a huge motivation for me, because I realised then that all the stuff we do here was worth it in the end. There are times when you question it, when you've lost a lot of big matches. But now I know it's worth it. It's made me want to work harder, to give myself another chance.'

'I still find it hard to believe all the things he can do,' Green said as we sucked at the air after a jog on what only a masochist, sun-worshipper or professional athlete would regard as a friendly surface. 'It's a tough time to be a tennis player. What you're seeing in this generation is a group of guys with incredible genetics: you can try to play like Roger Federer, you can imitate his footwork, but he is just born with something that sets him apart. The work you do as a fitness trainer is about trying to maximise that.

'Andy is naturally fast but he is also so strong: on his best day he can do twenty-seven pull-ups and push 300 pounds on the leg-press. He could probably run a fifty-second 400 metres if he trained for it. [Until 2012, Murray used to run successive 400-metre sprints, resting between each one for the time it took to run the previous one; he could do up to eleven of these in a row, an impressive mix of strength and stamina.] He is a big powerful guy, whereas Novak [Djokovic] has a wiry strength; his flexibility is extraordinary. Andy has lazy speed, by which I mean that he doesn't look as if he's moving that fast, but it's actually deceptive. He's been clocked at ten metres per second over very short intervals, maybe even as short as a single step, which is as fast as Usain Bolt. I'm not saying that he is that fast over 100 metres, but he has great acceleration when he is chasing down a drop shot. Even more valuable than his flat speed is his ability to stop and turn so quickly. He's putting three times his bodyweight through his legs in that moment, so they have to be seriously strong. But above all he is fast with his eyes: he picks up the cues so quickly and he knows where the ball is going that much faster than almost anyone else. All the guys in the top ten have that ability to some extent.'

But not all of them have the weight of an entire country on their shoulders.

Murray shook our trembling hands and headed for his apartment after what had been a relatively light work-out. He was preparing for another early night. We sought out a res-taurant with a good wine list. As we sat down to dinner, there was an unusual silence. Nobody said anything much for about five minutes. We were knackered. Speechless. The aches had not settled, but we knew they would arrive with interest in the morning. We had been given a glimpse of Murray's life away from the court, a merest suggestion of the sacrifice he makes in pursuit of success, and the experience was enough to render us mute. You could have got long odds about that ever happening.

4

Pain is Good

Melbourne, 12 January 2013

On the eve of the Australian Open, the first Slam tournament of the year, we are gathered in the main press conference room at Melbourne Park, a steeply banked, bowl-shaped space that resembles a small lecture theatre, and sitting behind a desk below us is a professor of the game, Andy Murray, ready but perhaps not eager to be quizzed. 'Does it feel like there's a monkey off your back?' is the first question for the newly minted US Open champion. Murray smiles. It has been a long journey, in more ways than one.

~

Having survived the intrusion of the British media in Miami at the end of 2012, Murray had much to be content about on the 9,000-mile flight across fourteen time zones in time for the start of another season in Australia. It was a journey he had made five times in pursuit of a Slam breakthrough, and it never got easier, whatever end of the plane he could afford, but he was relaxed, fit and confident. The weather in Australia at that time of the year approximated to that in Florida, and the courts would be hard, not dissimilar to those on which he had practised for up to two hours a day for nearly six weeks. He had long calculated that it was a good fit. But this time he was heading to Melbourne for the Australian Open in a markedly different frame of mind to that which had hindered his recent campaigns.

Until now, he had been an outsider looking in. His confidence at the upper end of tennis was sustained by self-belief, but with not enough evidence to give it substance, and he had found himself knocking too often on a door that nobody wanted to open. Now, in a January heat-wave, he came with a Slam title to his name and, still smiling, more than likely, at the image of overweight hacks hanging from a chin-up bar like limp fish, he reckoned life was looking up.

Going south from Europe in January – or south-east, to be accurate – always filled the heart with a glow. Unclipping the grip of winter, climbing into a flying tin box for a day and walking into a mid-summer furnace at the other end never lost its allure. I must have done it fifty times over the years, and 'going home' this time was gilded with the possibility of witnessing Murray start as slight favourite to win the first of the four Slams. The nature of his win over Djokovic in New York earned him that honour, or at least parity, especially given the absence of the injured Nadal and no convincing evidence that Federer had rediscovered his best tennis. Whoever won, Melbourne would be fun. The city – indeed the whole country – had changed out of all recognition since I first left there in the seventies, and the buzz of sophistication crackled the moment you stepped into an atrociously over-priced restaurant, of which there were enough to drain the deepest pockets. Our little band bivouaced in Rydges in Exhibition Street, on the edge of the city's Chinatown and no more than a pleasant twenty-minute walk across the bridge straddling the Yarra to Melbourne Park. The river got its name from a misreading of an unrelated Aboriginal phrase, Yarra Yarra – which means waterfall – giving birth to a misunderstanding not uncommon in Australian etymology. Over time, for reasons beyond cursory research, the word has entered the language as a mildly affectionate reference to madness, and is preceded by the all-purpose Australian adverb, 'dead-set'. On some days, with the Fahrenheit reading around 100, it seemed wholly appropriate a description of those pale (older) members of our little band who declined to wear shorts. And some of those who did could only be described as, well, 'dead-set Yarra'. How anyone had ever played here in long trousers is a mystery known only to Fred Perry and his generation.

If Melbourne Park – home to the Australian Open since it moved from the grass of Kooyong in 1988 – is a convenient stroll from the city's small but bustling centre, it also houses its product in a compact and accessible setting, the withering heat emphasising the cloying intimacy. The most comfortable place to watch the tennis on a sweltering day or night is not inside the excellent, roofed Rod Laver Arena, but outside in the middle of a sunken park in front of the obligatory large screen, with food and fine wine within touching distance. Australians have mastered acceptable decadence. But Murray had time for none of this when he arrived in Australia in January 2013. He had a bit of history to take care of.

On his first visit, in 2006, Murray's performance did not match his precocious ambition and his campaign lasted precisely 106 minutes. That was how long it took the twenty-seven-year-old Argentinian clay-courter Juan Ignacio Chela to put him out of the first round in three perfunctory sets. Murray bristled. 'If you guys expect me to play well every single match and every single tournament then it's not going to happen,' he said on his way to the airport. That told us. Nevertheless, it was a long way to come for a hiding, the one consolation being, perhaps, that he had displaced Tim Henman as British number 1. 'It's nice, but it doesn't mean anything to the other players,' he said, 'whereas if you're in the top ten in the world that's pretty special.'

A year later, Murray returned to Melbourne a tougher proposition altogether. We didn't expect the young British number 1 to win every match, but he had already recalibrated his sights. He had also muscled up a bit, in body and attitude, and, in the third round, he took just four minutes longer to beat Chela than he had done to lose to him, then gave Nadal five sets to remember before heading home. His Spanish friend was seeded second behind Federer, so this was something to build on. Jo-Wilfried Tsonga caught Murray cold in the first round in 2008 on his way to the final, where the Frenchman lost in four sets to Djokovic – not that it was much consolation to Murray. He reached the fourth round again in 2009 and, while he was a more complete contender when he finally put himself in sight of the title in the following two Opens, the occasion over-whelmed each time. He lost to Federer in 2010 and to Djokovic in 2011, both in three sets. His game was in place and he did not lack conviction, but these were defeats like none of the others in his career. Against Federer, he led 5–2 in the third set and had five set points in the tie-break, but froze. In the Djokovic final, he met an opponent whose defensive game was similar to his own, except a level better. The Serb hit an awesome peak that day, playing some of his best tennis in what turned out to be his season built in paradise. It was the year he won seventy matches and lost six, while hoovering up ten titles, three of them Slams. After Melbourne, he carved his way through the Tour, going on a win-spin of forty-three matches in a row. So it was rotten timing for Murray to catch him as he was cranking up in the southern summer. That said, Murray felt he had let himself down once Djokovic started producing some of his gorilla tennis. It was hardly a fight. And he didn't make a lot of sense in a loser's press conference he would probably have traded for two hours in an ice bath. 'I was in a much worse state last year than I was this year,' he said. 'I don't know why . . . That's it.'

That was, indeed, it – but nobody was sure what it was, least of all the man to whom it mattered most. Both setbacks left him devastated, that much was obvious. They nibbled at his faith in his talent, and he was not comfortable dissecting the gory experience in public. What he wanted was to get back on court and sort it out by belting the cover off a tennis ball. After each defeat, however, he went to the hard courts of America and lost with desultory performances against opponents he should have beaten, catastrophically in 2011, when Donald Young (ranked 143 at the time) put him out in the first round in Indian Wells, and Alex Bogomolov (118) sent him away at the first time of asking in Miami a week later. 'I've won a lot of matches when I haven't been playing my best,' he said, although he could offer no reason for two dreadful back-to-back performances in conditions that suited him. As he swirled about in a vortex partly of his own making, he had to fight the temptation of doubt, wondering if he could ever convert his effort and dedication into big wins in big tournaments, let alone swat away the distraction of players outside the top 100 in three-setters of far less consequence. Was he as good as he thought he was, as good as the extraordinary players who would not open the door to his insistent knocking? Could he ever beat them outside three-set matches and nail them in the final of a Major? He believed he could. He had to.

James Blake, who retired in 2013 after an injury-racked career that never properly delivered what it promised, spoke to Scoop Malinowski in his book, *Facing Federer*, about one match against the then world number 1 in which everything clicked for the American – but not well enough. 'I was playing my best and he sort of showed me a new gear,' Blake said. 'That was tough to deal with.' Murray had not shown Federer much more than first gear in 2010, so there was a mental escape clause; losing when playing poorly was a lot different to losing when playing well, as Blake articulated. But it was not an argument Murray felt comfortable with during a protracted stretch of troubling introspection. In fact, he lost all perspective and looked to be perilously close to meltdown.

His mood was low, irreconcilably so at times, the on-court demeanour even gruffer than normal, and he was a difficult interview, suspicious of the most innocent enquiries. There was a hint of the Henman Factor at work: what did anyone know about his game, if they had not been there and experienced what he was going through. How could they understand the depth of his disappointment and confusion? We tried, but there seemed no getting through to him. He was surviving when he should have been raising his game, and, for a scary moment, he made noises that sounded like he was falling out of love with tennis – which is exactly how some of the headlines portrayed his state of mind. It did not help. After Mardy Fish shunted him out of the Miami Open in straight sets in 2010, Murray said: 'I need to start enjoying my tennis again. This has been going on for a few weeks now.' He could please neither himself nor his inquisitors, and gave the impression that he was being consumed in a fog that seemed to grow thicker by the week. A year earlier, Murray had won the title in the city of his second home and was being hailed as the player who might make a dent in the hegemony of Federer and Nadal. 'I've been very happy off the court but just not on it, and that's where I need to be happy because that's my career, this is what I do. It's only me who can figure it out. People think sportsmen are different to other people but we're not.' These were the words of a troubled young man discovering the downside to his glamorous calling.

Quite apart from fevered bar talk among writers over his disposition, the ongoing debate about Murray in 2010 was whether he could find another gear, one that took him forward at speed to pose a threat rather than leave him stranded, an obstacle in the shadows of the back court. His tennis had become so rooted in defence he could go through an entire match and only get near the net on the change-overs. From deep and powered by strong, quick legs, he ferreted after the unreachable and returned what looked like sure winners with tougher questions. He was a wall with arms, moving back and forth across the baseline, breaking his opponents' resolve through a stubborn refusal to be outflanked or outfought. He played tennis like a boxer, like Evander Holyfield hitting Mike Tyson twice for every blow received, and standing over him at the end of the fight. Murray's movement, racquet skills and court savvy allowed him to wear players out. It was not always pretty, but it was usually effective. What was frustrating for those who had watched his development since he won the junior title at the US Open in 2004 was the fact that Murray had a tennis brain as sharp as that of any of his contemporaries, and he had the weapons to adapt his tennis to any situation. He had developed his tactical awareness as an undersized prodigy playing grown men in Dunblane, where he learned to win by cunning and craft rather than by power. It was a common scenario in the development of prodigies. Murray, who started playing when he was three and only briefly got sick of tennis – when his football skills attracted attention before he reached his teenage years – had the benefit of an astute teacher in his mother, Judy, a good player herself, and she shared all she knew about the mechanics and strategy of tennis. He avidly soaked it up – as did his older brother Jamie, who, when they began, was considered more likely to succeed. Andy and Jamie were the Rafa and Roger of their household, scrapping over every patch of turf. Their competitiveness, allied to talent, was deeply rooted.

So how did Murray's tennis go from all-out clever to predominantly reactive? He always had something extra, an inbuilt contrariness, an urge to prove people wrong and to do it his own way. He would not be bullied, an admirable trait that inspired him to make the sensible decision in September 2002, at just fifteen, to abandon the cumbersome domestic tennis structure that was producing zero talent in the UK and spend two years virtually on his own in Barcelona at the Sánchez-Casal Academy. It is there where he met Nadal and several other players and coaches who would have a profound influence not only on how he played tennis but on how he prepared for it. It was a brave choice that changed his life, a flash of independence that few players his age would dare have proclaimed.

Famously, when challenged to a match by the academy's co-founder, Emilio Sánchez Vicario, who considered him a bit of a wimp, Murray thrashed him in two sets. Sánchez Vicario had seen enough to convince him that not only was the skinny Scottish teenager no wimp, but he also possessed the sort of bloody-mindedness he would need to make it as a professional tennis player. However, Murray's education in Barcelona had side-effects, not all of them universally acclaimed as positive. Some said his Spanish education stilled his attacking instincts; he reckoned otherwise. Having been encouraged in Scotland to play quick-kill tennis because that was the most sensible thing for a light-framed young player to do against bigger, stronger opponents, on the clay of Spain he learned how to build a point and, if needed, extend a rally until his opponent grew weary of the argument. It is the way of the red dirt. Also, it was a philosophy that appealed to a player who just loved hitting a tennis ball, shot after shot. With the sun on his back and encouragement from wise mentors ringing in his ears, Murray felt warm and secure in an environment of elitism. Slowly, his body and his confidence grew stronger, as did his conviction that this was the way to play the game.

One part of his body did not hold up under the strain of his chosen trade. Two parts, actually. Murray discovered just before Christmas of 2003 that he had been born with a split knee-cap. 'I'd had a niggling knee injury for about two or three months,' he recalled later. 'It started at the US Open last year in September. Then I got an MRI scan in December, which showed I had a [right] bipartite patella, it was very inflamed, I couldn't actually bend my knee at all. So I had to take four or five months off of doing absolutely nothing.'

When he got back on court after seven months away, he was

refreshed and hungry. He brought with him to the courts away from his Spanish academy a game that was a lot different to those of other players of a similar age.

His guru was the Colombian Pato Álvarez, who had become something of a folk hero in Spanish tennis over the years. Álvarez drilled Murray in the virtues of his 'cube theory', which was based on painstakingly mastering the linked basics of defence, transition and attack, each dependent on the other, and none cultivated in isolation. It is possible the method overtook instinct and it became embedded in Murray's tennis, pleasingly so, he thought, especially when it brought him many good results. The part of the cube that Murray became most adept at was that which required the most doggedness – and the most number of strokes: defence. It was in his nature not to give in, so, while he developed skills of placement and ball control, he also was careful in his shot selection and where he found himself on the court. Preoccupied, perhaps, with defence, transition proved the hardest component of the cube for Murray to master – although he was not alone in that. Tennis during his formative years had changed. The serve-and-volley era had passed. The courts and balls got slower. As the sweet spot on racquets spread and string technology allowed players to hit the ball harder and deeper for longer, the rallies lengthened. The power tennis of Pete Sampras gave way to the Grind – and the gym sessions got tougher.

So, when asked years after his game had become a hard-wired system – particularly in the rough patches of 2010 and 2011 – if he had considered tinkering with his strategy, Murray answered with all the conviction of a First World War trench squaddie: he would continue throwing back grenades in the direction from which they came until they exploded. The transition, that part of the exercise in which a player converts caution to daring, diluting danger before heading for the net or the centre of the court and taking a risk that has been properly calculated, was his puzzle to crack. He was committed to doing so, he said, but not at the risk of giving up his obvious advantage from the back of the court. Murray, who was better equipped than most to switch quickly because of his speed of foot and mind, was reluctant to leave his fox-hole, especially against lesser players, as long as he kept winning. It sprung from experience, because his defence had more often than not been the difference between winning and losing. It was hard to argue with that, on one level. The longer he and his opponent stayed on the court, he reckoned, the more likely it was that he would prevail. He was a last-ball king. If he was fitter, stronger and more persistent in his safety-first tennis, they could not possibly win. They would wilt, because they did not have the patience, proficiency or the legs to trade shot after shot with him in long rallies. Fatigue and boredom would cut them down. He had his own problems with stamina while his body was growing, but he was steadfast in his refusal to change the way he played.

More often than not, Murray was right – except on those occasions when he came up against players who knew as much as he did about attritional tennis, and who would gamble more often and at the right moment. Murray struggled to conquer the tyranny of repetition: the more an athlete does something that works, the less likely he is to change. Repetition had become a religion in all sports, and in those involving the striking of a moving ball, it was considered non-negotiable.

In 2005, John Buchanan, briefly a cricketer of moderate ability with Queensland who found more fulfilment as a teacher than as a doer and who enthused over the teachings of the Chinese warlord Sun Tzu, entered the final stage of his employment as the Australian coach on their Ashes tour of England. Buchanan, tall, lean and bespectacled, could not have looked much more like the university lecturer he once was, and his fierce advocacy of repetition and drills did not sit comfortably with one or two down the back of the class. While Buchanan complained not about the lack of competitive warm-up games before the Test matches but about the lack of time in the nets, 'for executing our drills', Shane Warne, the finest wrist spinner the game had seen, was sniping behind his back. Warne just wanted to get out there and bowl England out. I spent a good deal of time with John on that tour, ghosting his column for the *Observer*, and it was clear that, while a majority of the players signed up for his philosophy, he could not convince Warne. The Blond was a maverick shouting in a room of conformists. Athletes had become modern-day versions of martial artists, moving only to the prompting of memory, almost in a trance of brain-to-muscle function, with not space for innovation. And, even though Warne's discipline demanded mastery of all of those skills, he did not want to be enslaved by method. He argued – rightly, in his case – that to take instruction from someone else would kill his creativity, the weapon he valued most of all in his battle of wits with batsmen.

In his thought-provoking examination of the phenomenon, *Bounce: The Myth of Talent and the Power of Practice*, the excellent *Times* sports columnist Matthew Syed, a former international table tennis player, makes a persuasive argument for the philosophy first posited by the psychologist Anders Ericsson in a study of violinists in Berlin in 1991. 'By the age of twenty,' Ericsson discovered, 'the best violinists had practised an average of ten thousand hours – more than two thousand hours more than the good violinists and more than six thousand hours more than the violinists hoping to become music teachers.' If Warne hit the 10K mark, it was not by design. Murray, however, went for the 10,000 hours – and then some. Could he have been an even better player had he ignored the method? We will never know. But he would not stay imprisoned for ever.

In the early days, however, if people kept telling Murray that he was wrong, that he should experiment with his shot-making, like any athlete whose sport was his living, he would want to know what the odds were, because there was much at stake, and he would need a skilled inquisitor to convince him that the thousands of hours he had spent honing his game could easily be disregarded. His problem was, while he stayed with his strategy, others just as good at defending exploited his reticence. He could see it happening, but seemed powerless to solve the riddle. He went to the Wall of Transition and did not always climb over it, perhaps because of something in his personality, an innate conservatism or distrust of too much outside noise. Federer and Djokovic were the sort of players, especially on hard-court, who found it easier to adapt to circumstances, and Murray suffered in their presence. There were moments in the 2010 final in Melbourne, for instance, when Murray was paralysed in mid-rally, refusing the chance to volley, and instead let the ball bounce and the exchange take its course. Federer, a freer spirit, seized on this nervousness, and his eyes lit up. He won in three sets when he should have been dragged into at least a four-set fight. Federer opened up the wound and, a year later, Djokovic added the salt.

Murray, deeply analytical, knew all this. And, by the time he returned to Melbourne in 2013, he was determined not to allow a repeat of those humiliations. If he lost, he would lose on merit, not through timidity. He was a Slam champion, Djokovic's conqueror in New York, and Federer's at the Olympics. He had, at last, invested in his gifts. Without totally abandoning his bedrock defensive game, he had picked the moments when to strike and had taken them. At Flushing Meadows, he waited until Djokovic was exhausted. It was exquisite torture – although the Serb, who put just as much store in his physical preparation, was reluctant to admit he had been outlasted, outfought. He gave credit to Murray for mastering the difficult conditions and throwing off a monkey that had been on the back of British tennis for seventy-six years (another Perry milestone knocked to one side), but not for being stronger or tougher. That would be too much. 'I think we both did a lot of running,' he said. But Djokovic can rarely have run so much as he did in the first set, which lasted nearly an hour and a half, about a third of the whole contest. He was right: Murray was the deserved winner; he was also the stronger. Neither of them would forget that.

Against Federer at London 2012, Murray hit hard and often from the start, sensing his opponent was worn out not just from the Wimbledon tournament a month earlier but during the whole Olympic tournament, and the win was almost embarrassingly one-sided. He was lifted, too, by a new audience of flag-waving Olympic enthusiasts let loose en masse in the sedate greenery of the All England Club. They made the most of it. So did the Scot, freed for the first time from the grip of the southern elite who wanted him to conform, to throw off his Caledonian cloak, be one of them. If there was a single moment of the final that moved Murray more than any other (and there were many), it might have been when he was soaking in the experience of being an Olympic champion on behalf of the whole country and an eleven-year-old Essex schoolboy, Henry Caplan, barrelled through the crowd to give his hero a hug. 'As soon as Andy Murray won I was crying with joy and hugging my dad,' he later told BBC Radio Essex. 'I told my dad to get off and the next minute I was gone. I was down by the royal bit in front of Federer's mum and dad. Then I hugged Andy Murray. I just thought I had to be there. It was cool.' Murray, whose tear ducts might never run dry, was visibly moved. Theirs was a hug that meant more than a thousand Murray Mounds or Henman Hills.

Now, in Melbourne, Lendl encouraged him to not only feed off these bursts of love but to trust the signals of self-determination that had manifested themselves at Wimbledon – and to understand that, if he applied timely pressure, he could inflict material and visible pain. Murray, it became clear, trusted Lendl more than he had trusted anyone in his career – except maybe his mother. The Czech also held the opinion that an Olympic gold medal was every bit as good as a Major – and he pointed out more than once that Murray's defeats in Slam finals had been against the best players in the world. Losing to them was no disgrace and, once he had wiped the disappointment from his memory, he could start to rebuild his game. Murray was now armed with proof that he could win seven matches in a row over two weeks against probably the best collection of players the game had ever seen. The wounds had healed at last.

Reaching the top of a mountain can do funny things to people. It is a rarefied place. When Christine Truman and Angela Mortimer met up at Wimbledon in 2011, fifty years after they had contested the title there, they revealed vastly different responses to the result of the last all-English final at the All England Club. Mortimer had lost in 1958 to Althea Gibson and now, at twenty-nine, was even more determined to win the ladies championship. When she did, she was sated. 'Once I'd won,' she told Ian Chadband in the *Daily Telegraph*, 'I didn't have any more ambition. Time to start living.' As for Truman, the 6-foot Essex girl who'd charmed the nation since winning the French Open as a bubbly eighteen-year-old two years earlier, defeat drained her of ambition. 'Until then,' she said, 'I'd lived, slept and eaten tennis. It doesn't take much – a few dates with boyfriends, a few other distractions and I never quite recaptured the way I was.'

Murray's reaction to winning was quick and unequivocal: he wanted more. He thrived on the buzz of victory, and he reckoned he had plenty left to prove, to others and to himself. If he had put that much effort in and finally won a Major, it was worth it. So he would keep doing it until there was nothing left to give. The repetition gene was working well for him. Whatever he had said earlier about being able to retire from tennis without a Major as long as he had given it his best shot could be put aside once he had delivered for the nation, and himself. Henman also used to say he could retire a happy man as long as he was convinced he had nothing more to give. Henman got close, but Murray got over the line and, once he had, he repositioned his goals. Would Henman have done so? Most likely, but we will never know. Murray did not want to be a one-Slam champion, as gratifying as that was; he wanted to at least give himself the chance to win more, to move closer to the numbers posted by 'the other three'. If he had played in another era, perhaps, he might have felt differently, but because he played alongside players of such unceasing excellence, he was incentivised to take his tennis further. They all were. There was only one gold standard. It was a matter of honour, almost: not walking away from the tests they set each other every time they were in the same tournament, big or small. The Big Four lived on because, as a phenomenon, it had an organic purpose. It was the club that refused to allow others in. As much as the new boy Murray was committed to keep going, so was the head boy Federer. Nobody wanted to be the first to walk away.

The challenge to keep going and not to rest brought a pressure of a different kind for Murray, neither more intense nor less, just different, and it lifted him, because all his life he has confronted and not shied away from challenges. From days chasing his brother Jamie around the front room of their family home in Dunblane, to beating up his Spanish teacher on the clay of Barcelona, to hunting down a well-struck forehand from Federer in a Grand Slam final, Murray has viewed any affront to his self-belief as something to conquer.

Primarily, he plays tennis for himself. He is not inclined to represent the hopes of others – yet, through circumstances, he has inherited the burden that is given to all athletes good enough to compete at international level. Some are not up to it. In Melbourne Murray most certainly was. That did not make it any easier. Indeed, his fierce competitive juices ensured he could not evade the challenge – as lesser players often do – by consoling himself that he had gone to his limit when, in fact, he might well have fallen short. The dilemma for Murray before his breakthrough in New York was he did not quite know what his limit was, so fine were the distinctions between defeat and victory against any of Federer, Djokovic or Nadal.

And what a waste it would be to give less than one hundred per cent as a reigning Slam champion after the sacrifices of 'our' Miami training camp. (I was not sure my left shoulder would be quite the same, but we move on . . .) First up was Brisbane, a hard-court tournament to get rid of the jet lag and build a bank of good feeling for himself with some solid shot-making in demanding conditions, in a country where the light is as harsh as the judgment. He could not have made a better start.

While the known obstacles were the players he was achingly familiar with, the lesser known were the ones provided by those who viewed him as he viewed those ahead of himself in the rankings: like a hungry wolf. Among them was Grigor Dimitrov, at twenty-one the youngest player in the top fifty, the sort of handsome, intelligent newcomer the game's marketing whizz-kids were crying out for. While he had made a fair impression on Maria Sharapova away from the court, Dimitrov was making an impact with near perfect timing as the Big Four began to show signs of vulnerability, a charismatic and stylish shot-maker who arrived at tournaments alongside the most glamorous player in tennis. Earlier in his young career, the dazzling Bulgarian was unsure of himself. While others were lauding his style and grace, he wondered if that would be enough to survive in the furnace of modern tennis. It was easy enough to move from number 500 in the world to near 80 or so, he confided. If you had the talent – in the space of five months in 2008, for instance, reaching the boys quarter-finals at Roland Garros, winning Wimbledon without dropping a set and taking the US Open title in a flourish before leaping into the Tour proper – that was a journey you would expect to make. From that point onwards, however, it got much harder, he said. The key was consistency – and he could not find it. It was fine winning occasionally and with style, but regularly threatening rather than beguiling opponents took more commitment. Life can be very pleasant for a handsome young man on the Tour; it can be very hell, as well, if he does not often deliver on his potential. Self-esteem is not an infinite commodity, although Dimitrov rarely seemed haunted by the sort of introspection that once had threatened to cripple Murray's ambitions.

In Brisbane, Dimitrov excited his many fans from the start, firing seventeen aces past the Austrian Jürgen Melzer to reach the semi-finals, where he took down the accomplished Marcos Baghdatis after a mid-match blip. The final against Murray reminded Dimitrov that he had a little work to do. The world number 3 blitzed him to love in a tie-break before closing out the final in an hour and a half to retain his title. Grigor accepted he was outclassed, but he was not despondent; he had made that promise to himself, that he would give tennis all he had. As for Murray, Lendl arrived with his golf clubs, professed himself pleased and they headed south for the real business at hand.

The draw is one of those rituals in tennis that has taken on a significance appreciated mainly by sports editors looking for a headline in previews to big tournaments. Still, the fall of the ball did not favour Federer in Melbourne and his fans flooded social media sites to complain he had been unfairly lumbered with having to play seven top fifty players to win the title. The notion that a random draw could be either fair or unfair is plainly nonsensical, but that is the way it was. And Federer had overcome exactly the same challenge once before in compiling his seventeen Slams: three years earlier in Melbourne. Would he be that sharp again for a fortnight? He knew better than anyone that if he were to win again rather than merely do well, then more than likely he would have to beat both Murray and

Djokovic, in whatever order. As it rolled out for him against the quality opponents his supporters feared might wreck his campaign, Federer made a storming start. Benoît Paire (number 46 in the world) lasted 83 minutes and the unpredictable Nikolay Davydenko (40) just under two hours. The faithful began to believe again.

Then came the first of several matches that would light up the tournament: Federer against Bernard Tomic. For so long a child striving against his juvenile tendencies, Tomic indicated he might have found some settling maturing. The combustible but talented son of a Croatian immigrant with a quick temper that would land him in serious trouble later in the year, Tomic had jumped twenty-one places in the rankings by winning in Sydney the week before. He was the legitimate Australian number 1 here, a status confirmed when Lleyton Hewitt, held together by a variety of metal pins, went out in straight sets in the first round, something he had not experienced since his debut sixteen years earlier. Tomic, meanwhile, was on fire. By the time he had secured his appointment against Federer, his unfettered tennis, rich with long-swept ground-strokes from deep and underpinned by a fast-improving serve, was all but irresistible, and he was quick to proclaim his own arrival in terms that allowed no room for self-deprecation.

Drawn in his section of the draw, did Tomic imagine he could beat Federer had been the question earlier in the first week. 'If he gets that far,' he said. 'You don't know what can happen. Tennis is a funny sport. So we'll see.'

That one candid remark – seized upon as arrogant, unfairly so, in my opinion – ensured his encounter with Federer would be more than just another third-round match. Tomic, whatever the power of his ego, had reason to feel good about his form and his prospects, having struck a career-high twenty-six aces past Daniel Brands to get this far for the second year in a row, and was unbroken in thirty-seven service games. He was dangerous – but for how long? Federer did not lose to players such as Tomic in big tournaments. Well, hardly ever. To that point he had won 249 matches in Majors, and lost only 37. In Melbourne, he was 59–2. The only players outside the top ten he had lost to in Slams since he won Wimbledon in 2003 were David Nalbandian (13), Marat Safin (86), Gustavo Kuerten (30), Tomáš Berdych (13) and Jo-Wilfried Tsonga (19) – all of them every bit as dangerous as Tomic.

Nobody born in the 1990s had ever beaten Federer – and young Tomic was not going to be the one to rewrite that little nugget of tennis history. Federer survived a tie-break fight in the second set to subdue his precociousness in just under two hours. When asked what he thought of Tomic's pre-match remarks, he reacted with the measured charm familiar to journalists who had seen him handle loud challenges in the past. It was a revealing response, nonetheless, and it would have added resonance later in the year.

> I'm only one guy out of hundreds out there, so it's important to respect all of us because we make each other better players. We should be thankful for that. I think in our sport, like maybe in golf, you usually do talk nicer about your opponents, about the other players, than in other sports like boxing, for instance. OK, that's an extreme example; I'm just saying we usually are pretty humble. It's just the way we are – because, at the end of the day, we are very friendly with each other in the locker-rooms, in the restaurants. We go for dinner away from the courts, stay in touch. It's a nice tour to be on. I don't know what he said but, when you're younger, you don't quite see that. You always see the opponent on the court, then you judge him just the way he acts on court. That's the way I did it as well when I was younger. I changed my attitude around over the years.

Federer's gift for diplomacy is peerless. He invariably says the right things at the right time. But there is a mannered, almost programmed feel to some of it, as if he is talking for all of

Andy Murray was indoctrinated in the two-fisted method from his earliest days in Dunblane. The determined grimace came naturally

Novak Djokovic, like Murray, was two-fisted from the start, and even as a four-year-old he had the balance and poise of a natural athlete

Young Rafael Nadal was originally right-handed but switched following encouragement by many including his uncle Toni, his lifelong coach, and his famous footballing uncle Miguel (pictured with him here in Mallorca). What a smart conversion it was

Roger Federer's rise as a prodigy arrived at Wimbledon, where he collected his first trophies in 1998, winning the boys' doubles title with the Belgian Olivier Rochus as well as the singles

Marian Vajda has coached Djokovic since June 2006. He grew weary of the travel, however, and so Boris Becker joined the player's staff on a short-term contract at the end of 2013

Football is popular among the leading players on the Tour, and Djokovic's balance and dexterity of foot on the tennis court are often on show in pick-up matches

Nothing lasts for ever in tennis. Just as Djokovic was letting Vajda take
a back seat, so Federer parted company with Pete Sampras's old mentor
Paul Annacone (pictured here), and brought in Stefan Edberg

Of the Big Four, Federer gives the impression of having to try the least, but
he trains hard in his own way, concentrating on flexibility and quick body
movement. Here he strengthens his deltoids, the muscles that drive those
tremendous single-handed backhands, by flinging a heavy ball

The core and back muscles form the engine room that players rely on for power and stability in the shot. Here Murray works on his upper-body strength at Queen's under the guidance of his former fitness coach Jez Green

Murray and Ivan Lendl formed a hugely successful partnership, working together from January 2012 to March 2014

Before the start of the 2013 season, Murray finally let a few tennis writers sample some of his brutal training techniques in Miami. Warming up on the soft sand, he is joined by Neil Harman (*The Times*), Simon Briggs (*Daily Telegraph*), Mike Dickson (*Daily Mail*), Colin Duncan (*Scottish Daily Record*) and, doing his best not to disgrace the *Guardian* and the *Observer*, the author

When Toni Nadal started training his nephew as a small boy, he made him play on rough courts with old balls to teach him how to deal with adversity. The facilities at Rafa's current Mallorcan base have been upgraded a little since those days. Toni, a jobbing pro as a player, oversees his shot-making, while physio Rafael Maymo and fitness coach Joan Forcades supervise his work in the gym

Djokovic tries hard to keep his family and coaching unit tight-knit. Not many are allowed into the inner sanctum, seen here celebrating his win over Murray in the 2011 Australian Open final

There was no hiding the announcement of his engagement to Jelena Ristic after eight years together, however. 'Meet my fiancée and future wife,' Djokovic tweeted in September 2013, with accompanying picture

Only one of the Big Four had married by 2013, and Federer values the company of his wife Mirka (a former Tour player) as well as, occasionally, his father Robert. Both of them are seen here watching him at the Gerry Weber Open in Halle, Roger's only title of the year

Nadal has said that the break-up of his parents' marriage in 2009 affected him deeply, and he was relieved when they were later reconciled. His sister Isabel, mother Ana Maria Parera, girlfriend Maria Francisca Perello and father Sebastian gathered in Rome in May to watch him play in the Internazionali BNL d'Italia, one of the ten titles Rafa won in his remarkable comeback year

Murray and Nadal have been friends since the Scot went to Spain to train as a teenager, and his mother Judy met up with Rafa's uncle Toni for coffee at Wimbledon in June

The Federer twin girls, Charlene Riva and Myla Rose, are often courtside with their mother. She gave birth to a second set of twins, Leo and Lenny, in May 2014

Andy and his left-handed brother Jamie, pictured at the 2012 Monte Carlo Masters, have enjoyed success in doubles but do not get the opportunity to play together often because of their schedules. When they were young, they were inseparable

Just as Nadal endured a parental break-up, so did Murray. But Judy and Willie (far left and second from the right) do meet at events, this time cheering Andy on at the 2009 ATP World Tour Finals in London, with Jamie (far right) and Andy's long-time friend Ross Hutchins in the front row

tennis, for the game's reputation and for the integrity of the Tour, the benefit of the sponsors and the all-round well-being of his fellow players. He is the game's ultimate ambassador. I imagine that one day, if he chooses, he would make a good politician – but not necessarily one of any radical tendency.

Federer's 250th Slam victory came, then, thirteen years after his first; and that was in Melbourne too, 'one of my favourite places', as he said later. Players always heap praise on tournaments where they do well. Federer's dilemma was he did well everywhere.

The third round also saw the exit of Gaël Monfils, always a sad moment, but again he left us with memories to cherish. While the Frenchman's eccentricities illuminate any tournament, they do not bring him a tangible dividend very often; in fifty-five matches in 2013, the Frenchman did not win a single tournament, although $634,168 in prize money probably eased the pain. Here he took away two wins and a five-set loss to his compatriot Gilles Simon, but not before sharing a seventy-one-shot rally in the ninth game of the second set, which ended with a weary backhand by Monfils sailing high and wide. He had the most curious of tournaments, even by his standards. In three matches that took 11 hours and 5 minutes, he struck sixty-five aces and forty-nine double-faults – including the rare double of twenty-plus of each (30–23) in his second-round win over Yen-hsun Lu. If there were no other incentive to watch tennis than the travails of Gaël Monfils, the sport would still be a top-drawer circus act.

Federer had not time for such fripperies. After seeing off Tomic and adding the rising Canadian Milos Raonic to his cast of dazzled opponents in quick time, he turned back the more stubborn challenge of Tsonga in the quarters. He felt good . . . and he looked good. There was fluency and power in his movement and a fresh sparkle in his eyes. Federer had rekindled his hopes of reaching a fifth final, comfortable in the knowledge that when he had done so in the past, he had won the title.

And there before him in the semi-finals stood Murray, whom he had so regally dismissed in 2010, leaving the Scot in a lachrymose heap. But this was a different man confronting him now, a player who had not let disappointment break him, however deep he had fallen three years earlier. This version of Murray was stronger physically and mentally, hardened by his experiences, not soured, and he had by his side a coach whose stare could crack a pavement, a knowledgeable rock of a man who remained impervious to scrutiny behind dark glasses, chin planted for hours on an out-turned palm as he leaned forward in the player's box like Nero overlooking the gladiators. There would be no tears this time, but there would be grief.

To understand Federer the man, as opposed to Federer the tennis player, a look at where he lives shines a little light. When he is not in a rented house in Wimbledon, a nice hotel somewhere else on the Tour or in the sports celebrities' low-tax haven of Dubai, he calls home Wallerau, a small town an hour's quick drive south-east of Basel, alongside 7,000 citizens who regularly return a conservative candidate to represent their canton and protect their pleasingly low rates of tax. Wallerau looks as peaceful as Federer's face. He has not always exuded serenity, of course. Famously, he was a volatile teenager, as quick to anger as tears, an impetuous and easily distracted student, but, once he had come through his ponytail stage, he found a calmness that would underpin nearly every aspect of his meticulously organised life and his equally tidy tennis. Federer Inc. became a market leader in good manners.

However, the quiet man from quiet Wallerau was moved to rare and angry animation at a crucial point in the twelfth game of the fourth set of the second semi-final of the 2013 Australian Open. This single incident was as revealing as any of the interviews I have done for this book. It lasted maybe fifteen seconds, but it echoed for a lot longer.

Murray was leading 6–4, 6–7(5), 6–3 and within a few points

of closing out the match in the fourth set. He'd played one or two unusually loose shots earlier, but had composed himself nicely after a tight second set and was building up to a solid finish. He sensed Federer was tiring. He had extinguished Djokovic's fire in New York; he could do the same to Federer in Melbourne. One more surge of concentration, a few more well-placed winners, and he would be back in the locker-room. Then he would head for an ice bath to soothe his weary bones before returning to face the press. Except it didn't quite work out that way.

Of the various interpretations of the incident, the most plausible is that Federer felt Murray had violated an unwritten code, the one that says a player should not try to influence line calls by any faltering stroke-play that hints his opponent's ball had gone out. Stopping in the shot is considered such a transgression. It began in the seventh game when, serving at 3–4 and ad, Murray had hit a half-hearted reply to a ball that landed at his feet, then motioned to the linesman, but was overruled on review for deuce. He protested to the chair umpire that he genuinely thought the ball was out. Murray held, but both players were stoking the fire, looking for any weakness, any advantage.

Federer held for 5–4, but not before being turned with an exquisite lob and sending an inelegant response into the stands, where it was caught by Shane Warne, the retired Australian cricket legend and still active gambler, who had backed the Swiss to reach the final. Warne smiled for the cameras but not for the bookies that night.

Having squandered his advantage, Murray was returned to a state of mild anxiety. He did not want to relive the experience of losing to Federer in Melbourne again. At 6–5 and serving for the match, he sensed he had him for the taking. Surely, it would not be long now. He fired a brutal forehand from the baseline with a last-minute flick of his powerful wrist, rifling the ball past the advancing Federer for a winner that left him stranded and bemused. The Swiss stopped and, loudly enough to be heard at courtside, issued the Scot a stinging rebuke: 'You fucking stopped.' The earlier indiscretion was at the forefront of Federer's thoughts. He was not going to let it go, even if the point had been lost.

Once the oath had been uttered, Murray, looking as pleased with the response as with winning the point, looked up at Federer from fifteen yards away as if challenged to a gunfight on the dusty streets of Dodge City. He said nothing. But, opening his chest and facing his opponent with all the aggression he could muster, he let a sneer cross his face that shouted, 'Want some? I'm here.' As the crowd craned forward to take in the building drama, there was enough electricity in the air to power a small town. The last time Murray had let his temper get the better of him was in Rome five years earlier during a night-match against Juan Martín del Potro, who during a change-over in the second set had taken a cheap shot at Murray's mother, who was cheering him on from the stands. That night, Murray gathered his composure and won. In this contretemps, however, his anger undid him, at least briefly. The placid man from Wallerau struck back, levelled at 6-all and took the tie-break.

Murray was rattled, but he got a grip on his nerves and, when they resumed in the fifth set, he clinically broke down the tiring Federer to wrap up the match in exactly four hours. It was the ugliest of their twenty contests and would not be quickly forgotten, whatever the platitudes afterwards.

Murray was relieved at winning and elated to be in the final again, and the last thing he wanted was to be drawn into a row that was over. But he saw the questions coming. 'I think Roger raised his game,' he said. 'Sometimes guys need to get emotion into the match. But it's not relevant. There are no hard feelings. I wasn't that surprised. Stuff like that happens daily in tennis matches. The stuff that some people say on football pitches and in basketball and all sorts of sports . . . it was very mild in comparison to what happens in other sports. It's just one of those things.'

It was a bit more than that. It was a conflagration of genuine bitterness between two athletes who spend more time in each other's company than is probably healthy for either of them. The release of emotion that Murray referred to was a volcanic moment, an eruption that had been building for some time. The pretence was over. It was not that they hated each other, but there was antagonism in that single exchange that bore testament to deeper, older wounds. At last, Murray could put the 2010 final behind him.

For Federer – who recently had been voted 'the second most trusted person in the world after Nelson Mandela' – the aftermath was a time for reconciliation and diplomacy. He was not going to let the fight drag on, either. 'It wasn't a big deal anyway,' he said. 'We just looked at each other one time. That's OK, I think, in a three-and-a-half-hour match. We were just checking each other out for a bit. That wasn't a big deal for me. I hope not for him.'

Djokovic, who beat Ferrer in the earlier semi-final, was already through to the final, without acrimony – although he had done well to recover from his earlier fourth-round war with Stanislas Wawrinka. Only Berdych had broken Djokovic's serve in sixty-three previous service games in the tournament; the Swiss broke him seven times – and still he could not win. The Serb's inner strength was phenomenal. For Wawrinka, glorious defeat probably changed his career and he went on to have his best ever season. He would play Djokovic three more times in 2013 – and come perilously close again to tipping him out of a Slam. Close means very little in professional sport, though. Djokovic had found a way to win again, just as Murray had found a way to play against him at Flushing Meadows. They could hardly be better matched at this stage of their careers.

Having despatched Federer, Murray offered a most curious critique on the prospect of playing Djokovic less than forty-eight hours later in the final: 'I'm going to have to be ready for the pain. I hope it's a painful match because that will mean it's a good one.'

Murray got what he wanted. For that matter, so did Djokovic. Except Djokovic got to enjoy the experience a deal more by lifting the trophy after 4 hours and 50 minutes of high-quality masochism. There was also the feather – the one that caught Murray's eye on the court during the second-set tie-break. He double-faulted. He lost the set. He lost the match. He also lost a good amount of skin on his feet from blisters, which everyone got to see in ugly detail on the big screen. But that did not bother him. Nor did he complain too much about the feather. He was as calm in defeat as I had seen him, a maturing rather than angry athlete, someone who had soothed the growling within his heart. He surely would be a better player for it. Murray limped away from court like a fighter who'd given a good account of himself, taken his licks, and, unlike his previous defeats in Melbourne, there were no scars. None that we could see, anyway. I found it hard, though, to forget his battle-cry before the final . . . Pain is good: a mantra for our times.

5

A Feat of Clay

Viña del Mar, Chile, 7 February 2013

Rafael Nadal is nervous. He is quite often nervous, be it against Novak Djokovic in the final of a Grand Slam, or facing an unknown wildcard in Monte Carlo. Today, about as far away from home as it is possible to be on Planet Tennis, his nerves do not belong to him. Nor do his legs, particularly his right knee, the body part he trusts least. Until it supports him with some degree of certainty, it is his enemy. What is about to happen to the Spaniard will determine if he will carry on playing – not just this year, but at all. He can afford to lose, but he cannot afford to collapse. He looks up at the warm skies, goes through his ritual shirt-tugging, gives his strapped knee one final rub and gets down to business.

～

A week or so after Murray and Djokovic flew out of Melbourne to recuperate in their respective torture chambers on the other side of the world, the tennis caravan rumbled on. On that first Wednesday in February, Federico Delbonis, a talented young Argentinian of ambition with little to show for it, stood on the giving clay of Club Naval de Campo Las Salinas in Viña del Mar, looked across the net and saw a legend in a purple shirt and grey shorts. While Delbonis hoped for a victory that would light up his career, he suspected, as well he might, that Rafael Nadal was going to win their second-round match in Chile's VTR Open, a low-profile 250 event on the ATP World Tour that would attract exactly zero interest anywhere beyond the enthusiasts' websites and local media were it not for the presence of the visiting Spaniard. Nadal had just logged twenty-nine different stamps in his passport, and he had a couple more to add before rejoining the main body of the Tour.

Delbonis, known to his friends back in Azul – a pleasant, medium-sized city 200 miles south of Buenos Aires – as 'Gordo', was determined to play his shots, to have his moment. He was twenty-three, stood 6 foot 3 inches and had a wicked forehand. South America was his home. So was clay. And Nadal, after all, had not played a competitive match in seven months, having lost shockingly to 100th-ranked Lukáš Rosol at Wimbledon the previous summer. After losing to Rosol, Nadal chose to rest his fragile knees in the company of anxious friends and optimistic surgeons. Now, 222 days after his unexpected departure from Wimbledon, he was not entirely confident the tendinitis that had plagued him on and off for years, worsening to the point of agony in 2012, had eased sufficiently to let him play with his old freedom and muscularity. There was no option but to try. Actually, there was an alternative: retirement. At twenty-six. So here he was in South America for the first time since 2005 – when he was a carefree teenager – contemplating the challenge of a player as unknown to him as he himself must have been to anyone else when he was finding his way on the Tour, a talent still to be nurtured. He would be merciless in his execution of young Señor Delbonis.

Nadal's long-ago compatriots, the conquistadores, brought railway tracks and sugar mills to the lovely Chilean valleys that wrap themselves around crisp, white beaches on Chile's Pacific coast. The former world number 1 brought a killer forehand, powered by iron wrists and more lethal than Delbonis's by a factor of at least five. His callow hitting partner for the day took just five of the seventeen games contested, although he did break

Nadal's serve once. So, 'Gordo' went home to Azul happy enough. He'd shared a court with the greatest clay-courter of them all, nudged his ranking up to 128 in the world and banked a cheque for $7,100. There were worse ways to be embarrassed in public. And there would be other days, other courts . . . and another legend to challenge before the year was out.

Without the vanquished, of course, there would be no conquistadores. Delbonis and several hundred like him were as important to the fabric of tennis as was Nadal, although that would be a hard sell to any of the TV executives and tournament organisers chewing fingernails that afternoon back in New York, London and Paris. They desperately wanted Nadal returned to full working order. He was too young to walk away from such golden times. There was, they hoped, still some juice in his rivalry with Federer, whose own roadshow had rolled lucratively through South America before Christmas. In six cities in Brazil, Argentina and Colombia, with the tournaments and their backers each stumping up around $1 million a performance for Federer to stage exhibitions of little consequence but much beauty, he had thrilled a constituency that previously could adore him only from a distance. Federer was bigger in South America than the Pope.

Now, Federer having returned to Europe after the Australian Open to prepare for the rest of the Tour, it was Nadal's turn to charm a new live audience. He did not win the tournament in Viña del Mar, but he beat his Spanish friend Daniel Gimeno-Traver in the third round and then overcame the dangerous Frenchman Jeremy Chardy, before losing to Delbonis's fellow Argentine, the 73rd-ranked Horacio Zeballos, over three tight sets in the final. He was content. He was back. And he would lose no more on his Latin clay comeback. He defeated David Nalbandian to win the title in Sao Paulo, with the Brazilian footballer Ronaldo an interested spectator (they later shared notes on injuries and comebacks), then made a mockery of

David Ferrer's number 4 ranking in Acapulco, winning 6–0, 6–2 in an embarrassingly one-sided final that took everyone by surprise. From the under-foot comfort of the red dirt, Nadal, encouraged now rather than anxious, headed for the hard courts of southern California, and from there he would launch the most extraordinary fight-back from adversity the game had seen since Andre Agassi rescued his career from self-destruction in the later years of the previous century.

Agassi, the flamboyant Las Vegan who played in an era that overlapped the current one, has a story, richly chronicled, that lends perspective and scale to the world inhabited by Nadal and his peers. Fighting on two fronts – against personal demons and a body he could no longer trust – he recovered from number 141 in the world in November 1997 to become top dog again in a little over a year and a half. Nobody has matched that scale of fight-back. It was a Mount Everest of a climb, without a rope. Agassi has revisited his struggle in an award-winning autobiography with the aid of an astute ghost writer, and one of his telling revelations (apart from the wigs and the drugs) is that he was born with spondylo-listhesis, the separation of the bottom vertebra from the rest of the spine. This condition gave him a pigeon-toed walk and an excuse, but, although lumbered with the former, he refused to use the latter. Instead, he did what champions do: he coped. Agassi had compacted nerves in the lower part of his back that had nowhere to move, inducing a sort of internal claustrophobia; on top of that, he suffered two herniated discs. He was a prisoner of genetic weakness, but was compensated by genius. Like his back, he would not bend. It was as well, however, that he also was gifted physically in other ways.

Brad Langevad, an Australian biomechanic who has worked with several leading players (and operated to a decent level on the American college circuit), told me once he had only ever come across two international-class athletes with near perfect body mechanics. One was the West Indian cricketer, Brian Lara; the other was Agassi.

> They have the sort of unthinking link of synchronised movement from toes to finger tips, all the way through their muscles and joints, and knees, hips, shoulders, elbows and wrists, that you could only pray for as an athlete. I call it unconscious consciousness, natural movement that an athlete just knows instinctively is there. He does not have to think about it. It is hard-wired into his very being. It is not the same as that which comes through muscle memory, which is grafted on, almost, through repetition [the now venerated '10,000 hours' that sports scientists talk about]. When Lara hit a cover drive, for instance, it started in his feet and rippled all the way through to his bat on to the ball in a second. Agassi, too. He did not have to think when he hit a tennis ball. It was built into his DNA. I have analysed the videos of Agassi's stroke-making and it could not be bettered, the racquet coming in a smooth, powerful circle nearly every time, hitting the ball with absolute maximum efficiency. It is a gift, wherever it came from.

As Pete Sampras remarked once: 'When Andre's on, forget it. He does practically everything better than anybody else.'

So, despite the malfunctions of his lower back, Agassi was, in the American parlance, a natural. Uncoachable, some might say – although his uncompromisingly tough father, Mike, who boxed in the Olympics for Iran, drilled young Andre for hours at their humble house on the outskirts of Las Vegas before entrusting his teenage jewel for polishing at Nick Bolletieri's famous Florida academy. They would all claim some input; everyone wants a piece. Anyway, I watched the videos of Lara and Agassi. What Langevad claimed, appeared correct to this untrained eye. These elite athletes were blessed in a way that makes mortals jealous. But what the videos did not show, certainly in Agassi's case, were the deeper, invisible fault lines, there from birth and ineradicable. As great a ball-striker and instinctive winner as he was, Agassi's major triumph was over his own body. Later, he would have the same fight with his mind.

As Agassi put it in his book, *Open: An Autobiography*: 'When the nerves protest their cramped quarters, when they send out distress signals, a pain runs up and down my leg that makes me suck in my breath and speak in tongues. At such moments the only relief is to lie down and wait.'

Famously, that fate befell him in the car park at Flushing Meadows at 2 a.m. one morning in September 2006, after he'd somehow beaten Baghdatis, the number 8 in the world at the time. Agassi was so racked by the pain racing through his spent body he could not complete the walk of a couple of hundred yards to the car of the Australian coach Darren Cahill. There he was, an ageing and crippled former world number 1, stretched out on the cold ground, staring at the night sky, immobilised and helpless, the very antithesis of a champion. He was paying the price, as he did for much of his career.

Agassi adds: 'Sometimes, however, the moment arrives in the middle of a match. Then the only remedy is to alter my game – swing differently, run differently, do everything differently. That's when my muscles spasm. Everybody avoids change; muscles can't abide it. Told to change, my muscles join the spinal rebellion, and soon my whole body is at war with itself.' Even allowing for the paid-for poetry of his skilled ghost – the distinguished *New York Times* writer J. R. Moehringer (who says he spent 250 hours talking to his subject and the same amount of time again reading Jung and Freud in order to understand him) – that is a vivid picture of the sacrifice that professional athletes are required to pay to take the prize. Coincidentally, it mirrors the experience of Andy Murray at both the French Open in 2012 and in Rome nearly a year later, when, on each occasion, his lower back seized up, rendering him temporarily and publicly crippled.

Agassi's last match – just after his victory over Baghdatis – was a defeat. In ninety-nine per cent of cases in any sport, however good the athlete is, that is the closing sentence, partly because defeat delivers the undiluted truth: it's over. Agassi was number 39 in the world rankings and thirty-six years on the planet. He'd played competitive tennis for twenty-one of those years. And that day, in the third round of the 2006 US Open, a title he had won in 1994 and 1999, Benjamin Becker, a German with a familiar name but no link to its other, more illustrious owner, proved too strong over four sets, and that was it for Andre. He had drugged himself up to the gills with painkillers, but it was not the waning of the magic pills and needles that made the tears well during the most emotional goodbye speech anyone present could remember. It was a beautiful farewell, and this is what Agassi said when he took the courtside microphone to address the New York crowd.

> The scoreboard said I lost today, but what the scoreboard doesn't say is what it is I have found. Over the last twenty-one years I have found loyalty: you have pulled for me on the court, and also in life. I have found inspiration: you have willed me to succeed, sometimes even in my lowest moments. And I have found generosity. You have given me your shoulders to stand on, to reach for my dreams – dreams I could have never reached without you. Over the last twenty-one years I have found you, and I will take you and the memory of you with me for the rest of my life.

Over the top? A bit schmaltzy, a bit American? Certainly. But heartfelt. Agassi, whom the veteran commentator and author Bud Collins once said had gone from punk to paragon, might not have had it exactly right about the long-haired rebel on either count, but Agassi was always someone tennis could not ignore.

Nadal saw only the remnants of Agassi's greatness across a net. He dropped a set, beating him in the final of the Montreal

Masters in 2005, and Agassi forced a tie-break before succumbing in three sets in the second round at Wimbledon the following year. But they spoke the same language of pain.

Nadal had no fight with recreational drugs, no existential inner turmoil, and no penchant for wigs or melodrama, but he would recognise the physical trauma that Agassi had to accommodate. For Nadal, his fault line resided originally in the ligaments that held his ankles together. They were not strong enough to reliably resist the torque his hugely physical game drove through his frame. When Nadal moved, so did the clay beneath his feet, violently. He was not a dancer like Federer, who is the Floyd Mayweather junior of their sport; he was a mini-Tyson, a quick-footed slugger, impatient to get from A to B and committed to full-blooded contact rather than feathered nuances.

When Nadal first consulted doctors about his problem in 2004 – after being forced to pull out of the French Open because of stress fractures to his left ankle – he was just eighteen (and had yet to visit South America). The inherent weakness would have to be managed because it was not going to go away, he was told. Three years later, his uncle Toni let slip a family secret, and Rafa was furious.

'It's very serious,' Toni Nadal said after Federer had thrashed young Rafa 6–4, 6–1 in the final of the Masters Cup in Shanghai, about an old injury that had flared again late in the 2007 season. 'I don't know [if it's career-threatening]. He's been affected by an injury to his foot since 2005. He has to learn how to live with it and so far he has managed for two years. His problem is that he has to play to maintain his physical tone and fitness levels. There's no other way to do it than by competing.' The heavy schedule was interrupted twice that year. Nadal had to pull out of a Davis Cup tie in March and was burdened by the injury throughout the US Open in September.

The player replied quickly to his uncle's revelations, however. 'This injury hasn't stopped me competing at the top level for over two years. The story that has come out is totally false.' Then his PR machine went into overdrive to repair the damage. 'This is nothing new, and it's not really serious,' said his loyal spokesman, Benito Perez-Barbadillo, who still speaks for him today. 'It's something he lives with. It's definitely not career-threatening. He's had a very successful year. He was the guy who played the second-most number of matches and he wouldn't do that if it was a serious problem. Rafa is not happy with what came out. He arrived back from a holiday in Egypt today and he starts training tomorrow, and plays an exhibition in Malaga at the weekend.'

That was a lot of protesting for a problem that allegedly did not exist. It existed, all right, and soon it would move from his ankles to his knees. When those pivotal joints gave up on him the following year, forcing him to quit in the quarter-finals of the Paris Masters against the Russian Nikolay Davydenko, he said: 'I felt the pain a lot when I woke up this morning. When I push [on my knee] I feel a sharp pain.' What he added was intriguing. 'I think with this calendar it's very difficult to play a lot of years in a row . . . I think the ATP and everybody have to think about these things happening at the end of the season.'

That night, Federer also pulled out of the tournament, after his quarter-final against the American James Blake, complaining of back pain. Nadal bumped into him in the locker-room and said, 'So, we're both going home early tonight.' They smiled, weakly, picked up their bags and went their separate ways.

Over the next four years Nadal had to play through the pain. He did not lack courage or commitment, but the evidence was building that he could not carry on indefinitely defying either the doctors or the insistent questions from tennis writers. He collapsed against Murray in the Australian Open in 2010 and, when he left Wimbledon grimacing after Rosol played the match of his life in 2012, he could deny the facts no longer. He bid us *adios* for a little while, although nobody was sure when or if he would return. Seven months later, he was back, rebuilt in body and spirit. It was a hugely impressive effort, a grand resurrection.

Although Nadal prevailed in that first comeback match against Delbonis in Viña del Mar, the vineyard by the sea, and nearly everywhere elsewhere on this road-trip, there was uncertainty in the air. People were worried. What had been whispered for a little while was growing into a disturbing crescendo in those edgy months at the beginning of 2013. The rivalry that had defined the sport for nearly a decade – that between Nadal and Federer – was, it seemed, either already over or coming to an inconclusive end. And it soon became clear that the unreliable element in the equation was not the player who had returned from the brink of retirement with a dodgy knee (or was it two?), but the ever-fit Federer, a player who had been unmoved by such earthly considerations as tendinitis. Alone among leading players, he had never quit during a match. There was that back twinge in Paris, certainly, and he had to cope with a dose of glandular fever which briefly cut him down – although not with such finality as it did Robin Söderling – but Federer was considered virtually immune from the physical demands of his calling. What ran counter to this view was the candour of the scoreboard. Nadal was winning. Federer wasn't.

The two had endured and enjoyed much together – but how many titanic collisions did they have left? Nobody could be sure. Rarely close – except when thrown together for commercial promotions – they did not waver in their respect for each other. As to who was the best, that is a debate that will rage until long after they have both left the stage, but what matters more, on balance, is their joint contribution to the sport and our universal entertainment. It is safe to say that neither would have been as good without the other. They lifted each other to Olympian heights in so many memorable collisions, and there was nobody to seriously challenge their hegemony for at least five years of the most amazing tennis any of us had been privileged to witness. Now, however, just as Nadal was putting himself back together again, Federer began to fade. At first his decline was almost imperceptible, then it came at a quicker, more insistent beat, as he lost inexplicably to players he should have been dismissing with regal ease.

The legendary Federer poise remained intact on court, but not always when he had to go through the compulsory post-defeat examination. These experiences could be irritating for him, and uncomfortable for all concerned. He was patient and courteous still, but less inclined to suffer what he regarded as premature and repeated suggestions that he was no longer the player who had quietly and elegantly terrorised his contemporaries. He still had a present, he maintained, to go with a glorious past. He was still hungry, still ambitious and still good enough to win more championships. Mostly, he was utterly convincing; occasionally, though, he sounded like an ex-champ, a fighter hustling for another shot at the title. Nobody enjoyed the spectacle. And nobody could think of a way to avoid it. This was human sporting drama unfolding by the tournament. Federer returned from South America considerably richer but not much wiser about his prospects for what promised to be another challenging campaign, perhaps his toughest yet.

Conquering South America, meanwhile, had been a cathartic experience for Nadal, although it was not without its moments of anxiety. The blood-thump in his heart was always strong; it was the ligaments, tendons and muscles of his creaking knees that took the pounding and they had come perilously close to disintegrating again. He was so scared they would give up on him that there were serious discussions with his closest advisers in the early days of his comeback about whether or not it was worth carrying on. Even when he had come through the fire of competition and added $313,100 in prize money to his account, alongside 900 ranking points, he did not feel entirely vindicated in his decision. In Indian Wells in March he revealed: 'Two weeks ago, two weeks before, I didn't really know if I would be here playing. After seven months I'm not gonna take crazy risks. But I am here.' Nadal had always been prepared to suffer on court; he knew that tennis had changed, demanded more sacrifice than before, because he had been part of that revolution. The difference was, he had looked retirement in the eye, and he did not blink. But it was a close thing.

Nadal spent as much time in the gym as his muscled peers. The days of the gentle game were vanishing memories. It was one of the sport's lingering paradoxes: the image and the reality. Tennis did not demand the life-threatening commitment of boxing but, in many respects, the disparate disciplines had grown closer. Tennis players were now fighters too. They did not bleed, but they bruised. And they fell. They quit on their stool sometimes, as well. They called more often for medical succour, battered warriors slumped at the side of the court, their hamstrings and back muscles crying for relief, old groin strains flaring, ankles and wrists burning under the strain of relentless rallying. Surrender became the chosen exit for an increasing number of players. There would be other days, they reckoned. This was a mantra especially attractive for those contestants who had gone up to the mark knowing they were not favoured to win. These were the pragmatists. They were *Mastermind*-level experts on airline schedules and had all the emergency cab numbers at hand for a quick exit. They knew the cheapest hotels and bars and restaurants. None stayed after losing. None. They all moved on. For the vast majority of the field, the whittling-down process at a big tournament was a familiar and dwindling humiliation. It was built into their psyche. Not that they did not give all they had. But all they had was rarely good enough to get them into a second week of a Slam or, some-times, the second round of a Futures tournament. Tennis had become unapologetically gladiatorial, and not a little ugly sometimes.

For Federer, the dilemma as he embarked on the 2013 campaign was neither entirely mental nor physical. Although he was the reigning Wimbledon champion, he had looked less imposing in the months since. The damage was done to his spirit, and it was done gradually and publicly. If it were hard for him to grapple with the possibility that his days at the zenith of the sport were numbered, it was virtually impossible for his disciples to accept that growing reality. Many refused to do so; they did not want to believe the evidence before their eyes.

As early in this process as July 2010, I received a letter from one of Federer's ardent fans, Professor Elizabeth Wilson. In part, she wrote: 'The views of political journalists and commentators may be challenged by letters pages, blogs, etc., but such avenues don't exist when it comes to sport, so I see no other way than by writing to you individually of voicing my dismay at your unfair reportage of Roger Federer. This has been evident for months, but my remarks relate specifically to your article in today's *Observer*, in which you append to your article on Tiger Woods an egregious repetition of the view that Federer was mean spirited, a bad loser etc. when he referred to injury after his defeat by [Tomáš] Berdych at Wimbledon.'

The point of Professor Wilson's letter, in short, was to challenge my contention that after Berdych had beaten Federer in the quarter-finals at the All England Club that year (to that point, the biggest win of the Czech's career), the Swiss broke the convention of complaining that he had been carrying an injury. Few players will be drawn into using this as an excuse in defeat, mainly because it does not play well in the locker-room and because it also hints at vulnerability. Perhaps I was hard on Federer for pointing this out; certainly Berdych did not think so when informed that his greatest win had been demeaned because he had secured it against a stricken opponent. He was, if anything, a good deal angrier than was Professor Wilson. 'We all get niggles,' he said.

There is not another player bar John McEnroe from the past few decades I would rather watch than Federer (hardly a contentious assertion, granted). His is a universally admired talent. He is, if you will, Fred Astaire to Nadal's Gene Kelly, a lithe, ethereal version of a more obviously robust and energetic counterpart. But it is not my job to be a fan. It is my job to be a witness. And that day I witnessed not only the earliest inklings of frailty in Federer's tennis at the highest level, but a dip in protocol. It was unlike Federer. It betrayed doubt and uncharacteristic tetchiness. That all passed, and he was playing brilliantly again soon enough. He reached the final against Murray in the Rogers Cup in Toronto, and beat Mardy Fish to win in Cincinnati, the warm-up for the US Open where, after struggling on early visits, he had already won three finals. At Flushing Meadows that year, however, Djokovic put him out in the semi-finals when Federer had the match in the palm of his normally steady right hand. It would prove to be a key result. Psychologically, it was devastating for Federer. Djokovic was making a serious move now and would soon hit a surely unrepeatable peak in 2011, when he went forty-three matches unbeaten. For Federer, there would be another finals loss to Murray, in Shanghai, revenge over Djokovic in his home town, Basel, then a concluding victory against Nadal in the season-ending ATP World Tour Finals in London. He had much to savour. He also had reason to wonder. Was he coming down from the mountain?

When Pete Sampras lost to Federer's relatively unknown compatriot George Bastl in the second round of Wimbledon in 2002, he found himself in the unfamiliar position of having to explain not only why he lost to a player then ranked 145 in the world, but also where it left his future. After pleasantries, one direct inquisitor finally stepped up and put it straight: 'You've always said that, no matter what happens in the season, when the grass courts come around, when Wimbledon happens, there's a spirit that comes to you, a fire. Are we going to see you back here, and are we going to see you in the winner's circle again? What's the future for Pete Sampras?'

Sampras paused, his brow wrinkling above those heavy eyebrows, and replied: 'Well . . . the future is flying home. That's the immediate future . . . But long-distance future? I plan on being back. You know, I'm not going to end my time here with that loss. And so . . .'

During that match, played out on Court 2, where so many good players had come to grief, away from the excitement of the show courts, Sampras pulled out a piece of paper in one of the more troubling passages of the contest and read it to himself. He has never disclosed what was written on that piece of paper, saying only, 'It was just some notes, just some thoughts and a letter that I was reading just to keep me positive and, you know, just to . . . you get your mind set on what's happening out there. It's nice to have something else to look at, think about. So it was something that I pulled out and read and it made me feel a little better . . .'

But he did reveal who it was from: his wife.

The Australian coach, Bob Brett, had suggested beforehand that Sampras had been pulled back to the field in 2002, that he had not grown his tennis to hold off the next generation (which included Federer, of course). Sampras said this: 'I still feel like my game is very dangerous. I always will have my serve. Players are better today, and I'm not as intimidating as I was five years ago. Players are better. I need to work on some things and start getting my confidence going. [But] I'm not going to give in to the critics. I'm going to stop on my own terms, not when someone else thinks I should stop.'

Sampras and Federer played each other just once in 2001, at Wimbledon as it happens, and Switzerland prevailed over five sets on that day too. This is inevitably how eras end, unexpectedly, with sorrow and doubt. Boris Becker had always said, 'If I go to a Slam I cannot win, I will stop.' Sampras went to one more Slam after Wimbledon, won it, and stopped. But it was tough to walk away that September in New York, after he'd beaten Agassi. Really tough. Privately, he wanted to carry on. But he didn't. Sampras pulled back and did what Becker suggested great players should do.

Now the dilemma belonged to Federer. The parallels were scary. Increasingly, he could not confidently rely on his genius to extricate him from trouble. Once he could swing his racquet with free majesty and the ball would do as it was told. In 2012, after the Djokovic hurricane had subsided, Federer regained his composure. He won sixty-four of seventy-six matches, briefly returned to number 1 in the world, and, although he lost again in the US Open semi-finals to Djokovic, he'd won a record eighth Wimbledon title and beaten Jo-Wilfried Tsonga to lift his sixth ATP World Tour Finals trophy; he reckoned he had no reason to believe that he could not challenge again. Tennis breathed a little easier. But for how long?

6

America

Edina, Minnesota, 21 February 2013

Mardy Fish has been off the Tour since September. The thirty-one-year-old American, a pro for thirteen years, misses the game. A lot. He picks up the phone and tells his agent, John Tobias, 'I want to play Indian Wells.' Fish, plagued by a rare heart condition that disrupts his sleep and brings on anxiety attacks so bad he cannot bear to be alone, is desperate to return to the world top twenty. His aim for the year is to play the US Open in September. It looks a tough ask.

~

When Nadal arrived in Indian Wells in March for the first hard-court test of his knees in nearly a year, he was not exactly shouting the place down. 'I don't expect a big result,' he said. 'Just happy to be here.' He would get happier as the week progressed. Under a beating sun and in a relaxed setting, he could momentarily forget about his recovering joints, pleasantly surprised that they did not collapse, like those of his opponents. His last hard-court match had been the previous March, when he lost to Tsonga in the quarter-finals in Miami, but the quality he had found again on the clay of another continent stayed with him. Others had to fight a little harder. Some didn't even make it to the line. The Argentinian Leonardo Mayer pulled out with a back injury when warming up, to gift Nadal a walk-over into the third round. 'That's the sport,' Nadal observed. 'When you push your body to the limit, these kind of things can happen.'

There was no physical frailty about his next opponent, although the same could not always be said about the state of Ernests Gulbis's mind. He was one of the game's most unpredictable characters. For too long an enigma rather than the influential player his talent suggested, Gulbis had fought through the qualifying tournament to make the main draw, alongside all fourteen winners of the ATP World Tour, a seriously strong field. There were forty-nine of the top fifty in the world here, and twenty-seven players were age thirty or older. If a young man was going to make an impression against the stars, would Indian Wells not be a good place to make a statement? The Latvian with all the strokes and plenty to say was on a roll, too, winning his thirteenth match in seventeen days by putting the world number 20, Andreas Seppi, out in straight sets to reach the fourth round . . . and a meeting with Nadal.

As if nature were in tune with Gulbis's volcanic personality, Indian Wells took a 4.7 Richter scale hit from an earthquake that rippled through southern California's Coachella Valley. The tournament survived the shake, although it was still reeling hours later from Neil Harman's on-air singing with Gladys Knight. The Pips' lead singer, a serious tennis fan who had been invited into the BBC commentary box, clicked with *The Times* man, who was immediately made an honorary Pip. For those who had heard him croon in Bill's, the New York bar opposite the Elysee on East 54th Street, his Manhattan home during the US Open, it was no more than he deserved.

There was the threat of more on-court turbulence, meanwhile, when Gulbis took the first set off Nadal. I had seen Gulbis at his best and at his worst, and the gap was noticeable. When he was uncomfortable in a contest, he could let his emotions wreck his best work and descend into the most ferocious funk, and you wondered if the hype about him was justified. But he was as imperious as his Roman surroundings when, in 2010, he gave Federer a tennis lesson over three sets in the Internazionali BNL d'Italia, one of the three Masters 1000 events on clay. Thereafter Ernie disappeared, but he resurfaced impressively in 2013. And hard-court was his favoured surface; it was here where he felt sure in the shot, letting his ground-strokes flow with full venom, his wrists turning late to find the most hurtful angles and depth. Now, facing a player who had promised nothing more than commitment at the start of the tournament, he had a chance to make a real statement, to move up a rung and do to Nadal what he had done to Federer three years earlier in Rome. Nadal, however, was mustering confidence and growing physically stronger by the day. He had not lost to Gulbis in four previous encounters; he would not lose to him this time, although the Latvian got to within a couple of points of the finish line in a tense third set. 'OK, if you want my match analysis, honestly,' he said later, 'I think that I played better tennis. I was more aggressive. I went for my shots much more than he did.' Gulbis rarely allowed the status of his opponent to intimidate him, on the court or in the press conference, although he conceded: 'He did incredibly well, as he always does, on important points. It's just really tough to beat the guy.' So, despite producing his best, he was denied a further test against Federer. That privilege would go instead to Nadal. It was their twenty-ninth meeting, and it would not be one of their most memorable.

They hardly ever met this early in a tournament. And it was unprecedented that two players with twenty-eight Slam titles between them would contest the quarter-final of a non-Slam tournament. Most had Federer a slight favourite to increase his hard-court count against the recovering clay-court master to 7–5; what we did not fully comprehend at the time was the trouble the Swiss was having with his back. It was nowhere near as serious as Nadal's tendinitis, but any back injury is a major worry for players as it can flare under stress, and Federer bore the mien of an anxious man. Nadal won going away – which is what Federer then did for seven weeks, pulling out of Miami to rest his injury.

Nadal beat Berdych for the twelfth time in a row to reach the final, and del Potro saw off Murray and Djokovic. So, on a warm Sunday afternoon three months into the 2013 Tour we were about to witness a final few would have predicted. Actors, singers and well-tanned celebrities from the gossip columns are among the thousands who trickled down from their mock-castles and condos to the desert oasis not far from Disneyland and were astounded to see Nadal, against all expectations, including his own, come from a set down to beat del Potro and win his first hard-court title since October 2010 . . . virtually on one good leg. It was his seventeenth win in eighteen matches in a month, and his third tournament victory. He had never started a season like this.

If Nadal really was back, where did that leave Murray, who had flowered in his absence? Where, indeed, did it leave Federer four months shy of his thirty-second birthday? Or Djokovic? Once fragile, he had become seemingly immune to the demands of their trade, yet his often impenetrable defence could also be dismantled on occasion, as Murray proved in New York, where he ran the Serb into the ground, and del Potro proved in Indian Wells, catching him in post-Slam ennui, perhaps. Was the Serbian superman starting to crack, too? Were all four not now slightly more human – paradoxically, because of each other's strengths?

The answer would seem to be yes. And no. Or maybe. Uncertainty abounded. Tennis, after a long period of exclusion and predictability, was volatile again.

In Indian Wells, Nadal ignored the throbbing discomfort in his knee. The pain had not disappeared; it had merely been calmed. He did not move with quite his old zip, but the power and precision were still there. How much longer he could continue to reproduce a rebuilt and credible version of himself we would only discover when he returned to the European clay. For now, he was defying all odds. But he had a warning: Mayer had fallen earlier, Federer was suffering, and the others did not look as if they could climb Mount Everest in a hurry. Injuries were arriving at any point of the calendar now, not just after several months of grinding, and Nadal was convinced the courts were to blame.

'Hard courts are aggressive for the body,' he said. 'If the next generations want to have longer careers and want to finish their careers, then we need better conditions physically – that's my humble opinion. The ATP have to find a solution and not continue playing more and more tournaments on this surface. It is a harder one for the joints and for the knees, for the feet, for the ankles, for the back, for everything.'

Not to mention the spirit. Nadal's, paradoxically, was in fine shape. He had just won the 600th match of his career, second only to Federer, whose tally of 891 at this point was nudging upwards, but far more slowly than in the past. Could he reach a thousand? He could not even make it to Miami – the next tournament. Nadal chose not to go, either. He was not going to press his luck on a surface he treated with such suspicion.

Florida made oranges juicy and Murray's tanned face smile. He had wintered here for six years, bought a luxury penthouse apartment in the Brickell district overlooking the bay; returning to Miami was like coming home. His Miami 'hood is a quiet, rich patch of the city's financial district, full of office towers, hotels and flash restaurants where once there were palatial mansions in colonial days. Crandon Park, twenty minutes away, is where he trains, and where he competes each year in the Sony Ericsson Masters, whose hard-working backers would like to regard as the fifth Open. It is an ambitious claim, but the tournament is still an essential part of the Tour, carrying

1,000 ranking points, and it is the last stopping point in America before the Tour heads for the clay of Europe. This, in a way, is the final examination on the hard courts until the Tour returns later in the summer, so a lot of players, especially those reared on the red dirt, view it with a deal of suspicion. It's a trial of their bodies.

Although he had not played particularly well in California, Murray was not struggling like some of his peers. He had a good vibe about a tournament where he had performed at both ends of the quality spectrum before. If he could win here – where he had gone out in the first round five times and reached the final twice, winning once, against Djokovic emphatically a year earlier – it would settle his nerves and put him in a good frame of mind for the return to Europe and the two northern Slams.

The draw presented him with two interesting tests in a row. He beat Bernard Tomic and Grigor Dimitrov – leading lights of the next wave, we were continually reminded – with the sort of irresistible tennis he normally reserved for finals. How did he compare them? 'It's tough to say,' he said, choosing his words carefully. 'Grigor is probably a better athlete but . . . tennis IQ . . . Bernard knows how to play tennis. It's tough to say who's better.' It was a revealing insight. Murray's commitment to the truth is strong, as he showed in the past with candid comments about drugs and match-fixing, as well as his infamous thoughts on the fortunes of the England football team. But, understandably in the fallout from some of those remarks, he has grown more circumspect. This, however, was straight-talking of the most informative kind. The sort Ernests Gulbis liked (and he was a time bomb waiting to go off).

Seppi and Marin Čilić fell in straight sets to the Scot, and his old friend, Richard Gasquet, took a set off him, so, by the time he reached the final, he was fresh and feeling good about his tennis again. But now it was time for a little more hell in paradise.

David Ferrer is one of the most humble players in tennis. It is not that he does not believe in himself; it's just that he is quick to acknowledge the merit of others – Nadal, for instance, whom he had beaten only five times in twenty-six matches; Federer, who had won all of their fourteen encounters; and Djokovic, who had eleven wins and five losses against him. As for Murray, they were closer. Before they walked on to the court in steaming heat for the final in Miami, Murray had won six of their eleven matches, most recently over four tough sets in the quarter-finals at Wimbledon the previous summer. But, if Ferrer were looking for reasons to struggle – as he often did – he need only ask the ATP's statistics guru Greg Sharko, who would have told him he was trying to become the first Spaniard to win the Miami Masters (that, and his own first final against anyone in the top five in twelve attempts).

After beating Haas in three sets to reach the final, Ferrer was his lugubrious self. Gloom follows him like a cloud and, in the absence of such fluff hanging over Key Biscayne, the Spaniard provides his own. He played well to see off the resurgent Haas, but you would hardly tell from his demeanour. 'I had to fight every point,' he observed, even though he gave up just eleven games, and had the German out on his feet towards the end of the match. He'd won his first Masters title in Paris but did not seem confident of winning another, especially here on this court. 'I don't know . . .' he muttered. 'I'm in the final . . . happy about that. It's going to be very difficult.' He knew that, win or lose, he would remain at number 4 in the rankings. Was that a comfort to him? 'No, nothing. I don't care to be number 4 in this moment. It's important when we finish the season in November.'

Ferrer's downbeat personality has its roots in a well-worn story that is worth briefly retelling for context, because his experience growing up as a teenage prodigy in Spain was to have a profound effect on him. During a spell at the Villena tennis academy of Juan Carlos Ferrero, Ferrer lost his enthusiasm for the game, especially when the repetitive drills favoured by his coach, Javier Piles, began to wear thin. He was only a kid, and he wanted to enjoy tennis, not have it shackle him as if he were prisoner of his own talent. That is exactly what he became: in what many people would regard as a medieval response, Piles locked the teenager in a tiny cupboard for several hours, occasionally passing him bread and water. If there was a pantomime element to the incident, it did not seem funny to Ferrer, and it had the desired effect. His immediate reaction was to give up the game and find work as a labourer. However, he was back within a week, keener than ever. To this day, his peers laud him above all else for his tenacity, his refusal to bow to either the pressure of the scoreboard or the stretching of a game that was methodical and workmanlike rather than imposing. Mr Piles, perhaps, knew Ferrer better than he knew himself. (By the end of 2013, Ferrer and Piles would part company after fifteen years. Enough was enough.) Every match Ferrer played was like a return to that little cupboard, where he would be asked to dig deep in his resources. He rarely failed to find an answer to even the toughest questions.

The final was a contest as fierce as the heat, with little to recommend it as a work of beauty at any point in the 2 hours and 45 minutes it lasted. Both players camped on the baseline and slugged. Of many such games in 2013, this Sony Open was as classic an exercise in dogged commitment to pain as any. Ferrer tried his best to mix it up with his inside-out forehand preceding the occasional dash to the net, but Murray was composed under the assault, and grindingly patient. Extending rallies rather than risk giving his opponent even the odd half-chance of a winner did not appear to concern him. He was metronomically comfortable heaving the ball back at Ferrer, as deep as he could manage, loaded with either topspin or slice, prodding as a doctor might a patient until he yelped. It was tennis of its age. Would Ferrer, the bull-terrier of the game, still be growling at the end of it?

Near the conclusion of a match that had started in the midday heat to accommodate college basketball on TV, they looked as if they were in a trance, hitting on auto-pilot. Ferrer got to championship point and then made a strategic blunder, challenging a Murray drive he thought was out but which had landed legally. The Scot gained strength from the moment and, having saved, forced a tie-break, with nostrils flared and legs and brain refreshed. It looked to leave Ferrer utterly spent and dejected, which was understandable. What we would learn later was that cramp was rushing through the Spaniard's body so virulently that he was barely able to stand up. And then it came, a freeze-frame second you would usually only see in a prize fight: Ferrer's knees gave way on him in the shot and he came perilously close to falling to the ground, his weak stroke a too-faint response. Murray had taken the tie-break 7–1, and with it the title. This was not just a win in a tennis match; it was vindication for Murray, proof that all the hours he had put in on this very court in preparation were worth it. This was the dividend. This reinforced what he already knew: the only way to win the big points in the big matches was to be the strongest, fittest player in that unforgiving oblong.

Murray was so disorientated afterwards, he struggled to put it in context. 'It was so tough physically and mentally, I was just trying to play each point,' he said. 'I wasn't thinking too much – because I was so tired. It was a brutal, brutal match. Both of us were on our last legs. Just as well it wasn't best of five because I don't know how the last few sets would have ended up. I don't think David gets the respect he deserves. Providing his body holds up, he'll be around the top of the game for as long as he wants.'

He added: 'Rafa and Novak played here a couple of years ago in a three-set match, and Rafa was in hospital after the match. The conditions in Miami are extremely hard.'

Those were interesting observations. Murray, as a fellow professional, wanted his beaten opponent to be recognised for his contribution to what for Murray had been 'one of my toughest ever matches'. And he paid tribute to Ferrer's physical strength, which has become the default currency of the era. Twenty years ago and more, few players would have felt disposed to make such a remark. Now, the ability to out-tough an opponent had become paramount. It was what separated champions from the field. Everybody knew it. To make Ferrer's knees buckle in the fading minutes of the fight felt to Murray like landing a haymaker in a boxing match. He had made him crack, something nobody else has ever done – not even Piles, his coach. He did not want to complain later. It was tough, he said, but, 'it is always tough against Andy'. When he got up to leave, his legs momentarily betrayed him. 'I'm OK,' said the toughest *hombre* in tennis, 'I'm OK.'

If we learned anything from this first hard-court swing of the American circuit, it was that Nadal had learned how to husband his resources on an unfriendly surface, that Federer would not risk aggravating an injury that plainly was troubling him more than he wanted to let on, and that Murray, who moved past him in his absence to number 2 in the world, was in decent shape. Djokovic? He had dipped. But, as he would prove spectacularly when the Tour moved to Europe, he had Nadal in his sights. The Spaniard was the player he wanted to beat most of all in the weeks to come . . . on courts that for nearly a decade had been his best friend.

7

Gladiators

Monte Carlo, 16 April 2013

Much has been expected of Grigor Dimitrov since he arrived on the scene, the embodiment of glamour and court artistry. Today, he delivers, putting Janko Tipsarević to the sword in front of Riviera's moneyed elite on the second day of the Monte Carlo Masters, after coming close to losing the first set. It is his first win over the cerebral Serb, who wears a quote from Dostoyevsky's The Idiot *— 'Beauty will save the world' — on his muscled left arm. Starting slowly is a habit Dimitrov has struggled to shake off, and it will plague him throughout the summer. 'I was just trying to hang in,' he said, in his near-flawless, melodious English. He would play well here this week, but 2013 was not to be his year.*

~

Professional tennis is not just about the four big tournaments that offer millions of dollars in prize money and enough instant glamour to satisfy a Hollywood extra. For journeymen, contenders and old guys hanging on, the game is about scrapping around the globe for ranking points – and money – in Acapulco (oh, the pain!), Bogota, 's-Hertogenbosch (surely the most misspelt place on the circuit . . . or anywhere), Memphis, Casablanca, Winston-Salem and forty-seven other exotic and/or dull destinations. There will be nobody there but the players, officials, a few friends and a smattering of hard-core fans. The cheers will echo rather than form a chorus. The interviews, such as they are, will be brief and, in all likelihood, ignored. There will be camaraderie to dilute the rivalry, as the troubadours of the game ramble alongside each other singing a song little listened to. It is here where all players start. It is in front of nobody that they strive to become somebody. If they are good enough, they might make it. But it is as far removed from Wimbledon Centre Court on finals day as the heart of the Gobi Desert. These tournaments are played in the big towns and small cities that are redolent with tennis lore and a thousand untold escapades, where players sleep in cars or on the floors of friends' budget hotel rooms, where complimentary (and rudimentary) meals are scoffed as if banquet feasts, where a lift to the airport in a taxi is as welcome as a limousine ride. These are the tournaments that receive minimal mainstream coverage, where players of all ranks swap forehands for small reward but much promise. And this is not even the basement of the game.

Beyond the comparatively bare landscape of the ATP 250 and 500 events lie Futures tournaments in faraway towns and cities with names familiar only to their residents, history students and itinerant tennis players, the gypsies of sport. A random trawl of the programme at the end of 2013 showed that Laurynas Grigelis, of Lithuania, justified his second seeding in beating Uladzimir Ignatik, of Bulgaria, 6–4, 3–6, 6–7(2) in the morning match of the MND Tour in Opava, an old city in what was once the Silesian capital in the northern part of the Czech Republic. Perhaps Mr Ignatik, a twenty-three-year-old pro from Minsk who had earned $275,000 in six years on the circuit, took the opportunity of enforced down-time to tour the sites of this thousand-year-old former capital of Silesia. Or maybe he got on a plane to Dakar, to make a grab for a slice of a $15,000 purse in the Senegal Open, held at the Olympique Club on Boulevard Martin Luther King Corniche Ouest. It is not an altogether unromantic existence.

But, for those who dream of more than old ruins and palm trees, there is tougher work to be had further up the chain. On an ambitious player's schedule, the ATP's 500 and 250 series sit just below the nine Masters 1000 events – Indian Wells, Miami, Monte Carlo, Madrid, Rome, Montreal, Cincinnati, Shanghai and Paris – that are positioned between the Slams, like obstacles on a race track, to give the stars a chance to rack up serious money and points. Although it is a frustrating life for those who fail week in, week out, it is also fair. If players are good enough, they will rise to the level that, in the end, they deserve to reach. It does not pay nearly as well as golf – but then they are not golfers. They have chosen their sport because they are good at it and, one would hope, they enjoy it. The trick is keeping that love of the game when serial disappointment might indicate they have not made the best career choice. That said, few drop out. Those still standing after even a few years are all the stronger for the experience and, like Gordon Forbes – the fifties South African doubles player who would go on to be a respected observer of his sport – what memories they have.

I had compiled a few of my own, much to my surprise . . .

Monte Carlo was my first gig as a full-time tennis correspondent. I wondered how my new colleagues might take to this arriviste from a grubbier street corner in Sports City. By inclination, circumstance and serendipity, I have been writing about fighting and fighters on and off for nearly forty years. But, when I woke up on the Riviera one crisp April morning in 2010 and looked out of my hotel window at what might have been Monet's *La terrasse de Sainte Adresse*, I believed I might, indeed, quite like being a tennis writer. There was a bit to learn. Climb into a ridiculously cheap bus at Menton not far from the Italian border and, within twenty minutes, you arrive at the Monte Carlo Country Club, which sounds like something F. Scott Fitzgerald might have written about in *Tender is the Night*. If it appears I am mining all my Mediterranean references in one paragraph, they were the first texts to hand when it became apparent that the thuds I would now chronicle for a living would describe the impact of a fluffy ball on a tightly strung racquet, more civilised perhaps than leather on slack, bloodied jaw but no less exciting, as it happened. It seemed appropriate to shift one's mindset from roaring fight venues to the gentle lapping of the sea on the rocks below one of the most beautiful landscapes it has been my pleasure to temporarily call an office. So, off to work I went . . .

Who were all these nice, rich people gathered on the Côte d'Azur for the first clay-court tournament of the summer, I wondered. They seemed oblivious to the purpose of their visit, and did not let the tennis parked below their champagne-glazed gaze on Court Central interrupt their afternoon tippling or gossiping on the terrace of the Monte Carlo Country Club. And who were these eager reporters, from magazines, websites and God knows where, asking players about cross-court winners and ATP points and groin strains in a variety of accents? Who were the beautiful women, younger and more convincingly tanned than their partners, babbling so elegantly on the terraces? And why wasn't anyone watching the bloody tennis? More importantly for an old fight writer, where was the buzz? Where were the villains to go with the heroes? I would find out soon enough.

I'd tracked Andy Murray's career from a distance since he won the boys championship at the US Open in 2004, but the first match on which I reported on him in my new job as an expert was against the not-bad German Philipp Kohlschreiber in this charming setting. It lasted 64 minutes. Murray was out of the tournament before I'd had a chance to check the tables at the casino. I asked a more experienced colleague what he thought of Murray's truly awful match and he said, 'Don't get carried away. It wasn't as bad as it looked.' Really? So I asked Murray. It was, he admitted, the worst tennis he had played since a similarly dire performance in Hong Kong three years earlier. Hong Kong and tennis were not on my radar in 2007, but I knew bad when I saw it. I accepted Murray's assessment over that of my colleague, and my first supposedly informed review of the player who was to be the hub of my professional existence for a few years to come was unreservedly scathing. I hoped he was not a *Guardian* reader. Well, not that edition of it . . . We would find common bond, it transpired, in our mutual affection for fisticuffs and, given a disparity in age and size, there was little chance of testing our relative proficiency. I imagine he might do rather well. For a round or two . . .

While some of the other British writers left a tournament as soon as Murray lost, my employers were enlightened enough to insist I stay to report on the rest of the proceedings in Monaco, and to take this tennis gig seriously. That evening, sitting with Mike Dickson of the *Daily Mail* and looking out on the still sea near our Menton hotel, with a glass of something agreeable in one hand and an expectant mobile phone in the other, I figured there were worse ways to earn a living. 'You'll get used to it,' Dicko said. What comforted me more than anything was this: although he'd collapsed like a pricked balloon against Kohlschreiber, Andy Murray was a significantly better tennis player than Tim Henman.

That lovely interlude seems such a long time ago. Maybe it is because so much has happened since, and so quickly. And here we now were, back in paradise in the spring of 2013, all gnarled and full of stats and questions and expertise, waiting to see if Murray could build on Miami, if Nadal could extend his long, long reign here at one of the outposts of his ochre empire, if

Djokovic had recovered from twisting his ankle in a Davis Cup match and if Federer was back to fitness after his wretched time in Indian Wells.

The first faint signs of change arrived in the third round, when Dimitrov battered Janko Tipsarević in straight sets, for only his second career win against anyone inside the top ten. The Bulgarian looked in sublime form . . . and happy. He had good reason to on two counts: his tennis was buzzing, and his relationship with Maria Sharapova, although officially off-limits in press conferences, seemed to be flowering in tune with the season. It was nice to see. The sponsors certainly thought so. Here was a couple that might be the golden duo of tennis, beautiful young things flitting from one tournament to another. It was a beguiling thought, but it needed one or both of them to deliver on court, and that was much tougher than being photographed hand in hand on a warm summer's night in Madrid (where their relationship was cemented in the imagination by the paparazzi).

Nadal was into his stride quickly, but not before a few laughs when the cheeky Australian Marinko Matošević tipped over his precisely placed water bottles on the change-over near the end of their match the following day. Nadal smiled. A bit. He'd won. Had he lost? Well, that would have been a headline to contemplate. If Matošević had monkey business on his mind, Murray had just plain business, and announced the addition to his team of the Indian doubles player and businessman Mahesh Bhupathi, a Tour veteran well known to British tennis writers. Bhupathi would later leak details of a quick-fire tournament of one-set matches at the end of the season across Asia and the Indian subcontinent, with Murray as a key attraction. Murray also had with him now as a business adviser, Juan Martín del Potro's manager, the astute and party-friendly Italian Ugo Colombini. 'The next four or five years of my life are going to be some of the most important for me,' the Wimbledon champion said in Monte Carlo. 'So you want to make sure you have the right people around you. That's why I made the decision to change some of the people I work with, like Ugo. I hope they do a good job for me.'

By September, Murray had set up a new management company, 77, with his long-time agent, Simon Fuller. There was further moving of the furniture. Matt Gentry, Murray's PR man for five years on behalf of Fuller's XI Entertainment, was appointed managing director, working with Bhupathi, who would oversee business and sales. Colombini was confirmed as 'responsible for tournament-related activity', while Murray's long-term relationships with financial manager Neil Grainger and business affairs manager Grenville Evans 'remained in place'. Industry estimates put Murray's potential career earnings at £150 million in sponsorship deals over the remaining stretch of his career through the rearrangement of his affairs. Meanwhile, he was looking for a sponsor for 'his left shoulder'. Shortly thereafter, his partnership with Bhupathi ceased. For the foreseeable future, there would be no end-of-year jolly in Asia.

On the Monte Carlo court, meanwhile, Murray looked good, getting rid of the Frenchman with an English grandmother, Édouard Roger-Vasselin, in his first match – but would fall at the feet of Wawrinka in the next round, winning only three games in his most disappointing performance of the season. Maybe Murray, me and Monte Carlo were a bad mix. He did not make excuses, but he plainly was struggling on the clay. After the high of Miami, defeat dropped him from number 2 to number 3 in the world. It never seemed to be an easy gig with Andy. 'I made a lot of mistakes,' he agreed. 'I've had tough losses on the clay before and I've come back well from them.' It would get worse, though. A lot worse.

Two days later, Dimitrov took a set off Nadal, the first time that had happened to the Spaniard in fifty-seven sets in a tournament that was virtually his personal property. But the king did not perish. That ignominy would come in the final when he met a surprisingly revived Djokovic, who, before the week started, had expressed fears that the ankle he rolled in a Davis Cup match a few weeks earlier might not hold up to sustained pressure. It did. Nadal had never lost on clay in April in eighty matches – one of the game's more obscure statistics – but it proved to be the cruellest month for him when he met the Serb for the third time in a Monaco final. The painkillers clearly were working a treat for Djokovic, who ended Rafa's forty-six-match-winning run on clay in straight sets and became the first player since Gastón Gaudio to beat Nadal in three separate clay finals.

For the rest of the scrabblers, this was a barely perceptible power shift: Djokovic's win meant twenty-six of the previous twenty-eight Masters 1000 events had gone to a member of the Big Four. For the time being, the revolution had been delayed.

Nadal's Wimbledon tormentor, Lukáš Rosol, meanwhile became the third first-time winner of the season in Bucharest, climbing to a career-high 35 in the world by beating Guillermo García-López in two whizz-bang sets. It was a monumental feat of resilience by the Czech, who, during his run to the title, held twenty-six of twenty-nine break points against him. His father had died ten days earlier, but he used his grief to give his tennis purpose and energy. It always seems an odd phenom- enon that death brings a form of life, especially in something as relatively trivial as sport. But this is a player's life. They are consumed by their sport. It dominates most of their working hours and it defines them. 'Before the second set started,' Rosol said, 'I was thinking about something else, my dad. I tried to just concentrate and finish the match in two sets. Before the last game, there were already emotions. I was shaking a lot before the match point, not because I was nervous, but because I was thinking about everything else.' Asked about his shock win over

Nadal the previous summer, he said: 'More people recognise me, but it didn't change me. Other players saw I can play good tennis, so they are more careful with me. People have asked for pictures and autographs. But I cannot live on this result for ever.'

In Barcelona, the king of clay had picked up his crown and plonked it back on his bobbing head. He dismissed Raonic with ridiculous ease in the semi-final, finishing him off with a quick bagel, then inflicted defeat on his Spanish friend Nicolás Almagro for the 10th time in a row without reply. Nadal is as ruthless with his own as he is with others.

Murray's loss to Berdych in Madrid a week later was not as total as his capitulation to Wawrinka in Monte Carlo, but there seemed to be a distinct lack of zip in his tennis, as if he were fighting his body as much as his opponent. He moved stiffly and his reactions were just a tick sluggardly, as if he had the Invisible Man on his back. Nadal powered on, stopping Wawrinka's run with a brutal exhibition of controlled clay-court power in the final.

Now for Rome, the home of the gladiators . . .

Glasgow seemed further away than the thermometer and the five hours on the plane to Rome were suggesting. The previous night I had been wrapped up in jacket and jumper in the Emirates Arena on the edge of Scotland's most uncompromising city, a place where it can be as easy to get an argument as a cup of tea. I was there watching Ricky Burns from Coatbridge hold on to his version of the world lightweight title through his own bloody-mindedness and the draining of that intangible commodity in his opponent, the previously unbeaten Puerto Rican boxer José González. Jose quit after nine rounds. As he sat disconsolate on his stool, a towel over his head, his cornermen begged him to continue despite the swollen left wrist with which he had been battering Burns for the previous 27 minutes. But he could give no more.

In the seventh round, Gonzalez had the local hero out on his feet, belting him from one side of the ring to the other, and he was on the verge of becoming a world champion, a result that would change his life. But the effort took its greater toll on the challenger. The Scot, whom I had described in the *Guardian* beforehand as 'polite as a bank clerk and harder than a Glasgow winter', thankfully did not make a fool of me, and in rounds eight and nine he found that reserve of almost superhuman will on which only a few fighters can depend without fail. All fighters believe they have it; some discover under fire that it is not quite as strong as they imagine. Burns has it. First he stopped Gonzalez's advance, soaking up the last of his heavy attacks, then he methodically broke the Puerto Rican's heart, as well as that throbbing wrist.

Something odd was at play, however. Just as Gonzalez was apologetically confiding to his seconds that he had nothing left to contribute to the entertainment after nearly half an hour of fighting, they advised him he was leading by three rounds on the scorecards of all three judges. That meant he had only to survive, jabbing and running with his one good hand for nine minutes, avoid being knocked out, and he should be assured of at least a draw. That decision would surely earn him a rematch, they said, and he would have another chance to be world champion. If, however, he also managed somehow to steal one of the remaining three rounds (and avoid being knocked out), he would edge the decision and take Burns' title tonight. The blood and sweat he had expended would have an instant dividend. He would be a world champion. There would be no cause to come back to Glasgow and try again. This was his moment. This was the time to make the sacrifice. For reasons that only a fighter could understand (or maybe he couldn't), he chose to quit. Many fighters have finished fights with broken fingers, knuckles or ribs, slashed facial skin, smashed teeth, fractured jaws, even a bruised toe – all manner of injuries mortals would consider serious enough to require immediate hospitalisation, or at least the comfort of a mother's kindly arm. But their business is different to ours. They deal in perceived immortality, legend, legacy, separateness. They are in the hurt business. They administer pain and they endure it. That was the deal that Saturday night, the contract with the opponent, the crowd and the people who were paying Burns and Gonzalez to fight.

Gonzalez, however, would surrender not another sliver of his spirit – for his seconds, for the strangers in the dark beyond the ring, for the title, for his sport. And so we left Glasgow the next morning, the fighter going home to Puerto Rico to wonder what might have been, the writer to a less dangerous place, once the home of gladiators but on this lovely spring day somewhere to play tennis.

As I looked out of the window of the plane on the approach to Flumenico airport, I felt deep sympathy for Gonzalez. He was highly unlikely ever to be invited back to Glasgow. If he were to receive another shot at a world title, it would not be the one owned by Burns. The champion, meanwhile, knew two things: that he deserved to lose, yet that he had found a way to win. Andy Murray, a friend of Burns through nationality and inclination, understands the ethos and morals of boxing. This does not mean he would love to box. That is a different proposition altogether. He has done a little light 'moving about', sparring with Amir Khan when the Bolton fighter was the world lightweight champion before Burns, and he has spent time with the former world heavyweight champion David Haye in his Miami gym, but they were observational exercises. Against Khan, there was no contact to speak of, just a bit of quality posing in the ring with gloves, extending the odd harmless jab, sliding in and out of range, feeling the pace of the exchange and wondering what it must really be like to be a boxer. Murray said he found the rhythm of the exchanges similar to those in tennis . . . without the bruises . . . or the anxiety.

Murray has the perfect physical equipment to be a fighter: long levers, powerful shoulders and big, strong fists, quick movement of hand, head and feet and the keenest of reflexes. He could have been a world-class boxer . . . except he doesn't like fighting; he likes watching it. And in that, he is among the majority on the planet. For all that abolitionists scream about the barbarity of the exercise, there is something deep in most of us that identifies with the need to defend ourselves against attack. It is in our genes to be aware of danger and to make a choice: fight or flight. Most, of course, choose the latter. Rightly so. It is nearly always the wisest choice. But the ego will demand the former. I have spoken to Murray about boxing many times. It is often our first point of discussion, swapping the odd bit of gossip or news. He has a wide-ranging knowledge of the sport and tracks the fortunes of British fighters at all levels, not just those who hold world titles or are in a position to challenge for them. David Haye, one of Murray's favourite boxers and someone who shares an understanding of the similarities between their sports, is eloquent on the subject.

In most sports, you'd find it difficult comparing stars from different eras, simply because they competed at different times against different opposition. Who's to say Mike Tyson was a better heavyweight champion than Joe Frazier, for example? Who would have won, Lennox Lewis or Muhammad Ali? You can make arguments all day, but it's tough to predict with any kind of conviction. These fighters are a similar breed, and even the fighters of today train pretty much the same way as their predecessors.

The sport of tennis seems to be slightly different, though. There have been huge advances in tennis, in terms of training and preparation, and this has created a gulf between the stars of today and those who came before them. The top players nowadays, the likes of Andy, Federer, Nadal and Djokovic, play the same game as Björn Borg, John McEnroe, Pete Sampras and Andre

Agassi — but they do it in 2013, and have benefited from years of development.

We've seen changes in equipment, changes in the way they train and also changes in style. All of this has combined to almost blur the lines between old and new. And so, hypothetically, someone like Borg, though rightly considered an all-time great, may struggle against an athletic phenomenon like Nadal, purely due to the way the game is now played and the kind of athletes it attracts.

I've watched some of these modern greats play at Wimbledon, live in the flesh, and am always amazed by the way in which they moved around court for hours on end, dipping, diving, running, stopping and starting. The agility on show is incredible. And, while it might not require physical contact, tennis remains an extremely physical sport, and those at the top of the game are some of the fittest sportsmen and women you're likely to find in this day and age. After all, a tennis match, often long and exhausting, requires its players to be strong and remain strong for the duration, game after game, shot after shot. Then, if they're lucky, they'll be playing again a day or two later.

Andy is a friend of mine and somebody who has seen his form greatly improve as a result of increased fitness and physical strength. If you look at Andy when he first came on the scene, he was basically a young lad, and, although tall and rangy, there was very little of him. Consequently, he sometimes struggled in longer matches and faded down the stretch. But, since sorting out his diet and investing in strength and conditioning, Andy has not only transformed his whole physique, but now has the strength to power past opponents in those gruelling five-set matches. It's no coincidence, therefore, that he's now considered one of the very best players in the world and won his first ever Grand Slam title at Flushing Meadows, and his second at Wimbledon.

Having trained with Andy on many occasions, I can vouch for his work ethic and fitness levels. In fact, I remember getting a call from Andy when he was playing a tournament in Abu

Dhabi and I was in Dubai, and the sole purpose of the call was to try and track down a Versaclimber. I had introduced this piece of kit to Andy and he now felt it was a vital part of his training regime.

So I put out a few feelers and eventually found what was probably the only one in the whole of the United Arab Emirates. It was in Dubai, though, not Abu Dhabi. Nevertheless, aware of the importance of getting the best training possible, Andy hopped on a plane and headed off to Dubai in order to use this one bit of equipment. A few years ago, he would have probably never made the trip and got by on just a treadmill.

Haye was still a working fighter when he shared these thoughts with me. He subsequently withdrew through injury from two big-money fights with the unbeaten Mancunian Tyson Fury and his future, at time of writing, was uncertain. By the end of the year, Murray would also have a good understanding of the career-threatening dangers of going to his physical limits.

On that 7.30 a.m. Sunday flight to Rome, I had time to ponder all of this. I saw also how proud Murray was of his compatriot Burns. 'Yessss @ricksterko big win! #andstilllllll!' he had tweeted from his hotel room in Rome, having yet again found an internet feed to watch the boxing. Burns responded the next day: '@andy_murray thanks a lot mate, hopefully see u at the next 1 in September'. This is how sportsmen communicate – remotely. Once, perhaps, they would cross at railway stations and stop for coffee, or even a beer. Now the reach of the social media has made us all instantly intertwined and privy to simple exchanges such as these.

In conversation with Murray, it becomes obvious he admires boxers more than any other athletes. He sees in them the primal imperatives that go beyond mere competition, the ultimate physical experience. He hears their breath leaving them under pressure, sees their limbs go limp, de-gassed by the effort of constant movement. He possibly also can look deeper, into their eyes and beyond, down into their soul, where logic locks horns with instinct. His fight with Ferrer in Miami was just that. They held tennis racquets instead of wearing gloves, but the longer it went on the more basic it became, the more removed from a game of tennis. They were trying to break the other's resolve, to hurt the other man, make him give up under a non-stop volley of loaded topspin, trying to drain his muscles of oxygen and his brain of judgment. That is what Murray did to Ferrer and he could hardly have felt more like a boxer.

Murray looks too at the geometry of their respective rectangular prisons: a square for boxing, an oblong for tennis. There is no escaping either of these spaces until the deed is done; no stepping out through the ropes into the comfort of anonymity with the watching crowd, nor slipping away from the court when, in critical moments, the familiar place of work might be the last space on earth one would want to be. Yet the sportsmen know the paradox: the battlegrounds that are their prisons are their homes, too. This is where they spend their most profound moments. It is where they become who they really are. That does not happen at press conferences, during magazine interviews or when they are celebrity walk-ons for television shows or someone else's premiere. The only performances that matter are the ones marked by a W or an L. It is in the ring and on the tennis court that fighters and racquet-wielders get to live most fully. It might be only entertainment for others, but these are the gladiatorial rings in which they judge themselves.

Some athletes have a trace of the Gonzalez in them. That is not to denigrate him or them. He had every right to quit. It is his life, his health, to be guarded as he sees fit. If he did not have the free will to make that choice, boxing would be a crime. And some tennis players also view their sport that way. There is only so much some of them are prepared to give and, as in boxing, there are ways to find the trap-door to quick anonymity.

Desperation springs from hopelessness and can deliver improbable victory or the temporary sanctuary of surrender. It is fascinating to see which players choose the softer option . . . and where that surrender to adversity is reflected in their rankings.

There has been an alarming tendency recently in major tournaments, nonetheless, for players to withdraw after starting a match, citing a wide range of injuries. Rarely do they quit while in front. It is usually when the cause is lost. Cynics would say that, in some cases, that is before a ball is struck. It demeans the contest and the beneficiaries, while grateful, are also left frustrated because it is their instinct to compete, not to surrender. They welcome the struggle; they do not want it taken away from them.

Ernests Gulbis is an intelligent, wealthy young man (his father is not only a former Soviet basketball star but, famously, the fourth richest businessman in Latvia), and he might be the last of the playboys of tennis. He has sometimes seemed as relieved to leave a tournament as to join it. When he beat Federer in Rome three years earlier, he was mildly surprised by our interest in the achievement; when he lost in the next round, to Nadal, he told us he was going out clubbing that night . . . in Latvia. 'If you'll excuse me, I have a plane to catch.' The plane was his own. This year, though, he promises to deliver on his considerable talent, to work harder, to give all he has got. But will he?

In Monte Carlo the previous month, he went into his match against Juan Mónaco surfing a wave of fifteen wins in seventeen matches. Would this finally be the year in which one of the game's true natural talents let us see what he was made of? Since February, only players in the top ten had tamed him: del Potro, Berdych and Nadal. In Monte Carlo, he began by beating John Isner. The run was turning from long to very promising. Gulbis looked to be untouchable against Mónaco after winning the first set to love, the fabled bagel. His strokes flowed like warm honey and his eyes burned with desire. There was energy in his every gesture, and that should have been a signal that the man for whom tennis had been a hobby was in danger of bursting a boiler if it all went wrong, because this was the sort of sustained success he had not tasted for a long time; this was his destiny once, and now it seemed as if he were fulfilling it. What could possibly go wrong? Within a couple of hours, after losing eight games in a row and failing to keep his discipline under no more than regulation pressure, Gulbis was on his way home again, a glowing ball of anger after losing a match he clearly should have won, with a smashed racquet left behind and bad blood too. But at least he cared . . .

Gulbis is not the only player who moves around the circuit under his own personal cloud – or in a private jet, for that matter, although Murray and Federer usually rent theirs (jets, that is). Murray flew to Rome from Madrid, personally chauffeured in the air so as not to waste a minute of precious practice time ahead of this tournament, the final work-out before Roland Garros, and gave Jo-Wilfried Tsonga a lift. Nice guy.

Once he had his feet firmly on the clay of Rome, it was time for work, time to organise his tournament. The players arrive at the gorgeous setting from their respective hotels, varied according to status and income, of course, but they are equal enough in the locker-room. Here they start from scratch. Notionally. It is before a ball has been hit that there are no losers or winners. It creates a false impression of parity, because what will unfold in the following week proves there is no equality. There are champions and there are those who sit beside champions in the locker-rooms of the game, from Rome to Melbourne, New York to Paris and Wimbledon. Here they are travelling companions of sorts; on the court they are enemies, and, no, very few times are they equals, whether they have flown here privately or with the rest of us.

Players will talk endlessly about levels. It means what it sounds like it means. It also describes how they have a calibration of intensity because, against lesser opponents, those in the upper reaches of the rankings can moderate their effort ever so slightly. They can get through early rounds playing with concentration and shape, wary of complacency, yet comfortable in the knowledge that they have more gears than the player at the other end. Ideally, in a Masters 1000 event, for instance, they would look to cruise past qualifiers and wild cards untroubled. It is when those lesser players reach deep and, inspired by the occasion of playing on a bigger stage, find a game they thought had long deserted them that the script is ripped up. They suddenly remember how good they were as young prospects, before the drudgery of serial defeat suffocated their ambition, reducing them to survivors, taking away their shots and their composure. But, sometimes, when hurled back into a big match, they use a cocktail of pride and adrenaline to give the big names of their sport a fright.

Rosol did just that at Wimbledon against Nadal. Rehabbed now, Nadal lurked in Rome until the Wednesday, then burst into the draw against the temperamental Italian Fabio Fognini. If ever there was a match-up between determination and insouciance, it is this one. The game lasted 61 minutes.

Murray, meanwhile, did not last at all. For only the second time in 529 singles matches, he quit during the contest. Each time, the misfortune befell him on his birthday: when his wrist gave up on him after he led the Italian Filippo Volandri 5–1 in the first round of the Hamburg Masters in 2007, an injury that kept him out for three months and forced him to miss Wimbledon; and here when, having fought back from a set and 1–4 down to level against Marcel Granollers, his back collapsed and he left the court in obvious agony.

When Murray arrived at the press conference, we were not aware of how serious his injury was. But it was obviously enough to make him quit, and that wasn't good. He is not a quitter – whatever Virginia Wade and others who reckoned he was 'a drama queen' imagined. He was, by instinct, a fighter. He was here to explain his predicament but he was short-tempered and sullen. When a reporter asked him to repeat a softly spoken answer, he snapped.

'I've pulled out,' he said again, slowly and louder, 'because there was a good chance I wouldn't be playing [in the third round on Thursday], even if I was to get through. I'll have to wait and see on Paris but I would be very surprised if I were playing there. I was in a bit of pain, the same sort of thing as in Madrid, when I took a few days off. It's not been perfect for a long period and I want to try to start feeling very good again. You always go into matches with little niggles and whatnot, but it is frustrating when for long periods you're hurting.'

He did not elaborate, but it would transpire this was more than a niggle or whatnot. It was a serious disc problem in his lower back. Pulling out of the French Open might have been the best decision of his career, because, had he played, the damage could have been far worse. Nobody could be sure – even the specialists who agonised over the decision to operate – but further aggrava- tion of the problem might have ended his career. The time for living with the pain had come to a halt. It was now in the hands of the surgeons. Murray hated losing control of any part of his life or his career. This time, he had no choice.

'You can have the injections,' he added, eyes downcast. 'They can help a bit with pain and they can take some of the inflammation away, but that also didn't make me feel one hundred per cent, and I want to feel one hundred per cent.'

Gulbis, meanwhile, was full of the joys of spring. For the moment. He had put together a run in Barcelona and was stopped in the second round in Munich – by the thirty-five-year-old Tommy Haas, who was constructing his own fine comeback and harboured thoughts of becoming the oldest player in the top ten for a very long time. Still only twenty-four, still volatile and still potentially brilliant, Gulbis arrived in Rome a mixed bag of tricks, buoyed by his return to form. However, trouble was never more than a bad line call away, and after that explosion on the Cote d'Azur he had the potential to explode again. He made short enough work of Jarkko Nieminen – for the second time in a fortnight – saw off Viktor Troicki and then walked into a war with Nadal.

It was a breathtaking, high-risk shoot-out. Gulbis thrashed fifteen aces past his astonished opponent – with none coming the other way – and took the first set for the loss of a single game, the fourth time in six contests Nadal had fallen behind against the Latvian. But Nadal's combative instincts carried him through. His competitive juices flowing, he saved thirteen of sixteen break points to beat Ferrer, then Berdych for the twelfth time in a row. He had now put himself into the lead in the race to the World Tour finals in London.

One player who hopes his Roman experience can maintain his rising spirits is Wawrinka, the second-best Swiss player of all time, perhaps – and possibly the best Swiss player of the 2013 season. Wawrinka does not, however, have the luxury of playing at fluctuating levels. He is one of those very good players who must play very well all the time. He does not have a reliable second gear. In Melbourne at the start of the year, he revved his engine to the maximum and came within a few points of beating Djokovic in the fourth round of the Australian Open. But he lost. Yet this most amenable of men does not want to mull too long over that experience, not in a negative way, at least. Losing is not exactly a habit, he told me in the players' lounge one afternoon in 2013, but it is a familiar experience. He is philosophical about what others might call his predicament; he accepts it as part of the deal, as unavoidable collateral damage. Tennis players, like golfers, come to rationalise defeat in a myriad of ways. Wawrinka's position is typical.

'Yes, losing can become a habit,' he says, as we chatted after an uneventful win over Carlos Belocq (and, although neither of us knew it at the time, shortly before he would be forced to retire from the tournament with a strained hamstring). 'That's what I find in tennis, almost everybody does. You need to . . . I'm not saying accept, but you need to give everything – then you can accept to lose, see what you can improve on next time. I don't know many players who just accept losing. In all sports you have better players. For some people, it's much easier to play well. Some people practise better. Some people want it more, so they sacrifice more to get there. It's not just about losing.'

Such a simple but clear view. Wawrinka is an interesting man, and very fine player – with a backhand every bit as potent as his compatriot Federer. But he often seems consumed by his own diffidence, as if he is expected to do very well but not very often. He has as much talent as most, certainly he is better on his day than Janko Tipsarević, for instance, who often is ahead of him in the rankings. But now Stan looks at the possibility of breaking back into the top ten and maybe staying there for a while, maybe reaching the ATP World Tour Finals. That surely would signal his re-emergence after a few years lurking outside the zone of his proper capability. And what of that match against Djokovic? Did he not feel shattered in defeat?

'For sure, I think I am playing better tennis than last year,' he says, eyes darting to the floor, then up again, like a wide-eyed kid. 'But then I think the Djokovic match in Australia helped me a lot. That match proved to me that I was at the right level, physically and mentally, to play the number 1 player in the world, to be so close to beating him. For sure it was a tough loss, but there were a lot of positive things to come out of that match for after.'

Wawrinka sees his dilemma in curious terms. He knows he is nearly as good as the best players in the world. Indeed, on his day, he is every bit as good and, for stretches, even better. Djokovic discovered that, almost to his cost. But Stan has such a history of struggle it can be difficult, or at least a challenge, for him to adjust to a run of success. He is more used to fighting hard just to stay in a big tournament, and so by the time he comes up against those better players in the later rounds, he feels he has less left in the tank than they do. It is an honest appraisal. Effectively, he is saying players such as Djokovic, Murray, Federer and Nadal have the luxury, almost, of being so good they can get to the quarters or semis of a Slam without leaving too much on the court.

'Last year in a lot of matches,' Wawrinka says, 'even when I played a guy who was behind me in the rankings, I was playing three sets or in some really tough matches. Then when you win two matches like this, you arrive in the quarters and you're already a little bit less fresh. It's tougher then to play the top ten players. For a few tournaments I had the chance to play really well at the beginning, that gives you more confidence to play the top ten players.'

Wawrinka should be a Buddhist. He is strapped to fate. It is not that he cannot do anything about this progression during a tournament, but almost that it is meant to be this way, because the others do not suffer as much as he does. He was not Burns. He was not Gonzalez. But nor was he Gulbis. He was just Stan.

Nadal beat Federer in the final. It was their thirtieth meeting and it lasted an embarrassingly brief sixty-nine minutes. Victory drew the Spaniard to within five career clay titles of the forty-six Guillermo Vilas had won. Not much more need be said about a duel that now had taken on the inevitability of a tidal wave.

As we said goodbye to the city of gladiators, there was blood all over the place. There would be a fair bit spilt in the months to come.

8

The First Break

It is three months since Rafael Nadal made his comeback on the clay of Viña del Mar in Chile. Today, he has accounted for a player significantly better than Federico Delbonis to win the Mutua Madrid Open in straight sets. Stanislas Wawrinka was on a roll up until Rome, when his groin went on him. 'I was not feeling that well and maybe not 100% physically and mentally,' the Swiss said. 'Even if I'm playing my best tennis and am completely fresh, it's really, really tough to beat him. If you're not completely there, then he's killing you.' This is the clearest sign yet that Nadal is close to full rehabilitation. If he can win at Roland Garros, maybe he can get revenge for that embarrassing first-round loss at Wimbledon the previous June.

~

When Jim Courier lost in the Wimbledon final to Pete Sampras in 1993, he was at least partly consoled by the fact that he had become the youngest player, at twenty-two, to reach the finals of all four Majors. It is a record that still stands twenty years later and is likely to last for a little while yet. Courier won four Slam titles and, just four years after turning professional, he was ranked number 1 in the world, a position he held for fifty-eight weeks. After he successfully defended his French title in 1992, the handsome 6-foot-1-inch all-American boy from Florida with the sandy hair and the big smile charmed Court Philippe Chatrier by delivering his victory speech in French. All his significant success came in a rush at the start of his career, so he knows better than most about the blizzard of quick celebrity and how tough it can be to upset the natural order of things. If it wasn't Sampras in front of him, it was Andre Agassi or Stefan Edberg. Courier retired at age thirty with twenty-three singles titles to his name, and was inducted into the International Tennis Hall of Fame five years later. Five years after that, he married Susanna Lingman and was named captain of the United States Davis Cup team. He leads what appears to be the most contented and fulfilling existence, the acme of a successful, well-executed career. Seamlessly, he took his smile into media work and he now earns a living as a charming TV frontman and commentator, sometimes simultaneously for different networks. His play-to-the-gallery air and an incurable weakness for appalling jokes disguises one of the keenest brains in the game.

Courier was adamant on the eve of the 2013 French Open. 'I don't see anyone breaking through in Paris,' he said over the phone from what sounded like the back of a New York taxi. Having won the French twice, he was worth listening to. 'Realistically, it's difficult to see anyone other than Rafa, Novak or Roger lifting the trophy. The younger players have a problem because these top players are so good offensively and defensively that they can get by in a bad game with just defence alone. In past years, players like Becker and Sampras, if they had an off day offensively, they could be vulnerable. That's just not the case with these guys. They are so well rounded and just so physically strong and, for the most part, durable when it comes to the best of five sets, as the records clearly show.'

It was as succinct a critique as I had heard, addressing strategy and technique as much as pure talent. It spoke to the seemingly obvious: if you could not hit the last ball against these great players, you were dead; against previous legends, there was the possibility of cracking their defence. This was not anti-tennis. This was new tennis.

'Eventually, Federer is going to retire,' Courier said. 'Nadal as well, and there are going to be opportunities, and these younger guys are going to win some of the big ones. It's hard to say who or when, but they are starting to see some daylight, because physically we've seen some cracks in the top four. Federer is playing less, Murray [*hors de combat*] is clearly suffering from a substantial back issue, and Rafa's knees kept him off the Tour for quite a while last year. The game has changed substantially from my day, because of the slower balls and courts. Now players have to be prepared to grind, day in, day out. Players need time off. From Andy's point of view, if he was feeling concern about his back, the French was a good one to miss.' How right could one man be . . .

As Courier pointed out, the key to the on-court power of these players was defence. The question was: how long would it be before an ambitious slayer of dragons cut one of them down, either through audacity or desperation? When would the wall begin to fall? None of them claimed to be unbeatable, even though they mostly were. They did lose in smaller tournaments – but not often – yet hardly at all when it counted. At the start of 2013, all four were so far ahead of the field that even consistently good players such as Ferrer, Berdych and del Potro could only hope that the draw, upsets or injury would allow them to be occasional intruders in the deciding weekends of the Grand Slam tournaments. Djokovic had the first in his pocket, but he might have guessed that adding the French, even after beating Nadal in Monte Carlo, would be his biggest challenge of the season. The last person to win the Australian and French back-to-back? Jim Courier, in 1992. It was every bit as tough a double as the French–Wimbledon, which are rammed up against each other in the schedule and require such an instantaneous adjustment from clay to grass that good players are often derailed.

Sport is not all about the score line, though. It is as much a part of the human experience as sweeping the roads or running a country. When we see these exceptional tennis players performing minor miracles every few weeks, it is easy to lose track of their fallibility. Djokovic, more than the other three, it always seemed to me, was a child of his emotions. There was a beast in there that roared when poked, but he also could be funny, scary, domineering, smart, intuitive, calculating and just plain crazy, all in the space of a match. He was also intelligent – and intelligent athletes sometimes are the most vulnerable, for all the right reasons. They think a lot. Although he had beaten the physical handicap of a rolled ankle to overcome Nadal at Monte Carlo a little while before the French Open, when he lost to him in that tournament twelve months previously, he was physically near perfect but emotionally wrecked after the death of his grandfather.

'I definitely don't want to take away anything from Rafa's win,' he said at the time. 'But it's a fact that I didn't have any emotional energy left in me. I just wasn't there. I've never been caught up in this kind of emotional situation before. It's been a very difficult week for me to go through mentally. I won three matches since the news. I mean, I think I did pretty well.'

Nadal recognised his rival's dilemma and sympathised, but he could not resist delivering him an unkind cut. It shocked many people on the Tour – the players, officials and journalists who regard the Spaniard as a good guy. 'Djokovic wasn't the real best Djokovic,' he said. 'But in other finals that I played against him, I wasn't my real best, either.' He was referring to the break-up of his parents' marriage in 2009, which coincided with a worsening of his tendinitis in both knees. He lost his world number 1 ranking and was as low as he had ever been in his career. 'My knees were the immediate reason for my loss of number 1,' he said back then, 'but I knew the root cause was my state of mind.' Later he told his biographer: 'They were the mainstay of my life and that pillar had crumbled. I was depressed, I lacked enthusiasm. I had lost all love for life.'

Given Nadal's own experience, then, his crack at Djokovic was a doubly cheap shot, and totally out of character. Yet it hinted at the ambivalent relationship between the two players, one which Djokovic's father would later claim was a lot less amicable than people imagined. By the end of the year, however, the two would be holding hands in front of a glacier in Patagonia.

In Paris, one of Nadal's many clay citadels, Djokovic was again struck down by a personal loss. His childhood mentor, the inspirational Jelena Genčić, died during the tournament, but he was not told until he had won his third-round match against Dimitrov. Djokovic, who had been to see Genčić at her home in Belgrade a few weeks earlier, cancelled his post-match press conference. When he emerged to address the media the following day, he expressed his sadness with the most moving and eloquent speech any of us could remember. Press conferences can be numbingly dull; this one was numbingly spellbinding.

'Jelena was my first coach,' he said, 'like my second mother. We were very close throughout my whole life, and she taught me a lot of things that are part of me, part of my character today, and I have the nicest memories of her . . . She worked with kids between five and six years old, to twelve, thirteen years old, and she was dedicating all her life to that generation and to tennis. She never got married, she never had kids. Tennis was all she had in life. She was seventy-seven years old and last week she was giving lessons to kids. She didn't really care about the nature of the illness. She had breast cancer. She survived that. She's one of the most incredible people I ever knew.'

In one short eulogy, conducted in the context of a mandated exchange with strangers bearing notebooks after a mere tennis match, a man better known as an iron-willed professional athlete brought a degree of humanity to the triviality of sport, and it left everyone present speechless.

Sentiment lingered in the locker-room for an appropriately decent time, but everyone had to get down to the work of trying to win a tennis tournament sooner or later, and there was a feeling at Roland Garros – just a small register on the Richter scale – that a tremor could be about to rip a fissure through the fabric of the game. After all, did Nadal not just lose to Djokovic in Monaco, stopped dead in his tracks there after eight titles on the spin? And was Murray not laid up in London, nursing his crumbling back? As for Federer, he had been out of sorts for so long that here, on a surface where he had only prevailed in the absence of Nadal, he was again going to be outside the core betting group.

There were early hints of rebellion. Three Americans qualified in the main draw for the first time since 1982: Denis Kudla, Steve Johnson and Jack Sock. It had been a wretched time for the American men since Andy Roddick retired . . . actually, before he retired. For now, they looked spent as a force at the top of the game – so this was, at least, encouragement for the future.

If we were looking for young players who might make an impact – and we were, desperately – Jiří Veselý, the only teenager in the top 200, qualified for his first Slam tournament. Pablo Carreño, who had had back surgery the previous June, and of whom good judges spoke warmly, was back and in the draw – but he had the misfortune to run into a rampant Federer in the first round, and went home after three sets. This was the Swiss's fifty-fourth straight Major. What must young Carreño have made of that? The Australian Nick Kyrgios was the youngest player in the tournament at eighteen, and marked his arrival with a debut win over thirty-five-year-old Radek Štěpánek (who also lost to Murray at Wimbledon in 2005, when Andy was eighteen; it might be cruel to call the former world number 8 Radek Stepping Stone, but sport is a cruel place).

Kyrgios had 'something about him', as the Australians say. The son of a Greek immigrant father and a Malaysian mother – with a lawyer for a brother and an actress for a sister – the smart young kid from the national capital, Canberra, was building a profile after winning the boys' title at the Australian Open. He was officially the best junior in the world – which can mean little to the grown-ups on the Tour, although there was not a lot Štěpánek could do to blunt his energy or determination in three straight tie-breaks. Kyrgios had arrived with a bit of a thump in Australia, winning a Challenger aged seventeen at his second attempt (and without dropping a set) when stepping up from the juniors. Only fifteen players in the Open era had won at this level at his age, which sent stats analyst Jeff Sackmann into a frenzy of research at his blog, Heavy Topspin. He discovered that five of those players went on to win Majors, four of them more than once, while also reaching number 1 in the world. Two had recently finished the calendar year in that spot: Djokovic and Nadal. All but four were ranked 9 or higher in their careers. The fifteen players have won 192 titles and twenty-two Majors between them.

And here is the list of the blessed prodigies since 1992, which Kyrgios joined: Gabriel Silberstein, Nicolas Kiefer, Marat Safin, Lleyton Hewitt, Mikhail Youzhny, Mario Ančić, Jimmy Wang, Richard Gasquet, Rafael Nadal, Tomáš Berdych, Nicolás Almagro, Novak Djokovic, Evgeny Korolev, Juan Martín del Potro and Bernard Tomic. It is a starry collection. Whether or not those numbers would mean much to Kyrgios was way too early to tell. But he was in good company. Marin Čilić, who still had no inkling that his refusal to take a drugs test in Monte Carlo would soon return to haunt him, took a little over an hour and a half to send young Kyrgios packing. He headed for Nottingham, where Jordan Kerr, a thirty-four-year-old Australian doubles specialist who had long stopped dreaming, put him out in the second round of qualifying.

The old guys were not exactly idling at Roland Garros. Tommy Robredo, who nearly gave tennis up because of injury, had returned in good spirits and full health; otherwise, there is no way he would have been able to save four match points and come from two sets down to start his campaign, then do the same in his next two matches. Nobody had won after giving up the first two sets in three straight matches in a Slam since Henri Cochet at Wimbledon in 1927. The same day that Robredo was seen wearily leaving the court after doing the hat-trick, Federer won his 900th career match, also in five sets (the first since Lendl in 1990), and Djokovic won his 500th. What are records for if not for shattering with such memorable symmetry?

And yet the British press corps pined for a bit of Murray. What was our boy up to? Well, not a lot. He was back in London mulling over his future and taking advice from all quarters on whether to get his back fixed straight away, for once and for all, or carry on at Queen's and then Wimbledon on painkillers. For now, he kept hitting. And hoping.

We did keep up one sacred ritual in Paris: dinner with Ion Țiriac. For as long as any of our little band could remember, the eccentric and engaging Romanian, whose outrageous moustache was a perfect match for his personality, had entertained us at a restaurant of his choice when we came to town. Occasionally we reciprocated, which could be financially bruising but was always worth it. The evenings were never dull. Usually Țiriac, who runs the Madrid Open and was about to be inducted into the International Tennis Hall of Fame, would regale us for twenty minutes with high-grade gossip about the people who ran international sport (some of whose names we actually recognised), and without fail would select wine and food we imagined would not look out of place in the Palace of Versailles. Keeping this appointment often taxed our ingenuity, given the late finishes to some matches, and the reluctance of Parisian taxi drivers to even pretend to understand where we wanted to go, but we got there. Few tasks galvanise a journalist like an invitation to a free meal. It would be impertinent to share some of those dinner-table anecdotes, but it is safe to say one or two of them might not have made it on to *Woman's Hour*. The man who briefly gave tennis blue clay (at Madrid the previous year) could also relate the odd blue story.

The tournament, meanwhile, was moving towards an inevitable climax. Wawrinka hung tough for five sets against Gasquet in one of the best matches either of them played all year to reach the quarters, but the Swiss could not get past Nadal. Federer also was dragged into a five-setter against a Frenchman, Simon, and looked weary, losing in less than two hours to Tsonga, a Frenchman too far. Given their history, the Nadal–Djokovic semi-final shaped up as the confrontation of the fortnight, and it did not disappoint, the Serb cursing a mysterious mid-match collapse that allowed the champion to grind him into the dirt over five enthralling sets. It was Nadal's thirteenth win over Djokovic on clay in sixteen matches – and Rafa's forty-eighth consecutive semi-final win on clay since he lost to Carlos Moyá at Umag (in Croatia) ten years earlier. That is scary dominance.

In the other semi, it surprised none of Ferrer's many admirers to see him beat Tsonga, who for so long has cast gloom over his chances at a tournament where a Frenchman has not won since Yannick Noah, in 1983. There was a frisson surrounding that seemingly innocent fact: two years earlier Noah had savaged Spanish sport in a newspaper article, hinting strongly at the widespread use of performance-enhancing drugs. 'Today if you don't have the magic potion,' he said in *Le Monde*, 'it's hard to win. How can a nation dominate sport virtually overnight like this?'

He added: 'When I still milled around on the courts with my racquet, we weren't ridiculous, far from it, against our Spanish friends. It was the same on the soccer fields, the basketball halls or on the roads of the Tour de France. Today they are running faster than us, are much stronger and only leave us the bread crumbs. We look like dwarves. Did we miss something? Did they discover some avant-garde techniques or training facilities that nobody before them had imagined?'

Nadal was livid. 'He knows better than anybody that to say that today is a totally stupid thing because you know how many anti-doping controls we have during the season, year by year. So in my opinion, the article that he wrote was from a kid and when one kid says something it's not painful for us. What he said is completely stupid. This guy does not deserve to write in newspapers anymore.'

Nor, reckoned Nadal, now on the eve of the 2013 French Open final, did the French hero deserve to be in the frame for presenting the trophy to the winner. He was a strong and obvious candidate – especially if Tsonga had managed to reach the final – so the argument was diffused in the end. When I wrote this in the *Guardian*, it did not go down well with the Spaniard's team and I received a sharp, short phone call later asking who my source was. That, of course, was not information I felt inclined to share. But I was sure of my facts. I asked Nadal's man, if the story was not true, would he, indeed, have accepted the trophy from Noah? After a silence, I was informed that this was irrelevant.

As it happened, apart from a tie-break in the second, the all-Spanish final – the sixth at Roland Garros – proved to be a disappointment as a contest, although Nadal was back to his wonderful, grunting best. Ferrer, sadly, seemed to shrink in the presence of his friend in three quick sets. While Ferrer adopted his hang-dog mien afterwards, Nadal could not stop smiling. He had just become the first player to win a Major nine years in a row and now had twelve to his name, just five behind Federer. He wanted more, though. The hunger had returned with a vengeance. And, receiving the Coupe des

Mousquetaires from the world's fastest man, Usain Bolt, Nadal knew he would have to make the most of every minute left to him in his career.

There was a footnote to the tournament that would not easily be erased. Ernests Gulbis, not influential with the racquet, hit an ace with his sharp tongue. This is what he told *L'Equipe* shortly before Gaël Monfils put him out of the second round after four thrilling sets.

> I respect Roger, Rafa, Novak and Murray but, for me, all four of them are boring players. Their interviews are boring. Honestly, they are crap [*chiants*]. I often go on YouTube to watch the interviews. With tennis, I quickly stop. It is a joke. It is Federer who started this fashion. He has a superb image of the perfect Swiss gentleman. I repeat, I respect Federer but I don't like it that young players try to imitate him. When I hear them answer like Roger, I am terrified by phrases like, 'I had a little bit more success at certain moments and that is how I won.' If I win, the guy on the other side of the net, I have sent him home. That is the reality. I do not want to hear in an interview a guy – who I will not name, but who I know well, that he thinks all his opponents are arseholes – putting on an act. I don't care [what people say]. I have no interest in appearing nice. On the court, it is a war. Off court, no problem. I have a good relationship with most of the players. But I want to say what I think. And if my prognosis is that I am going to win the match, it doesn't bother me to say so. I would like interviews to be more like in boxing. OK, maybe those guys are not the most brilliant on earth but, when they face each other down at the weigh-in, they bring what the fans want: war, blood, emotion. All that is missing in tennis, where everything is clean, and white with polite handshakes and some nice shots, while the people want to see broken racquets and hear outbursts on the court.

John McEnroe, who knew a thing or two about confrontation in his playing heyday, had his five-cents-worth too. 'I don't disagree that it would be nice in a way, people going at it a little more viciously,' he said. '[But] it's, like, it's not their styles. I guess they find it hard to show it. I'm not sure what there is underneath the surface. I don't see it the way it was when it bubbled over between me and [Jimmy] Connors or [Ivan] Lendl.'

Before Roland Garros, Murray touched on the subject of candour in an interview with GQ magazine, when he said: 'Whether people like you or not should be irrelevant. But, to be honest, over the years I have found it difficult to open up and be a bundle of laughs in press conferences, or interviews. I always try to give honest answers, but they are fairly boring so I don't have to deal with the aftermath of any scandals. I would say that I am different from what a lot of people think I am like.'

Djokovic gave substance to Gulbis's core argument with a monumentally boring reaction. 'I haven't heard about his comments,' he said, stretching credulity as the row raged across all forms of traditional and social media, 'and I haven't talked with him about that, but everybody has their own opinion, so that's difficult to judge. We have certain rules and ways that our tennis is functioning, and that you have to respect. I try to look at it on a positive side. I think that especially the top players are very respectful toward the sport and toward, you know, people who are appreciating and following the sport, to the media, and also to each other. This is very important. Even though it's individual sport, we still have very respectful and healthy relation-ships. It sends a good message out there. In some moments it can be more entertaining, yes, it can. But, again, there are good things, a lot of good things. There is always something you can find and say, OK, that's something that should be different. But I agree with one small fact [which] is that maybe we are lacking more enthusiasm and maybe more entertainment in the players, so more creativity in the players.'

This was filibuster-level snooze material. Gulbis will have laughed his head off reading it on his way home from Paris in his private jet.

As for the man attracting the most opprobrium, Federer tried desperately hard to keep a dignified silence but eventually made a brief response. And, to the surprise of many, he did not totally disagree with Gulbis. 'I understand what Gulbis said,' he told us just before Wimbledon. 'He is partially right. Our interviews are often boring. But it's the machine. We often have to give too many interviews. Also, if you criticise others, you get torn apart by the others – so that's why we all are nice to the others, although tennis doesn't lack for characters.'

So diplomatic and reasonable was the Federer reply, one was tempted to imagine here was a man who could solve almost any of the game's complex issues (perhaps one day, he will be in a position to do so). And that, to an extent, is what annoys the other three . . . if ever they were to be open about it.

None of these allegations is especially shocking, but the wound that Djokovic's father opened up for all to see did give weight to the words of Gulbis, as well as to other whispers on the Tour. Some of it will have been inspired by jealousy, of course, and might well have been exaggerated, but it is unlikely all of it was made up. While they were 'professional friends' of varying degrees, it is fair to speculate that any two or even all of the four might have spent as much time together locked in battle on the tennis court as ever they have over a quiet meal. Their pact of mutual respect was genuine and, inasmuch as they ever acknowledged it, low-key. None wanted to waste words on it. It existed, and that was enough, even under irritatingly persistent questioning. They did well, sometimes, to stay patient. Not everyone was convinced about the enduring politeness of these intelligent and articulate athletes. Maybe Gulbis had a point. There were slivers of evidence that all was not as it seemed.

9

Wimbledon

> Immediately the lark mounted with a loud trill from
>   Felpham's Vale,
> And the Wild Thyme from Wimbledon's green and
>   impurpled Hills,
> And Los and Enitharmon rose over the hills of Surrey.

That little grab of mystic vision by William Blake, attached to his four verses of 'Jerusalem', could be the answer to one of the minor puzzles of British sport: why are Wimbledon's colours (the most famous in sport, alongside the ham-and-egg red-and-yellow of the ancient Marylebone Cricket Club) dark green and purple? It is the sort of arcane question that would fascinate only the most fiendishly obsessed, and I will take it on trust that Stephen Woodley, scholarly in such things and, relevantly, a member of the All England Club, might not mind being so described. It is his theory that Blake and Wimbledon are linked, not an association that might immediately spring to mind to devotees of either the revolutionary poet or the club, one of the foundation pillars of the British establishment. The club's original colours of blue, yellow, red and green too closely resembled those of the Royal Marines, apparently, and Mr Woodley surmises that, forced to change (this would only happen in a country so grounded in military history), the committee might have been influenced by a member familiar with the above passage. It is as good a theory as any, and one to which John Barrett is happy to subscribe.

Nobody, surely, knows more about Wimbledon than Barrett. He is the keeper of the faith, a man whose own talent and passion for the game has ensured a lifetime association with the revered home of tennis. He reached the third round four times, got as high as number 5 in Britain and captained the Davis Cup team between 1959 and 1962, before diving into a long media career with the BBC and the *Financial Times*. He has chronicled every single result in the history of the club, and says it is his joy to live 'a stone's throw' from Wimbledon with his wife, the 1961 champion, Angela Mortimer.

The first time John visited the green lawns of the All England Club, they had not seen any tennis for six years. It was in the summer of 1946, when, as a fifteen-year-old schoolboy, he travelled down from Mill Hill in north London to share in the post-war euphoria that gripped a country still weary from the rigours and sacrifice of global conflict. In 1940 a German bomb had levelled part of Centre Court (where the players used to sit), and it still had not been properly restored, so there was an air of sticking-plaster make-do about the championships. This was in keeping with the national mood, as people continued to master the intricacies of the ration book and a still-creaking infrastructure. The car park had been given up during the war to growing vegetables, and, as Barrett recalls in his all-embracing official history of Wimbledon, 'the main concourse echoed to the marching feet of London Welsh and London Irish Regiments'. And so one sport's traditional base was married to the fortunes of the nation. Not surprising, then, that it was to Wimbledon that young Barrett and thousands of tennis fans hurried back for a glimpse of unalloyed British sporting life that some of them had feared they might not see again.

There were eight seeds that year, none of the forty-seven British entrants having been honoured (although the top-rated player, the Australian champion Dinny Pails, was born in

Nottingham). Jack Kramer, the glamorous American, was seeded second but he was the crowd's favourite, a crew-cut Yank with a big, confident smile, the epitome of New World hope and ambition, the Jim Courier of his day. They had saved the world, hadn't they? However, struck by blisters on his right hand, this gleaming champion of post-war modernity had to play wearing a glove and was cut down by the bespectacled Czech left-hander, Jaroslav Drobný, in the fourth round. Before the Iron Curtain completely clanked shut across Europe, there was a strong sense of commonality among the Allied nations, and it was manifest at Wimbledon that year, driven by relief at being alive and an urge to celebrate every second of it. In the final, over five sets, the giant Frenchman Yvon Petra – one of whose booming serves broke a net during the tournament – defeated Australia's smaller Geoff Brown, who could hit with either hand. Petra was not only the last Frenchman to win Wimbledon; he was the last finalist to wear long trousers. It was a match – and a tournament – about as far removed from the two-fisted wars of today as it is possible to conjure up in the imagination. Although Blake would have given it a good try.

On the fourth day of the 2013 edition of 'the championships' – as they are fondly referred to, tongue-in-cheek by sans culottes, with grim seriousness in the clubhouse – there seemed no more appropriate authority to talk to than Barrett, for an historical overview of the game he loves and which has changed beyond recognition in the sixty-three years since his first visit. As a player, commentator and writer, Barrett has seen all the game's ebbing and flowing, with a critical but never jaundiced eye.

And there was much to talk about midway through the first week.

On Court 1, a thunderbolt ripped through the championships. Nadal was beaten. The villain (and hero to all Belgians) was Steve Darcis, who, like Lukáš Rosol a year earlier, was inspired by the company he was keeping to reach rare heights of excellence.

He won in straight sets. 'Today for me was not a lot of things good,' Nadal observed. Asked to compare this defeat in the first round to the 2012 shock in the third round, he could only say, 'I really don't know how to answer this question.' I had not seen him this devastated since he arrived at the World Tour finals in 2011 lacking what he called 'passion' and losing before the semi-finals to Tsonga. It is tougher now to apply total commitment to every single match than it was in Barrett's day.

'The only time I've missed a day since I first came here was when my son was graduating,' he says as we share a pot of tea in the media lounge overlooking Courts 14 and 15, which would be carved up and relayed in the winter as the club embarked on a wholesale rebuild of the premises, due for completion in 2019. For an institution long considered to be stuck in the past, the All England Club, inspired by the commercial clout of its product and gingered up by competing sports, had developed pleasingly progressive tendencies. This was not quite the club John Barrett visited for the first time in his school uniform.

'Every year since 1951, and the four years before that, I was here at least for one day, as a schoolboy. I played here eighteen years. Home was Mill Hill, so I had quite a journey, but it was no hardship.'

Today's journey for himself and Angela is a stroll. But is the experience as pleasant? Barrett gives the impression that it doesn't matter what you do to tennis, it will fundamentally be the same entrancing experience, for those who play and those who watch. Nevertheless, it is not as it was, and he does regret that.

'What has happened to tennis,' he says, '[is] it has become so much more a physical sport, simply because of the racquets and the strings. Now it's a topspin sport from the baseline, where the angles are sharper, the ball is hit faster and therefore the players have to move more quickly to get there. It is part of the evolution of the sport. If they had banned metal racquets – as cricket banned metal bats – then we would be able to compare eras. I'm not saying this isn't a great era. It is. It's a wonderful era. But it's a different era. It's a totally different game. Everybody now plays with western grips and open-stance forehands. It always used to be eastern grips, put the other foot forward and swing through the shot. Not now. It's topspin, topspin, topspin.

'When Borg made his comeback to play in Monte Carlo, he asked Slazenger's – who had made wooden racquets for him originally – if they would reopen their production line. But it was too late. By then, nobody was using them. Then he tried Donnay, his last racquet-maker; they couldn't do it. But Gray's of Cambridge came up with one. They were still making wooden racquets for racquets players and squash players. I went to see him practising at Queen's Club, the week before we went down to Monte Carlo, and he played Chris Wilkinson. Chris was using a modern Slazenger graphite racquet. I remember watching the rallies develop, and the ball pinged from Wilkinson's racquet, then ballooned softly as Borg hit it back with his topspin. I went home and I said to Angela, "I've just spoken to Björn and his intended return to tennis next week. I don't care who he plays, he will lose. He will be eaten alive." And sure enough he was.'

On 22 April 1991, after five years away – during which time he had cut his locks and descended into some unhappy places with drugs and personal relationships – Borg emerged from his Monte Carlo residence, his hair long again, and returned to the courts he had once terrorised with his crushing ground-strokes. In 78 minutes the Spaniard Jordi Arrese, ranked 52nd in the world, fulfilled Barrett's fears. It did not get any better for the Swede. Borg then lost, in succession, to Olivier Delaître (43), Wayne Ferreira (22), Goran Prpić (34), Thomas Hogstedt (157), Chris Pridham (112), Nicklas Kulti (77), Lionel Roux (196), Jaime Oncins (46), João Cunha-Silva (113) . . . and, finally, thankfully, when he had nothing left to give but his name to sponsors, he went down in flames against Alexander Volkov (17) in three sets in the Kremlin Cup in Moscow on 8 November 1993. He fought to the end, though, losing the third-set tie-break 6–7. There can hardly have been a more poignant withdrawal from the drug of sporting celebrity than that . . . except by George Best, perhaps. A couple of months later in New York, Borg's compatriot, Mats Wilander, would share his theory about this revealing period of Borg's life.

The composition and quality of the hitting implement is a source of obsession for nearly everyone in tennis. There are those who understand the mysteries of the modern weapon down to the finest millimetre. Barrett does – but he has a similarly profound understanding of the consequences of the technology.

'There is no room anymore for the sort of tactical game that demands subtlety. So, we'll never see another [Nicola] Pietrangeli, [Ilie] Năstase, we'll never see another [Manuel] Santana . . . all those artists. They can't exist now. Having said that, there is a lot of artistry in what some of the hitters do. They can play that way. Nadal is a lovely volleyer. His drop-shot is first-class. But it doesn't pay them to play that way. If it did, they would. In a professional sport where money matters, everybody plays the most effective game to earn the money. And you can't blame them for that. It's absolutely normal. So everybody is playing with these racquets which allow you to hit with fizzing topspin. They are incredibly hard to volley.'

Which brings us to the defeat of Federer in three of the worst hours of his career. What Sergiy Stakhovsky did to the seven-time champion in the second round, two days after Steve Darcis of Belgium had executed Nadal in the first round, was to put his hand inside his chest and rip out his heart. He did it without fear, almost without thinking. His willingness to live or die at the net at first annoyed Federer, then bewildered him.

Even though there was only a single point between them after four sets, it was the Ukrainian who left the court walking tall. The rest of the tournament, from the media centre to the lines of fans wandering home, was an emotional bombsite.

For the first time since 2010, Federer had opened Wimbledon as defending champion on Centre Court, his personal stronghold in the course of gathering seven previous titles. There was a collective urge for him to do well, and he did not disappoint, giving up just five games to Victor Hănescu. Surely, his disciples reckoned, the Messiah had returned with a fresh cloak and his halo at just the right angle.

'I pack my bags anyway for five sets every single time,' he told us later. He was confident, nonetheless, that he brought more to the championships at age thirty-one than he did on his early visits. He was happy in his matured state. 'I'm stronger, because I have the experience. Because I've played so much, I'm just overall a more complete player. In those ten years, many things have changed, racquet technology, strings, balls, court speed. All these things have a big impact on the game.' He could have won with a toothpick. There was no reason, yet, to have blasphemous doubts.

The defeat of Nadal on the Monday was shocking, but of a different type. Those who'd seen him bundled out by Lukáš Rosol had almost been immunised against the effects. Less certain was how the player himself was taking it. There was a stunned disbelief in the main interview room. This was not déjà vu, it was a recurring nightmare. It was not how it was meant to be. 'I don't gonna talk about my knee this afternoon,' he said, grumpily, but he did allow a glimmer of insight into his physical condition when he confirmed, 'I gonna try my best for the next couple of years.'

But what of his twenty-nine-year-old conqueror, Darcis? This was his greatest day, yet, inevitably, it would be framed in the context of his illustrious opponent's embarrassment, and he pretty much knew that would be the case. He was ranked 135 in the world at the time (and would slide further after pulling out of his second-round match against Łukasz Kubot) and had become used to the role of sparring partner. He did not often live up to his nickname of 'shark' but on this fine day he was that lurking enemy, szhumping from the deep to cut the Spaniard down at the knee. (His hobby is fishing.) He won behind a strong serve, a teasing slice that drew Nadal on to his punch, and a cool nerve, wary of his wounded prey until the last stroke of the match. 'I don't know if he was injured,' he said. 'Physically, he looked OK. He was running, he was moving good.' Thus he punctured the jury's case. Yet it was unreliable evidence. Darcis, whatever the merit of his excellent win, could hardly be expected to concede he had beaten a diminished version of a player with eleven Slams to his own meagre haul of two Tour titles, in Amersfoort six years earlier, then Memphis the following year, when his talent plainly was in its fullest flower. 'Of course Rafa didn't play his best tennis,' he agreed. 'I could see it, so I took advantage of it. I tried to fight.' This was revealing. Had Darcis not sensed a weakness, would he have been as combative, or would he, like many of Nadal's opponents, have bowed to the inevitable after a brief, spirited challenge? Darcis had played many fine players before – he beat Berdych in the first round of the Olympics – but, invariably, he had lost to them. This glorious triumph, to be cruel, was a one-off. He probably realised that, but could not say so and it would have been unreasonable to expect him to. That, however, was the reality. That is what we had just witnessed, a cold blast to leave a chill, not a hurricane. On day three, Darcis withdrew from the tournament, his magic moment captured for ever in his own head (although he immediately sought out a DVD).

There was a collective wish, meanwhile, that Nadal would not leave us for another seven-month refit. He did not let us down. Federer we were less sure about. When his moment of truth struck like a left hook, he reeled in front of us. The Swiss struggled for composure but was his usual accommodating self, even if desperate to leave the scene of the accident and be with his own thoughts. Reaching for the best shine on a dull day, he said: 'I appreciated the standing ovation I got leaving the court, no doubt about it. I'll be OK.' It was, he said, a 'normal day, normal warm-up, normal match'. Clearly it was anything but. This was award-winning abnormality: the greatest player of all time losing to an unseeded opponent in the second round of a tournament he had won seven times. That is not normal.

Then, the howitzer question you could have heard coming from a mile away, the same one we had tormented Nadal with: did this feel like the 'end of an era'? It had to be asked, even if it had been proffered many times over the previous year or so. And he had to answer it. 'No, because I still have plans to play for many more years to come. It's normal that after all of a sudden losing early after being in the quarters thirty-six times, people feel it's different. You guys hyped it up so much, me playing Rafa, and we're both out. So there's a let-down clearly. Maybe it's also somewhat a bit disrespectful to the other opponents who are in the draw still. I think it sends a message to you guys as well that maybe you shouldn't do that so often next time around.'

Now we were on an antagonistic footing. Now it was partly our fault. Why didn't we back off, give the other guys some credit? Well, there was a very good reason for that: the other guys weren't normally fit to carry the bags of Federer, Nadal, Djokovic or Murray – well, not guys who couldn't break into the top 100 in the world. It was not, as Federer insisted again, 'normal' for him to lose to Stakhovsky. He was giving him respect, which was all well and good and very noble, but he was whistling in the dark on this one. He should not have lost to the 116th best player in the world if everything was 'normal'. The exchange had drifted into a weird place. There seemed no point in extending the mutual discomfort, but we ploughed on, because Federer had something to say and we had plenty to write.

'He was uncomfortable to play against,' Federer offered. 'He served and volleyed really well. It was difficult to get into that much rhythm clearly against a player like that. But I don't mind it, to be quite honest, playing an opponent like that.'

And Stakhovsky, it transpired, did not mind playing Federer, even if it had not totally sunk in a couple of hours later. 'When you come here, on the cover of the Wimbledon book is Roger Federer,' he observed. 'You're playing the guy and then you're playing his legend, which is following him because he won it seven times. He's holding all possible career records here, winning matches and everything. You're playing two of them. When you're beating one, you still have the other one who is pressing you. You're saying, "Am I about to beat him? Is it possible?" It's just psychology. You cannot run from it. It's just how it happens. When I was a break up in the fourth, you think about it. "Really? Is it happening?" I hope I can come out with a great performance the next round.' Two days later, he was packing his bags and heading home to Bratislava.

'The remarkable thing yesterday,' Barrett says as we survey the wreckage of the tournament, 'was that Stakhovsky was hitting so many good volleys against Federer's attempted topspin passing shots. It was refreshing in a way to see the basic values of what we all regarded as clay-court technique had been restored. It was lovely. It was a little visit from the past. When was the last time Federer played a serve–volleyer? There's only a handful of them left.'

Barrett recalls with a deal of wistfulness Tim Henman's inspired run at Roland Garros in 2004, when he decided he would play grass-court tennis on the clay of Paris – virtually a heresy. It got him all the way to the semi-finals, and was among the most thrilling runs in a Major by any British player. He was, at times, irresistible, combining grit with inspiration to come from two sets down against Cyril Saulnier, beat Lars Burgsmüller in three very quick sets, do a similar job on Galo Blanco, struggle from behind again over five sets against Michaël Llodra (himself a prince of the serve–volley game), then dismiss the Argentinian Juan Ignacio Chela in three sets.

'Do you remember that, against [Guillermo] Coria?' Barrett says, taking a quick sip of his cooling tea. 'He should have beaten him. Extraordinary match. The element of surprise in any sport is good, and that is what Tim did in that tournament.'

Barrett recalls another piece of tennis theatre that left him – and everyone else – astonished: Rosol's win over Nadal at Wimbledon the year before. 'It was the most remarkable experience I've ever had watching a tennis match. It was staggering. He just hit clean winners at will. Unbelievable. And he didn't choke.'

What Barrett cherishes about tennis is the game's in-built capacity for the unpredictable. He sees victories such as these as the player's 'golden day', when all the required ingredients for an upset converge at the right time. We revel in the achievement of the German-Jamaican Dustin Brown, who, the day before, had put out the former world number 1 Lleyton Hewitt with the sort of carefree tennis you might see in the park, but not in an important match in a Slam tournament. 'What a refreshing character,' Barrett observes.

That said, you have to sustain the quality of your tennis. You're working in a profession, and your job is to win. When Murray, for instance, was working his way up, he was building his game, getting his confidence and all that was missing was that last piece. He actually knew he could play an attacking game. He was just a bit nervous doing it often enough. He used to try to extract wins, instead of imposing them. Now he imposes them. He has Lendl a lot to thank for that – plus the fact that he's older, he's had more experience – and two great wins last year, plus two great finals, one here in the Olympics, then in America. So he now believes he can do it.

Barrett has as keen an eye for the minutiae of the game as anyone and saw in Murray's win over Yen-hsun Lu in the second round the previous day details to wonder at. 'What a beautiful tennis match,' he says, a smile growing across his face. 'High-quality rallies of eight, nine, ten strokes – and Andy was imposing himself, that was the difference. Really good players have another gear. But Federer couldn't find his yesterday. As he said afterwards, he was disappointed when he got close he could not find a way, as he usually is able to.'

He compares Federer's defeat to another loss that left the tournament utterly flat: the last appearance at Wimbledon of Pete Sampras, in 2002, when he could not find a worthwhile answer to the inspired play of the rank outsider George Bastl, whose fame is secured for ever in the numbers from that second-round match: 6–3, 6–2, 4–6, 3–6, 6–4 in 195 minutes. The previous year, Sampras had gone out to Federer in the fourth round, 6–7(7), 7–5, 4–6, 7–6(2), 5–7 in 221 minutes. Losing to Switzerland with diminishing resistance in successive Wimbledons sent undeniable signals of doom to the American, not to mention encouragement to his rivals. That he managed to win another Slam in his last match on the Tour, against Agassi in the final of the 2003 US Open, was testimony to his gift for conjuring up magic from nowhere. Were there not obvious parallels between the two, I ask Barrett.

> Well . . . that was another sad day. It's a good point, though, the comparison between the two events. They were very similar. And of course they become irritated when we keep asking them about it, about when they might call it a day. As for Roger, I hope he doesn't play on for more than one or perhaps two more years. We all want to remember him as the great champion he has ever been. There has been no greater. Nobody will ever, ever achieve what he has achieved in terms of consistency. Nobody.
>
> You can't compare eras [which, of course, is no impediment to our doing it all the time]. But what you can say is this: [Rod] Laver missed twenty-five opportunities to play Grand Slam

tournaments, when he was a pro in those years. And [Ken] Rosewall, who was the best player in the world at that stage, having beaten [Pancho] Gonzales in the pro game, missed something like forty-three chances. And Gonzales himself missed seventy-five Grand Slam matches, yet came back in '68. So those three would sure have won more championships.

But it's always sad when a great champion begins to lose. And the manner [of his loss to Stakhovsky] was so sad. If he'd gone out with a great fight, it would have been different. But it was a rather dismal loss. He shanked I don't know how many shots. It was ten years ago here when he first amazed us with his artistry. But it's got to happen some time, that it comes to an end. Nothing goes on for ever. I don't think he will win another Major. The surprise is that it has lasted as long as it has, really, at such a high level. His consistency has been quite staggering. Nothing even remotely approaches it. And I don't think there ever will be. In nineteen consecutive Grand Slams, he reached the final of eighteen. That is absolutely phenomenal. If Nadal hadn't been there, he would have won a whole lot more, because he was easily the second best clay-court player in the world at that stage of his career, when Nadal kept beating him.

But tennis always needs rivalries. They have produced the great finals of the past. And I think Djokovic and Murray are the natural inheritors of that mantle – but don't write off Nadal just yet. We were all worried when he had to miss seven months of tennis after Wimbledon last year. It was clearly very serious. From football, we know how tricky knee injuries can be – probably more than any other part of the anatomy.

If new rivalries, new contenders are emerging, they are not yet so established as to encourage confidence in their longevity. Barrett sees some cause for encouragement, though.

We all think Dimitrov has got potential. Whether he'll work hard enough and build on what he's got, we don't know. But he has got talent. I thought Raonic was going to break through – but he's lost again today [to Igor Sijsling in straight sets]. Now

Janowicz [who had just put out Štěpánek and would make much more noise before the tournament was over], there's a promising player.

We might also remember that the '01 final between Rafter and Ivanišević was one of the last great serve–volley matches. Then we had Hewitt and Nalbandian in the final the next year, the first of what we have now come to expect as normal, which is a baseline final. That's when it all changed. It would be nice if we could find a really good serve–volleyer to test the players of today. But they've all been phased out, even on fast courts . . . It's a bit boring, to be honest with you . . . The variety is no longer there. It's all the same, every match. I'm told if you run your fingers across the strings of Nadal's racquet, you draw blood. I think the ITF have failed the game in not controlling the development of racquets and strings properly. It's condemned the game to be a one-dimensional slug-fest from the back of the court, which is wonderful in one sense, because they're so good at what they do, but it's the variety that I miss. You'd have to be a bit of a dinosaur to understand that . . . It all seems like such a long time ago.

Whether Federer will be part of the next evolution in tennis is up to him. Although unlikely, it would be wondrous if he were to somehow do it. But, as Blake said in an entirely different context, 'You never know what is enough unless you know what is more than enough.'

10

At Last

The Hurlingham Club, 22 June 2013

There are two bottles of mineral water lined up on the table in front of Andy Murray as we settle down to talk in the decorous surroundings of one of London's most exclusive sporting clubs, on the banks of the Thames near Fulham – one sparkling, the other still. He has just finished his final work-out before Wimbledon, an encouraging if undemanding win in an exhibition match against Kei Nishikori. A small wager with a colleague on which water Murray will choose is down; Murray chooses still. I should have known: athletes do not drink fizzy water usually because it interferes with digestion, and Murray is as meticulous about these details as he is about any aspect of his tennis. Besides, he has brought his own special mixture. Of course he has. Murray is late for the interview after 'precautionary' treatment to his back. He says he feels 'fine' for the challenge ahead.

~

After Federer and Nadal had been shipwrecked, Andy Murray sailed with serenity into the second week of Wimbledon. These were much calmer waters than he was used to in a Slam. He had negotiated the brief, testing challenge of Mikhail Youzhny in three sets on the second Monday and there was no sign – or complaint – that his back was causing him trouble. However, by the time the already weakened field had been further filleted, it was time for the tough to get going. And Murray, whose gift for making life difficult seemed endless, could hardly have made the going tougher for himself on Wednesday than by falling two sets behind to the combative Fernando Verdasco in what turned out to be a quarter-final worthy of a title-decider.

Sir Alex Ferguson, heading for retirement and now a fully paid-up, world-travelling tennis groupie, was there again to support his countryman, a comfortingly robust presence in a sometimes stuffy and slumbering royal box. This time he was here with his son, Mark, rather than Sir Sean Connery, his party partner in New York the previous September. There was tennis royalty here, too: Nicola Pietrangeli (a foot soldier from Barrett's treasured past), Rod Laver and Manuel Santana.

Wimbledon pulls in old legends from all eras and countries; it is the go-to celebration of the sport. While the other events also have their five-star guest lists, none matches the quality and depth that the All England Club manage to put together every June and July in the English summer. The well-heeled, the titled and the comped mingle in the champagne bar beneath and, when summonsed, move up to be ogled alongside a varied list of minor royals. It is as much a part of the tradition of the place as are the strawberries and early exits of local hopefuls. There is fun to be had on a warm day in betting on which guest will nod off first. There have been some big names asleep during very important points on Centre Court over the years, but it would be cruel to name them.

On this second Wednesday, it was hard to miss our old friend, Ion Țiriac, his moustache looking more like an ancient motorbike handlebar by the day. Roger Taylor, he of the heavy, dark eyebrows and for years Britain's best player, was there too. His was a gentler age by a distance, and he is remembered still for sportsmanship in the 1973 quarter-finals that probably will never be repeated. Playing Björn Borg on the Swede's debut at seventeen, Taylor was declared the winner when the teenager's final shot was called out. Taylor thought otherwise, asked for the point to be replayed, won it and went on to reach the semi-finals. He thought nothing of the gesture, incidentally.

Back in slaughterhouse 2013, Murray was having an altogether terrible time against Verdasco and clearly needed a moment of magic. When it mattered, he invariably found one, which seemed perverse to those watching who could never dream of emulating even a bad Murray ground-stroke – a feature of his game that, although not as bad as it used to be, lurked like a fluffed line. Often the badness came when least expected; a slump following a break. Here, he had played pretty well but struggled to tame Verdasco, who was playing near to his maximum in every point. A set down, Murray was in real danger of going out, a parlous situation made worse when it looked as if he could not stop the Spaniard's energetic progress. And then he slowed it in the final exchanges of a rally after an hour and a quarter with a single shot of such magnificence that the dividend in the third would be enough to rescue the result and his Wimbledon campaign.

Verdasco struck a dozen killing forehands on Murray to pin him perilously behind the baseline, then teased him with a sliced backhand in the deuce corner that stretched him to the point of surrender – not a word the Scot gives house space to. Murray chased down the shot and, under immense pressure on the run, found a cross-court forehand that not only left his opponent helpless but brought Centre Court to its feet. It was the turning point everybody missed at the time. Verdasco held, but he had been put on notice, and he sensed it. From that point in the match, Murray had his measure. The fight drained visibly from Verdasco's tennis as Murray ground him down with a stream of exquisite topspun torture, forcing one mistake after another. By the time Murray had secured the victory, he looked ready to go another five sets. It was stunning tennis, but, had he not hurt Verdasco with that single stroke of brilliance in the second set to start the disintegration of his spirit, Murray might not have made it to the final. As with all significant achievements in Majors, the ultimate prize is won in a thousand minor skirmishes.

The longer they play at this level, the more the game's elite players are reinforced in their faith in the dictum that tennis is a collection of small, accumulating wounds. They are matadors, slashing at their prey's sense of comfort, making him sweat in every rally, won or lost, weakening his legs, his concentration and his will until his head drops and he is ready for the insertion of the finishing blade.

A point lost now can easily be a game or a set or even a championship won later on . . . if not today, next time. There are players on the circuit known for such doggedness; and, as Courier identified, four of them are rulers of our era. If a player semaphors the message that no point is a hopeless cause (even when logic suggests it patently is), confusion spreads in his opponent's mind about what really is a winning stroke. This induces panic and daring, leading to high-risk shots that stray closer and closer to the lines and, eventually, on to the other side. It is akin to a great boxer making a challenger swing and miss, then discover too late he has left his chin exposed.

No player on the Tour can match Murray for sowing such consternation in an opponent. Part of that arises from his personality, because, as some complain, he often looks as if he is ready to collapse, only to spring to life like some inspired jungle insect. His mood is almost impossible to read. His defence also is astonishing, and, as he was putting his game together in recent years, he felt vindicated playing deep, to give himself the best chance of recovery. He knew that against a certain level of player, he only had to keep getting the ball back and his opponent would disintegrate sooner or later. He also knew, though, that he could not hug the back of the court for ever against quality opposition, as Lendl reminded him, and, once he emerged from the shadows, the nature of his game changed, especially when in trouble against the very best. It was then that we saw the real Murray.

With the sun on his back and the net more of a friend than a distant puzzle, the Murray forehand came into play, hurting rather than teasing. The cuts went deeper. The intensity rose. His challenge was to marry both aspects of his game and, against Verdasco, they were manifest. The Spaniard was rendered helpless when in the ascendancy. That is what separates the great players from those who end up as their hitting partners.

'Today, I did put a lot of effort into chasing every single ball down,' Murray said later at his press conference. 'But I don't feel too bad.' That is why he suffers in Miami in December: to collect at Wimbledon in July. Someone pointed out that Ferguson was watching and (redundantly, perhaps) was famous for coming back from 2–0 down. Did Murray see any parallels? 'Yeah, when you play so many matches, you understand how to turn matches around and how to change the momentum.' But he did not want to get into a Fergie love-in; he had interrupted his post-match warm-down to talk to us, and that was where he wanted to be now. As he got up to go, he looked a little bit more exhausted than he let on.

Murray is impressively single-minded about his preparation, right down to the smallest details – actually, they are a lot more important than that. Such 'details' are a player's weapons and equipment, his racquets and strings, his tapes and towels, even the bandages for feet that can swell and bleed in the heat, or the prepared liquids he stacks up alongside his courtside seat to ward off dehydration. It is the hitting implement, though, that a player tends like a soldier's rifle. It has to be just right to the milligram of weight and correct tension in the strings. Depending on your point of view, the advances in racquet technology have either ruined the game as a spectacle, turning players into baseline robots, or given them the ability to play shots with power, accuracy and consistency that previously would have been out of reach. While retired players express occasional consternation, you will hear no dissension among the active ranks. When Murray destroyed Verdasco in that single point in the second set, it was in part down to the trust he had in his racquet.

'I've been playing with the same racquet [a Head YouTek Graphene Radical Pro] for eleven years, and I've been playing with the same strings [Luxilon Alu Power main strings, crossed with Babolat VS Touch] since I won the juniors at the US Open, which was in 2004,' he told us once. 'The racquets have obviously changed. I've hit balls with wooden racquets before, but that's a completely different game. In the last ten to fifteen years, I personally don't see a huge change in the racquets. But I've watched matches from twenty-five, thirty years ago. I saw the racquet my coach used to play with. It had a very small head, so it's difficult to generate a lot of topspin with it. You have to hit through the ball a lot more. So, the technology has definitely changed – but not so much in the last ten, fifteen years.'

It might be presumptuous to observe, but Murray could be in for a surprise. The evolution of racquets, as he is obviously aware, is so far advanced they will soon be fitted with microchips to measure the weight and direction of shots, later to be analysed in depth. This is turning a racquet into the tennis equivalent of a Formula One car, computerised by a team of scientists and driven by the hired gun, who responds to a series of instructions. When I asked Babolat, the French company who have designed this new whizz-bang wand, if I could examine one, I was told they were 'still under wraps' until their launch in the UK in 2014. This, of course, has the effect of adding mystery to science, an intoxicating combination. Had I not been overly bothered before about this super-bat, I was now intrigued to bursting point. So I spoke to Eric Babolat, whose family have been making racquets for other sports in the French factories since 1875 but have been involved in tennis only for about twenty years. Nadal and Tsonga are among their star clients. Monsieur Babolat rejected the notion that the manufacturers were imposing products on players. The desire for change and innovation, he insisted in quicksilver English that was as tough to track as a Nadal forehand, came from them.

First of all, the players themselves have changed since a few years now, in terms of physical abilities, training and so on. It is not that they were not professional before, but they were not training all year long as they are now. They are as complete athletes in tennis as in other sports. And that is a big change. They are bigger, taller, stronger. Tennis is a game where you have to win more points than your opponent and they are all looking for that balance of control and power, which can be on the shoes or the racquet, strings – all the same thing.

You might think that the size and the power of the player make the [equipment] not an issue but it is our duty as manufacturers to find the right combination for them. One of the first Babolat racquets that sold well in the market and on Tour was the Sure Drive, which was designed for ladies: very light, very powerful, light blue colour. Then it came to the point where players who were watching the game told us the game was faster. They wanted it so that the extreme shots of yesterday were the normal shots of today, like playing in front of the ball, not turning, making pretty shots. They asked for racquets that were powerful, easy to manage, easy to move through the air. The traditional competition racquets were heavy, a problem to just control. The first player to use this kind of racquet was Carlos Moyá, and now there was a completely different way of playing the game.

The tendency increasingly now is for topspin. The players wanted to hit a big ball – and not just to hit a straight, flat shot, but to give rotation to the ball, to make it uncontrollable by the opponent. A lot of technology in racquets and strings has been going in this direction for six years. That is what we are working on. For us, innovation always comes from observation – and listening to the players.

As a demonstration of how important equipment can be to players, take the slightly odd case of Serena Williams and Roger Federer. Early in 2012, Williams made the big decision to tamper with her strings after resisting repeated calls to abandon the all-gut strings she had used throughout her illustrious career. Nearly everyone else had moved on; Serena saw no need to, and who could blame her. Now, as she got older, she wanted insurance. But first she needed to know what equipment Federer was working with; he, after all, had won more Majors than anyone in the history of the game. He must know what works best. Having been one of the last players on the women's circuit to stick with the old-fashioned strings, she wasn't satisfied with the new ones from the Federer range when she tried them out, and so demanded more experiments. Finally that summer, she switched the strings on her Wilson racquet from gut, made from the fibres of a cow's intestines, to a combination of gut and synthetic. The cow contributed the vertical strings, and they were crossed vertically with Luxilon 4G. This, she was told, would increase control and power – as if any of her poor victims would notice the difference. In the fifteen months that followed, they might have noticed. Serena won ninety-four matches and lost four, picking up three Slam titles and an Olympic gold medal among a total of thirteen trophies. That, you might think, would be fair evidence that she had made the right choice. 'I just love playing with them,' she said.

By the time she got to Wimbledon in 2013, her confidence was sky high. And then she lost to Sabine Lisicki. Federer had already gone out to Sergiy Stakhovsky. Very soon, he would turn to his sponsors and tell them something he never thought he would say: find me a new racquet. If anyone thought anxiety resided only on the fringes of the rankings, here was proof that the two greatest players of the men's and women's game in modern times were suffering just those palpitations, and their response was to break the old maxim: a good tradesman doesn't blame his tools. That is the extent to which racquets and strings have come to dominate tennis. For some, it was depressing; for those making the gadgets and using them, it was the natural order of things. Was this paranoia, insecurity or common sense? Nobody knew. Williams carried on, Federer changed his racquet for a slightly bigger one – and kept losing – then temporarily abandoned it. In reaching for perfection, it seemed, great players had become blinded by science. No doubt they would have played just as brilliantly with an old Slazenger made of wood and weighing probably twice as much, but they had been brought up to expect and demand perfection. This was the new age of sport. This was their addiction. Nobody relied on instinct alone any more. Everybody needed help, even the great players.

Monsieur Babolat described the process of negotiation with the players.

We change the aerodynamics of the racquet to penetrate the air, to make the swing quicker. The player's movement is completely different. We give it to them to try and, if they feel it is OK, we work on it. This racquet was created for Nadal [the AeroPro Drive GT Babolat, with RPM Blast strings weighted at 55 lbs] nearly ten years ago. Nadal started with the Pure Drive. But we said we could accommodate his swing better, so we did a proto-type, tested it, he liked it and now it's his racquet. Players want their racquets all to be completely identical, to the millimetre, to the milligram. For commercial products, the difference can be maybe six grams. For Nadal, two grams difference is huge. We would give him six test racquets and he could tell, after two shots, that one was half a millimetre stronger and he would go, 'That's enough.' It is that exact. The racquets have to be completely identical when he changes them during a match.

I was lost in a cloud of numbers. No doubt it all added up and meant something profound. But I came to the game from innocence, as do most people. I did not want to know that these amazing scientific advances had contributed so much to the genius of these players. I preferred to dream on, believing it was their gifts alone that separated them from the rest. Nonetheless, an important and obvious point had been reinforced: it was the players who were driving change as much as the manufacturers. Like Formula One drivers, they could sense and feel how their equipment was responding in different situations. It is also a never-ending process. 'Usually,' says M Babolat, 'we take November or December to adjust the racquets, the tensions, as they work out what they need on different surfaces, in different weather, whether it is colder, warmer, then outdoors or indoors.'

To leaven the growing tension in the tournament – not to mention the anxiety over tension in racquets – we needed some levity. It came in the form of Serena's backside and a spat between Annabel Croft and the *Daily Mail*'s esteemed sports diarist Charlie Sale. It started in the Lawn Tennis Association's sponsors suite underneath Court 1, where Croft was speaking at a corporate lunch, the sort of harmless function that has become part of the fabric of modern sport. Charlie, an Old Reptonian who had taken quickly to the demands of Fleet Street and whom I had known for many years, was respected for his ferreting skills. His eyes lit up, no doubt, when he came across a version of what Croft had said, originating from one of the guests present at the shindig, and the *Mail* went with it. 'Annabel said all Serena's dresses were very carefully designed to hide her bulk,' the offended diner apparently told him. 'She then moved on to concentrate on what she termed Serena's huge backside. She said she was in the ladies' changing room and wondering who was going to wear what looked like a wedding dress. She then saw Serena getting into this dress and that the train had been carefully designed to wrap around Serena's huge backside. It was quite offensive.'

And Croft certainly took offence at Charlie and the *Daily Mail* for giving credence to remarks allegedly made at a private lunch. Normally the very picture of Home Counties decorum, the former British number 1 stormed into the media centre the following morning, found the unsuspecting Sale idling at the coffee machine and gave him both barrels. 'I'm very, very, very, very angry with you, Charlie,' she told our gobsmacked hack, who, it has to be said, took his medicine from nurse with admirable sangfroid. He had heard worse. Annabel, meanwhile, sought to check the embarrassing furore with a measured statement: 'I apologise to anyone who might have taken offence, but it was meant as a harmless piece of banter. Serena has a magnificent bottom that every woman should aspire to.' It was just about the perfect end, so to speak, to a perfect tiff. Williams said she 'did not care to know what she said; I'm here to play tennis'. She was . . . and she was growing weary of off-court distractions.

Serena had already had a far more acrimonious row to deal with, a proper stand-up with another lovely flower of tennis: Maria Sharapova. This one had its genesis in the women's final in Paris, where Williams won the title when she handed Sharapova another beating in their long-running rivalry, which stood at 13–2 in the American's favour. The Russian's only significant victory over the American had been at Wimbledon when she won the title as a seventeen-year-old in 2004. There was a subtext, though. There nearly always is.

Williams earlier in the year had given an interview to *Rolling Stone* magazine during the course of which – unknowingly to her, she said – the reporter overheard her talking on the phone about someone assumed to be Sharapova and her boyfriend Grigor Dimitrov – who once had stepped out with Serena. Apparently. Whatever the truth of that, this is what appeared among her quotes in the magazine: '. . . she begins every interview with "I'm so happy. I'm so lucky" – it's so boring. She's still not going to be invited to the cool parties. And, hey, if she wants to be with the guy with a black heart, go for it.'

Whether or not 'the guy with a black heart' was Dimitrov, Sharapova now felt compelled to retaliate. And she chose to target Williams's own private life: her alleged romance with her French coach, Patrick Mouratoglou, who had once coached Dimitrov. Sharapova, whose inner Russian steel is not easily hidden under her glamorous façade and who was still smarting from her defeat at Roland Garros, took the first opportunity she had to hit a return that brought up the chalk on the baseline. 'If she wants to talk about something personal, maybe she should talk about her relationship and her boyfriend that was married and is getting a divorce and has kids.'

On her next serve, Williams replied: 'I feel like Maria, unfortunately, was inadvertently brought into a situation she should have never been brought into.' The words 'unfortunately' and 'inadvertently' might have been open to all sorts of interpretation, given how the row started, but Serena pressed on. 'I'm the first person to apologise. I'm the first person to reach out to individuals and people if I feel that something may have hurt them or something may have been misconstrued. I personally talked to Maria at the player party. I said, "Look, I want to personally apologise to you if you are offended by being brought into my situation. I want to take this moment to just pour myself, be open, say I'm very sorry for this whole situation."'

Did Maria accept the apology? 'We always have great conversations, so I believe that she definitely did accept it,' she said, keen to 'move on', as celebrities say when cornered. 'I'm not really gonna comment on her reaction, whether I'm disturbed or not. I know she also said that I should definitely focus on the tennis here, and I feel like that is another thing I can definitely take her advice on. Maybe I wasn't focused enough in the past on tennis. I'm definitely gonna try to focus on that for the next two weeks.'

The press conference – if it can be so defined – was so brilliantly laced with sarcasm and innuendo, it might have been constructed by Dorothy Parker. There has not been as entertaining a public spat at Wimbledon since . . . well, Croft and Sale.

As for the men's singles championship, that was going to a more straightforward script, with a couple of twists. Poland had been on the fringe of tennis since Wojtek Fibak reached the quarter-finals in 1980, and now two of his countrymen were there: Łukasz Kubot, who put out Adrian Mannarino in five sets, and Jerzy Janowicz, who also took five sets to beat Jürgen Melzer. Janowicz, growing in stature (as well as inches, perhaps; he looked immense alongside a gate), ended Kubot's Wimbledon to book a place in the semi-finals against Murray, while Djokovic made his semi-final arrangements by accounting for Berdych in a flat quarter-final.

Djokovic had to go to the limit to hold off del Potro over five pulsating sets in the semi-final, probably the best match of the tournament. Janowicz gave it his very best shot against Murray, mixing up power serves and drop-shots to give the US Open champion fits and take the first set in a tie-break, but he could not sustain the effort and faded in the closing stages. So the old order remained intact.

And we ultimately got the final we wanted: Murray vs Djokovic. It was, after all, supposed to be the rivalry to replace the one that had just started falling apart: Nadal vs Federer. There was an excitement building up that weekend unlike any other I can remember at Wimbledon. I am certain, also, that it was more absorbing than when Fred Perry stepped on to Centre Court for his last final in 1936, blowing away the injured German aristocrat, Gottfried von Cramm, 6–1, 6–1, 6–0. This was going to be a proper fight . . . wasn't it?

There is just no telling where sport will take us. On the face if it, the scoreline of 6–4, 7–5, 6–4 in only three hours and nine minutes with no tie-breaks suggests as clinical and straightforward a Wimbledon final as we have had in many years. There is little indication of struggle in the numbers. But, for all that tennis is a game imprisoned by numbers, this time the drama existed not in the overall struggle for numerical supremacy but in the very last shoot-out. The theatre of the entire match was condensed into the final game of the contest. There was plenty to admire in what had gone before, certainly, but there was an edginess to it that never let either player fully express himself.

'Winning Wimbledon is the pinnacle of tennis,' Murray said later. 'The last game almost increased that feeling. My head was kind of everywhere. I mean, some of the shots he came up with were unbelievable. Mentally, that last game will be the toughest game I'll play in my career.'

Unforgiving types who have never swung a racquet in anger might think that serving for the title at 40–love against an opponent who had plainly been beaten up in his long semi-final against del Potro would be the sort of assignment any tennis player would sign up for. They would be wrong. It was that very scoreline that delivered a unique pressure. Murray could not afford to lose from such a vantage point for the very reason that it was such a good one.

To lose from here would make defeat almost unbearable – and that pressure quickly transfers itself to his shaking right hand as he prepares to serve out for history. Murray had secured the second set with an ace and would love to have sealed the championship with another, but somehow he realises that is not going to happen. This is going to be hell. He knows he is on trial unlike any stage in the match up until then. Just as he had to splash water on his face to wake himself up after the fourth set against Djokovic in the final of the US Open, now he needs to find invigoration from somewhere. But there is nowhere to go, no bathroom to run to. He has to do the job here, now, as quickly as he can, with probably 20 million people watching him on television sets all over the country, as well as those packed into Centre Court almost too nervous to breathe.

Djokovic, exhausted but now in animal mode, saves three match points, then threatens to break. Murray saves for deuce. Djokovic clips the net – in his favour. Murray saves again. The collective intake of breath sucks almost all the available oxygen out of south-west London. A Djokovic diving shot gives him another chance to break. Murray saves to give himself a fourth championship point. The match is entering the realm of the surreal. Centre Court is going mental . . . and that is just in the press box. Murray steadies himself for what he hopes will be the last time in the tournament, hands, arms, shoulders and head trembling. In some respects, he would rather be anywhere else in the world; in another, this is his destiny, the place he was always meant to be. He sucks at the warm air, mightily, and exhales. He eases his body back in a motion he has executed a million times and more, and trusts his strong right arm to come through the familiar arc on to the ball tossed with as much steadiness as he can muster. The serve goes in, they trade, then Djokovic, going for a winner down the line, nets a backhand . . . It is done. It is bloody well done.

There are no more words to add in that moment, and we stare around at each other, at the frenzied crowd, at Andy's mother, Judy, and all his team, his crazy coach, the ball kids and the favoured few in the box . . . and, finally, Djokovic. He is seated now, staring ahead without blinking, devastated but somehow relieved that the pain has gone. The ordeal is done. There will be other days, but today, most definitely, does not belong to him.

11

The Second Break

Wimbledon, 7 July 2013

Everyone wants to talk to winners. But losers are often more illuminating – especially when they are as articulate as Novak Djokovic – because their emotions are not clouded by the adoration of others. It is a tough gig, honouring obligations to talk to the media after losing a match as important as the Wimbledon final. But the Serb is up for it. In the room where he celebrated victory in 2011, Djokovic nails the essence of a frantic encounter: 'It was a very long match for three sets,' says the man who has made long finals his preferred method of crushing opponents. He did not get the chance to extend the fight this time, although there was a near universal theory that, had Murray not wrapped up the title with his final service game, Djokovic might well have recovered strongly enough to take the set – and maybe even the match. That thought sustained us as we reflected on probably the most fraught ending to a British sporting victory any of us had been privileged to witness.

~

Life after Wimbledon for Murray was very heaven . . . and, briefly, a short spell of hell. After his media commitments, he warmed down properly, left for home, and briefly collapsed. 'That was a massive fight out there today, just managed to squeeze through! Lying on my bed treating myself to a Milkybar to celebrate . . .' he tweeted at 11.19 p.m. But there was the champions' ball

186

to attend, and he somehow squeezed his aching body into a dinner suit, arrived as late as was fashionable at celebrations that had been underway for a couple of hours, and hugged the women's champion, Marion Bartoli, who looked sensational in her figure-hugging dress and outrageously high-heeled shoes. It was a moment among many to savour, and he was happy to share it with as many people as wanted to be there. There were many hands to shake, backs to slap and photos to be taken. But, really, where he wanted to be was home.

Just before 3 a.m., Murray, Kim, mother Judy and a few friends and family members arrived back at Murray's home in Oxshott, a twenty-minute drive south of Wimbledon and a haven from the attentions of the world. 'We were all so exhausted,' Judy said. 'But the thing about it was that Andy could not remember a single thing about the end of the match. Nothing. So we turned on the recording on the TV and watched it again. He just sat there, staring at it. It was as if he had seen it for the first time. Incredible.'

As he watched his own history unfold on the television screen in front of him, the adrenaline drained ever so slowly from his body and tiredness took its grip at last. But he did not sleep easily. He reckons he might have dropped off for an hour or so, but around dawn he was up again and heading back to Wimbledon. At 6.45 a.m. he tweeted: 'Can't believe what's just happened!!!!!!!'

It was a curious loop, as if there was no escaping the event and the rolling celebration and the venue. Murray looked surprisingly refreshed for the TV cameras when he got there and was not at all disturbed by the attention. Everyone in the building embraced him, from staff to members, and just about anyone who was left to clear up after the most momentous day in the club's history for seventy-seven years.

We, meanwhile, were not done with him, and he did well to both sound coherent and keep his patience, I thought. As we gathered in the main interview room at Wimbledon, there were priorities to sort out. The international press were there for the first open-to-all scrum. Then there was a session for the British writers at large – but an international colleague from scrum number one claimed squatting rights and was reluctant to leave. The point was made to him – a little forcefully, perhaps – that it was in his interest to go. Now. He did. Scowling. And, finally, those of us who dared to call ourselves tennis experts had some time with Murray after the hubbub. What is enduringly daft about this whole process is the idea that Murray can compartmentalise his thoughts and satisfy such disparate media demands. He has become very good at it, because it is part of the deal, but sometimes it is counter-productive. Demanding that he compress his emotions into slightly different gobbets of quotable fluff demeans the process of communication, and he is aware of that. On this day, however, he just let his words flow, and there was no disguising the enormous joy and pride that he felt. Murray had already deflected questions from one newspaper about when he and Kim Sears might marry. He also had to constantly sidestep the issue of Scottish independence. Now, he could talk tennis for a while, and there was plenty to talk about.

If there was one point he wanted to make clear, it was that winning Slams was his priority, not the world number 1 ranking. It was an interesting take, because getting that top spot mattered a lot to Djokovic, not quite so much to Nadal, and had disappeared from view in Federer's scope. What is certain is that, in sight of that peak, Murray would be more aware of the possibility of ruling his peers. For now, he was not getting ahead of himself.

'I don't think the ranking system always reflects a player's qualities perfectly,' he said. 'You are more remembered for the Slams you win. I would rather win one more Slam and not get to number 1. The top ranking would be a great thing to do but, if I was picking, it would be another Slam.'

Could he have won without Lendl, we wondered. This was a

ticking bomb question. If he said yes, his trainer would be unamused. If he said no, he would sound too reliant on his influence. He paused, then said: 'I don't know the answer to that. It was a combination of a lot of things but he has helped me a lot and results suggest that. But, I have also done a lot of hard work with the other guys in my team and I have had a lot of people coach me in the past. I've had Darren Cahill, Alex Corretja, Mark Petchey, Miles Maclagan and Brad Gilbert. These are top-quality knowledgeable people. I wouldn't say it was purely down to Ivan but he has made a big, big difference.'

You half-expected Nelson Mandela to step from the wings and hand Murray a gold cup for diplomacy. But he was right. All of those coaches had contributed to his development – and he had the necessary ruthlessness to ask them to leave when he needed to move to another level. In that respect, he might well have been able to make it without any coach at all. But it might have been a bit uglier.

As for the 'Scottish question', Murray's footwork was equally adept. 'When the time is right I will probably say something about it. I'm going to get asked about it all the time. I will think about it, speak to some people and try to see what is best for the country. But I haven't thought that much about it.'

The question for some was: which country? All his career, he has had to deal with this duality. Even now, it refuses to go away. The only reason some people want to know what Andy Murray thinks about Scottish independence is to reach for the next headline. It can hardly be to inform the debate, and is a curiously English phenomenon. The world champion boxer and former Olympic silver medallist Amir Khan, the son of Pakistani parents but as rooted to his birthplace of Bolton as his accent suggests, has struggled for acceptance as 'English' among a minority. Murray's dilemma – if it is one – has been subtly different. It is as if he has to give up his Scottishness before he is totally accepted. It is an absurd notion – perhaps one he gave fleeting consideration to on his way home from Wimbledon to Oxshott.

After we'd done with him and he'd done with us, there followed another slew of radio and television engagements. Murray had to be photographed, of course, in front of the Fred Perry statue at Wimbledon. How he stayed awake, let alone patient, is a mystery. Later, he was ferried away to accept BBC Radio 1's Teen Award for Best British Sports Star, an honour that allowed him to be pelted with tennis balls by a load of screaming kids. 'Thank you to everyone who's voted for me,' he shouted over the row. 'It's been a great year on the court and I'll try to be there next year so I don't have to deal with this nonsense. Thank you!'

For the next two days, with the world clamouring at the door, Murray locked himself away in his house. For a week, he was waking at 5 a.m. or a little later. For more than a month, he could not face picking up a tennis racquet. Winning the title had struck deep at the core of his emotions, which some might interpret as worrying and others as the way it is meant to be. There could be no doubt Murray cared. He cared so much that it put his normally organised life totally out of kilter. The place he found refuge – apart from at home with Kim and their dogs – was the place at the heart of the disturbance to his regime: Wimbledon. He had always felt an affinity with the place, ever since his debut there at eighteen and his advance to the third round, before collapsing because of lack of strength and stamina against the clever Argentinian, David Nalbandian. Nalbandian would soon announce his retirement, and Murray was Wimbledon champion. That was a nice, rounded circle.

In the summer of 2012, before he lost to Federer in the final and then beat him in the Olympics, Murray would return to Wimbledon, unnoticed, and sit for long stretches in the seats looking down on Centre Court. After nailing the title, that's where he went again, for solitude and, maybe, a little reassurance that it really had happened. Something as simple as staring at the scene of his greatest triumph and drinking in the memories of the past at this most history-laden of courts gave him comfort. He is an intense and fascinating individual.

After years of struggle, he walked in the sunlight of his sport. Everything seemed golden. The player who once was doubted was now embraced. The release of admiration and affection was palpable everywhere he looked, and, in a way, it stuck in the craw because of its late arrival. Unlike so many previous British sporting heroes, the love for Murray was conditional on his winning something big, not just losing gallantly. Andy Murray was not Frank Bruno – although the two shared a determination and, in the end, Murray got there, he got his world title, he proved he was good enough at the highest level.

After he had shaken up the tennis world, Murray's thoughts turned to where it had all started, Dunblane. When he won Olympic gold, he posed beside the gold postbox that had been erected there in honour of his Wimbledon triumph, and then he took off his medals and placed them around the necks of schoolchildren sitting nearby. The streets of the town that had endured so much thronged with happy, smiley faces; none beamed more than that of their favourite son. Perhaps that was his real prize, just coming home. This time, he had to tend to urgent business: his back. But the spectre of what happened in Dunblane on 13 March 1996 – when a local man, Thomas Hamilton, walked into a school and shot dead sixteen young children and their teacher – would never disappear. Andy and Jamie were at school that day, and both have struggled to talk about it. In a BBC documentary broadcast shortly before Wimbledon, Murray struggled to contain his tears when recalling the massacre. He paused, gathered his thoughts, and said, simply: 'It's just nice that I've been able to do something the town is proud of.'

The impact Murray has had on British society by winning

Wimbledon has gone beyond sport. Our culture, surely, was enriched when Andy appeared in the *Beano*. Then there was the striking of a stamp with his face on it. A Scottish dance called 'The Pride of Dunblane' was quickly put together, soon augmented by 'Wee Andy Murray', a song the author described as 'a punchy number', and another, 'He's a Winner', by a musician who calls himself One Man and his Beard. Three female Humboldt penguins at St Andrews Aquarium in Fife were named after Judy and Kim and Andy's grandmother, Shirley. A fourth, incongruously perhaps, was named after Andy. And on it went . . . crazily and non-stop. The department store John Lewis complained that sales were down during Wimbledon as shoppers turned into stay-at-home tennis addicts in front of the television. The Scottish Tourist Board chose to disagree. Andy got into the swing of things by banning foie gras from Cromlix House, his luxury hotel near Dunblane. In early October, however, he would take on board the best young chef in Scotland: presumably to be on foie-gras-watch.

Wimbledon 2013 proved to be the single most significant turning point in the realignment of power in men's tennis since the decline of the serve–volley game. It was not just the early departures of Nadal and Federer that shook the status quo; it was the prospect of their sudden disappearance from the game. Surely the two players who had so dominated their opponents for so long would not simply limp away and lie down. They were, after all, in the opinion of many respected observers, the two greatest players there ever had been. But the clock ticked without pause. Nadal's knees, whatever his reassurances, would never be as strong as when he was sweeping all before him three and four years earlier, a fact which makes his efforts of 2013 all the more phenomenal. Federer's back had worried him since Indian Wells and now the pain resurfaced on a worryingly regular basis and at just the time when his hitherto unbreakable self-belief came under siege and he kept losing to players he once would have beaten without bother.

Federer was to suffer further pain, and from an unexpected quarter. After Wimbledon, he sought comfort on the canopied clay of Germany's biggest court, the Am Rothenbaum tennis centre in the middle of Hamburg. But, after an encouraging start, he again was disappointed. It was doubly cruel that his tormentor several months earlier had given Nadal encouragement in his comeback match on the far-away clay of Viña del Mar in Chile.

Since his two-sets loss to Nadal, Federico Delbonis, not surprisingly for a player on the lower slopes of the game, had experienced a mixed season. In his next match, he lost in the first round of qualifying for the Sao Paolo tournament that Nadal would go on to win. Gordo's conqueror this time was Teymuraz Gabashvili, a Russian ranked 195 in the world. From Brazil, Delbonis travelled to Buenos Aires, where world number 11 Nicolas Almagro put him out in the quarters in two sets. There followed further early setbacks in Santiago and Pereira, then a tournament win in Barranquilla, Colombia. He flew to Panama City, losing in the second round, then headed for the clay of Europe. He had moderate success in a Challenger-level tournament in Rome, went out at the first time of asking against the Brazilian João Souza in Bordeaux, lost in qualifying to the well-travelled Dustin Brown in Düsseldorf, bombed out in the second round of the French Open, the quarters of Caltanissetta in Italy, the first round of Queen's, the quarters of Braunschweig in Germany . . . and then he arrived in Hamburg.

After fighting his way through the qualifying tournament against similarly unfancied entrants, he played his best tennis of the year to that point to beat the excellent and experienced Spaniard Tommy Robredo and reach the fourth round of the main tournament. There he played well again, refusing to buckle to the subtleties of the seasoned Russian Dmitry Tursunov, and shocked everyone who saw it by defeating world number 34 Fernando Verdasco in three tough sets in the quarter-finals. That would have capped his year in any other season, but there was more to come: a semi-final against Federer.

There was not a reliable witness in Hamburg who gave Delbonis a chance against his second former world number 1 opponent of the season, but the Argentinian thought otherwise. In seven minutes under two hours, and in front of 13,200 disbelieving spectators, he outplayed Federer, controlling his nerves to limit his double faults to just a couple, and manufactured seven break points. Six times, Federer resisted him, but, in two tie-breaks, Delbonis held his game together and could not be denied the biggest win of his career.

The soundtrack to this drip-drip slide by Federer was a raucous and unexpected breaking of silence by Djokovic's father, Srdjan, who disturbed for ever the myth that the Big Four were also the Big Four Friends. He reserved his vitriol for Nadal and Federer, his son's chief source of grief before the arrival of Murray, pouring mental salt on to their physical wounds. While the players might not have paid a lot of attention to the row, it cannot have helped their composure in a difficult stretch of the Tour, with the US Open not far away after the brief, tough second hard-court swing in the USA.

Srdjan surprised everyone when he told the Serbian newspaper *Kurir*, in July, that Murray was fine with Novak, but that Nadal and Federer could not hide their supposed jealousy of the world number 1. '[Murray and Djokovic] cannot be best friends as they fight for the most important titles and lots of money,' he was quoted as saying. 'But they are more than correct rivals and, after they finish their professional careers, they will be great friends. I have never, not even for a second, felt jealousy from Andy's family. Andy's mother went into the locker-room in Rome to congratulate Novak, his team and his family.'

He then tore into Federer, one of the most popular athletes

in the world. 'He is perhaps still the best tennis player in history but, as a man, he's the opposite. He attacked Novak at the Davis Cup in Geneva, he realised that he was his successor and was trying to discredit him in every way.'

Djokovic senior was similarly cynical about Nadal, who, he said, 'was his [Novak's] best friend while he was winning. When things changed, they were no longer friends. It's not sporting.' Nadal responded: 'I've always got on very well with him and I still do. I've lost lots of matches against him and vice versa, but we've never had a problem.'

Clearly, this was going to be an interesting conclusion to the season. And, however deep or lasting the feelings in the complex arrangement were between Djokovic, Nadal and Murray, it seems none of the three was especially close to Federer, who was not only older than them, but stood apart in other ways. He was not aloof, but he was superior, in the real sense of the word. He attracted parody, as on the sometimes hilarious Twitter send-up, @PseudoFed, which enraged his followers.

Back on the hard-courts of North America, Federer's struggle continued. A week before his thirty-second birthday, he withdrew from the Rogers Cup in Montreal without explanation after his third straight loss to an unrated opponent. He was in a quandary of his own making. His loss to Delbonis had knocked his confidence in his new 98-square-inch racquet and there was little time left before the US Open to experiment further. 'So far, I'm happy with this change, but I need many hours on the court to see if this is a good decision,' he said. 'I haven't yet taken the decision on whether to use it in the US Open. I still need to think it over. There are players who have experienced problems when they changed racquets, Fernando Verdasco and, to some extent, Novak Djokovic.' But Djokovic had resolved that issue. Federer would too. He stayed with what he knew. Would it be enough to save his season?

12

Sweat on a Wine Bottle

Mason, Ohio, 12 August 2013

When Mardy Fish played the Cincinnati Open in 2010, they put him in a hotel overlooking a fast-food outlet called Five Guys. That was cruel for a player who used to be known as 'Lardy Mardy'. Thirty pounds slimmer, he resisted the call. Still, he reeled off his favourite local restaurants for the media: 'Embers, then McAllister's for lunch; Jimmy John's for lunch . . . IHOP for breakfast.' Three years later, Fish is a different player. Now he's fighting his unreliable heart. He'd made his tentative comeback at Indian Wells. Today he doesn't feel so good, and he loses quickly to Philipp Kohlschreiber. 'This is not an easy game,' Fish says. A week later he quit against Jarkko Nieminen in the third set of their second round match in Winston-Salem, and did not play again in 2013.

~

Of the many days and nights on which I watched tennis in 2013, one was different from all the others. It was not at Wimbledon or Flushing Meadows, or any of the big cathedrals of the sport, but in a prosperous conurbation on the outskirts of Cincinnati. I am glad I was there, because it was one of several significant turning points in the story of the season. Something else happened while I was in Mason, Ohio, that September that lent me a perspective I had not anticipated.

The eminent American music critic Albert Murray once said a fine thing about his chosen love:

> I think it's terribly important that jazz is primarily dance music, so that you move when you hear it – and it always moves in the direction of . . . elegance, which is the most civilised thing that a human being can do. The outward extension, elaboration and refinement of effort is elegance, where just doing it gives pleasure of itself. That's about as far as we can get with life. It is equivalent to what Ernest Hemingway called the sweat on a wine bottle: if you don't enjoy how those beads of sweat look, when you pour the white wine out and you taste it, how your partner looks and how the sunlight comes through, well . . . you've missed it.

Murray was talking to the American film-maker Ken Burns about swing, the effervescent offspring of jazz, which took a hold during the Great Depression and, for a decade and more after that, was the soundtrack of a generation. As Duke Ellington once said, it don't mean a thing if it ain't got that swing. What has this got to do with tennis? More than you might imagine.

Tennis, of all the sports that involve the striking of a moving ball, has a laid-down rhythm that drives the exchanges within agreed parameters, much as a well-constructed symphony might keep an orchestra in time. There is similar movement in football, but it is haphazard. Cricket and baseball also have a disjointed and unpredictable beat. In tennis, a player serves and his opponent has no option but to hit the ball back immediately, thus giving the exchange an internal coherence, or rhythm. What happens after that might be considered a riff, a familiar repetition of a pleasing sound. In its best moments, tennis mesmerises the audience with the insistence of those exchanges, with heads moving side to side, eyes fixed on the ball, then the shot, the ball then the shot, everyone entranced by the cadence of the action until the inevitable crescendo and crash.

So, if you will forgive my stretched musical indulgence, I like to think that Albert, Ernest and the Duke would have enjoyed watching Roger Federer play tennis, because nobody, surely, has swung a racquet with such sweet syncopation as the Swiss. He has unshackled elegance, like Johnny Hodges' saxophone or Cootie Williams's trumpet. Federer doesn't play tennis; like Duke Ellington, he conducts it. Because he does so without concern for the short-term consequences, he could be said to be more jazz than classical, an improviser working within a roughly agreed framework. It is why he inspires devotion in a mechanical age, whereas his contemporaries generate awe. We can almost hear the music in his tennis. You can't miss it. It is sweat on a wine bottle.

The day Albert Murray died – 18 August 2013 – he did not make major news. He was ninety-seven and time had parked him by the highway. There possibly was a mention in the *New York Times* or the *Village Voice*. I couldn't be sure. I was in Mason, watching Rafael Nadal beat John Isner in the final of the last significant warm-up tournament before the US Open. The Western & Southern Open, for several years now a no-miss event for the game's best, began life more than a century earlier in the Avondale Athletic Club without sponsorship but with the approval of the city's most solid citizens; a low-key occasion once located on the campus of the Xavier University. Membership was reserved for 'gentlemen in good standing in the community over eighteen years of age', most of whom, according to the *Cincinnati Inquirer* of 1897, lived in 'the fashionable circles on the hilltops'. After a circuitous journey over several decades, the tennis component of Avondale's athletic diversions was significantly democratised and arrived in the more prosaic surroundings of the Lindner Family Tennis Center in Mason, forty minutes' drive from town, financed by a local insurance company with assets of more than $60 billion. That's some journey.

How decorous the tennis must have been in the tournament's

brief life at the Avondale. The final this latest September, meanwhile, was 115 minutes of tough, clean hitting, and the sound on the strings was more military than melodious. The rallies were uncomplicated, brutal. Nadal beat Isner in two tight sets, needing a tie-break in each one, the second five points shorter than the first, as the striving young American's best was no match in the end for the Spaniard at just a tick under his own maximum.

It was Nadal's fifteenth straight hard-court victory of 2013 and, coming after his success at the Rogers Cup in Montreal the week before, was his first back-to-back tournament win on a surface that over several years had been unkind to a body more comfortable with the demands of clay. He had done well to test himself on it, let alone win two tournaments in a row. But surely, we thought, he could not go to New York the following week and win the US Open for a second time, away from the reassurance of his beloved ochre. Nadal reckoned otherwise.

It was not just beating Isner on Cincinnati's quick Pro Deco Turf II courts (the fastest on the Tour; the same as those in Canada the week before) that buoyed his spirits. Two nights earlier he had scored a far more significant victory. In turning back the briefly mesmerising challenge of Federer in the quarter-finals, Nadal had made an emphatic statement. It was about both of them, and it was like Wynton Marsalis going up against Miles Davis: nobody really wanted a loser, but the younger man would do what young men often do. He won.

For those of us lucky enough to witness the match – a lovely prelude to the more raucous main score – the memory lingers not so much of Nadal's ultimate victory in the third set but of Federer rediscovering his genius in a first set that took the breath away. He was untouchable. He sprang up on his toes again like Nijinsky and, twisting in flight, bull-whipped his cross-court forehand with silky venom, out of the reach of his exasperated opponent, shot after shot, like a lash. The backhand, too, with just one hand on the racquet, clicked like a clock.

He served with precision and cunning, the weapon that for years had driven opponents crazy, suffocating their efforts to get into a rally. When Nadal did manage to draw him into a fight, Federer cut it short at the net. His volley, not so much of a threat in recent years (Pat Cash, for one, considers it the least reliable weapon in his armoury), was firm and deadly, leaving Nadal marooned behind the baseline, where he often did his best work. Not in that golden hour, though. Federer moved with the ease of an athlete at the height of his powers, and only someone similarly gifted could have stayed with him. But there would be a downbeat ending to the contest.

Federer, reborn for one night, converted seven of nine break points and several times looked as if he would make Nadal crack under the nagging drip of his genius. This was the Federer that tennis loved and would never desert. Yet he lost. He could not sustain his effort, as those among us not constrained by hero-worship feared might be the case. We were not blessed with insight denied others; we had just sniffed decay, because that is the nature of our trade, forever poking about in other people's misfortune. Romantics preferred to enjoy the experience for what it was, and there could be no wrong in that. This is elite sport, however, and winning and losing are the enduring currencies. Federer lost the second set and, with increasing helplessness, gave way in the third. It was like watching Joe Louis being propelled through the ropes at Madison Square Garden on the end of Rocky Marciano's young left hook, except Joe never fought again. Federer was a long way from finished. As the final bell got closer, it looked as if he had the punch but could not throw it. Nadal prevailed for the twenty-first time in their thirty-one contests. 'Do you reckon that was their last match?' I asked my colleague from *The Times*, Neil Harman. 'Who knows,' he said. Nobody knew. Not even Federer. Eight days earlier, he had turned thirty-two. Time, which in the execution of his shots once was his prisoner, now was his captor.

Nadal, five years younger, was rampant before that US Open, pushed to the limit by opponents of contrasting gifts in the space of a couple of days. That is not to disrespect Isner, who was having a good season. But while the crane-like contender's uncomplicated forehand, struck hard and clean on the march at every half-chance, gave the impression he was some sort of serve-and-volley monster, he was not. He was a big guy – the only player on the Tour who could look 6-foot-10-inch Ivo Karlovic in the eye – with a big serve and a big forehand. His tennis did not resemble the art of Federer. While the Isner strokes flow through long, whizz-bang arms at frightening speed, Isner's method and strategy are simple: hit it hard, early and flat. Despite his best efforts, Isner would not be a significant part of the discussion at Flushing Meadows, where no American had won since Andy Roddick in 2003. This time, Nadal would be awesome; Federer – who had won five US titles back to back – less so. They had never played each other at Flushing Meadows. They still haven't, and they probably never will.

On the day of the Cincinnati final, several time zones away on the banks of the Volga, the Ukrainian Sergiy Stakhovsky was collecting $7,200 for beating 424th-ranked Valery Rudnev in the final of a Challenger tournament in Kazan. Federer, who had just banked a cheque ten times bigger than that for losing in a quarter-final in Cincinnati, might have spared a private smile for Stakhovsky. They would finish the year with at least something in common: a single trophy for their troubles. Federer's came on the grass of Halle, where he fought back from a set down against Mikhail Youzhny in an edgy final to lift his first cup since beating Andy Murray at Wimbledon the previous summer. Kazan was Stakhovsky's single success of 2013 – and his fourth tournament win in ten years on the Tour.

He will be remembered for none of these modest achievements, however. Eight days after Federer beat Youzhny in Germany, Stakhovsky beat Federer on what would come to be known as Wimbledon's wild Wednesday. Steve Darcis, ranked 135 in the world and who had put Nadal out in the first round, retired himself that day with a shoulder injury. Joining him were Jo-Wilfried Tsonga, Isner, Radek Štěpánek and (in a mystery that would take months to unfold), Marin Čilić, among others. The women's second seed, Victoria Azarenka, also limped home, and Maria Sharapova lost to the reformed Portuguese screecher Michelle Larcher de Brito.

None of these calamities matched Federer's. This was his turf, the place where he had bathed in the high-summer warmth of Centre Court to celebrate victory in the championships seven times. So his losing in four sets to a player whose name casual observers struggled to spell let alone recognise was tough to believe at the time, as if there had been a big mistake, as if we would all wake up at the same time and rub our eyes, put the kettle on and get back to reality. Stakhovsky – the deep-thinking son of a urology professor from Kiev and whose mother, Olga, once taught economics at university – rarely figured in the universal imagination of the Tour. He was probably as well known for his advocacy of the rights of lower-ranked players as he was for his tennis. And he did well to contain his bewilderment. He said defeating Federer at Wimbledon was like 'beating two men'. He was talking about the man and the myth.

To put Stakhovsky's achievement in context, consider this: before his monumental performance against Federer, he had lost four matches in a row. No sooner had he shocked the world than he lost again, in four sets to Jürgen Melzer, just outside the seedings at 37 in the world, in the third round. After beating Rudnev in Kazan, Stakhovsky went out in the first round of the US Open to Jeremy Chardy in five sets, and, as if spent by his efforts, then capitulated 0–6, 0–6, 4–6 to Nadal in the Davis Cup. Stakhovsky was the loosest of cannons. For the obvious lack of an alternative, he remained devoted to coming in behind his powerful serve at every opportunity, good or bad, the very antithesis of the tennis intellectual – or maybe he was an instinctive anarchist. Federer, as cerebral a player as the sport has seen, just happened to be standing still on his favoured turf at Wimbledon that summer when the Ukrainian's aim was the truest of his career.

For most of his career, Federer rarely had to deal with defeat by players of Stakhovsky's level. There had been unexpected losses, certainly, but they were followed by a string of stirring victories, an aria to follow a cough. Players such as Stakhovsky had laboured with diligence around the top 100, sometimes venturing deeper into the rankings, grateful for the occasional upset, and Federer had dismissed them from his court with a regal sweep of his backhand. Not any more. Now, he could indeed lose to Stakhovsky. And Stakhovsky that year could lose to players rated below him, even in the game's far-flung outposts: 4–6, 0–6 to Albano Olivetti (ranked 235 in the world), Adrian Ungur (108) and Malek Jaziri (169), all in low-level Challengers; and, on the Tour proper, to Michael Linzer (352), Cedrik-Marcel Stebe (178), Jan-Lennard Struff (109) and Marc Gicquel (132). Those losses – each of them in the first round to players outside the top 100 in front of a handful of friends and strangers for small amounts of money – always left Sergiy enough time to catch a quick car to the nearest airport and another flight back to Kiev or to go on to the next disappointment.

That's what would have pierced Federer's heart in the darkest moment of the most wretched winter of his career. A smile was never far from his handsome features, though, as he charmed the media and comforted those close to him. Do not be alarmed, he said. This is sport. It happens. I will be fine. But he was losing to sparring partners, not contenders. And that is why going down valiantly to Nadal in Cincinnati brought at least a quick glow to his cheeks. He reckoned he was still in contention. He might yet wear his crown again. The story was not over. By the end of the year, Federer would rediscover enough slivers of self-belief to reassure us he was far from finished.

This was not a monologue, mind. The other participants in the most interesting debate tennis had entertained in a long time included Nadal, Djokovic – whose 101-week reign as world number 1 the Mallorcan would later interrupt – and Murray. The Scot had put a flutter in British hearts by winning the 2013 Wimbledon title nine months after winning his first Major, the US Open, and the nation now climbed on to his shoulders, demanding more. What it was to discover was that the weight of expectation, as well as Murray's own, had filtered down to the base of his spine, where it briefly threatened to end his career. His fight against the sport's physical stresses would mirror that of his friend Nadal.

These four players had identifiably unique styles – although Djokovic and Murray, born a week apart and raised separately on a diet of science-led physicality, were not far apart in their method and philosophies. Nadal would emerge from his island hideaway, Mallorca, like a one-man raiding party, his jagged English sometimes clouding the sharpest understanding of the art of tennis. If these were the three musketeers of the game, Federer was d'Artagnan, the aristocrat separated from the others. There was mutual respect between them, but warmth was conditional; they put a civilised public face on their four-cornered rivalry, while secretly hoping the others would collapse in a heap. For a while, they were huddled at the summit of the game to regularly test each other, a closed-shop fight more fiercely contested than any other in the sport's past. At the end of 2013, Nadal, Djokovic and Federer had thirty-six Grand Slam titles between them, and Murray had secured the first two of what he and others hoped would be a growing list. No other quartet playing at the same time could match that. And it is likely their aggregate will edge towards fifty by a couple of victories before you have finished reading this book (if that is not too rash a presumption on either count). But only a purblind romantic could fail to see that the gilt on this precious egg was starting to crack.

The golden era, then? It is an apposite description, for all that it is the most dilapidated of clichés. The one we are all living through glitters nearly every day with performances that astonish and delight. Yet all eras are golden to some degree, shining a little brighter than those that went before, or so we imagine. There are writers and commentators alive who will tell you there can be nothing to match the post-war tennis of the fifties and most of the sixties for sheer joy and freedom, when the Davis Cup was still a dominant event – and when money (or rather the lack of it) was an impediment to having a good time, not a goal in itself. Gordon Forbes was one of those troubadours. The South African, a player of decent talent, wrote *A Handful of Summers*, wherein he chronicled that innocence with such charm that Michael Atherton, the former England cricket captain, rates it his favourite book about sport.

Recalling his first tennis excursion to Britain in 1954 with his compatriot Gordon Talbot, Forbes wrote: 'In Sutton, for instance, Gordon and I each received a return rail fare from London (about 35p), cold lunches each day, private accommodation with warm-hearted local families, and £2.50 for "expenses". If you won the tournament, you received prize vouchers: £5 for the singles, £2.50 each for the doubles, and these stated that you could spend them only on "white apparel". Usually at Simpson's, where white lambswool cost £2.50.'

Pleasures do not come more unadorned, although that did not stop Forbes and his mates from exploring the possibilities. 'I suppose I might have made more of the pretty girls I came across in all those friendly old European towns where we played,' he wrote. 'They're cities now – not nearly as simple and friendly as they used to be. To this day, I still suspect that we had the best of them, in spite of our lack of ready cash and worldly ways; two of the main reasons, I suppose, why we allowed so many pretty girls, both tennis players and others, to go to waste.'

Of those whose recollections stretch back to before the Second World War, there was gold to savour in the tennis of Don Budge, Fred Perry, Ellsworth Vines and Baron Gottfried von Cramm (who risked death and Hitler's ire by declining to sign up for the creed of Aryan supremacy) and other noblemen of the court. And what of von Cramm's American mentor, Bill Tilden, the first tennis superstar? Certainly, the tennis that some of them played would look quaintly out of place today, but they were the guardians of their own excellence, the best they could be.

One player characterised it thus: 'In no other game with which I am acquainted has there been such development in the mode and style of play as in lawn tennis. A Rip Van Winkle would rub his eyes and wonder whether it were really the same game that he had learnt some thirty years ago.' The author is Anthony F. Wilding, who was a pretty fair player about a century ago, as you might have detected from the language. Wilding added in his lovely memoir, *On the Court and Off*: 'The old style of gently lobbing the ball over the net into the middle of the court is, among those who consider themselves tennis players, as extinct as the Moa.' (If you're wondering, the Moa were the flightless birds that once inhabited Wilding's native New Zealand.)

So, there was tennis before it became warfare. There was no chance, however, that it would ever be constrained in the gussets and parasols of Edwardian England. Its growth was steady and irreversible. By the time ocean liners arrived in New York from Europe in the 1930s, laden with smiling amateurs and their lovely admirers, the game had morphed into more serious competition, not at all resembling the supposedly revolutionary days of Wilding, with a distance to go yet before it embraced Nadal, Federer, Djokovic and Murray. The sunburnt Californians of those gentler times would cross the continent to mix with their sophisticated east coast Ivy League cousins to contest the US Open, a tournament that still had a seductively country-club feel to it at Forest Hills out in the genteel part of Queen's. Newspapers would report on the doings with a light touch and without rancour. The game was quicker, getting quicker still, but it had yet to become frantic. In an age of telegrams and trains, tournament schedules mattered less. Matches rarely went beyond three sets. Few lasted more than an hour or two. Most were filled with glorious shots, the rallies guileful and wickedly short, but not hurried. The heroes were timeless, with time on their hands.

At first glance, Fred Perry epitomised the period, and up to a point the stereotype fits. His dark hair was slicked back atop a lean face, his Roman nose an unmistakable centrepiece. The creases of his pristine white trousers were as sharp as his killer forehand, and his knowing eyes were ready to twinkle at any female encouragement. As the world lurched from economic chaos towards global war, he was a star in a sport that was as much a gilded sanctuary from life's awfulness as it was a testing ground in a rarefied sporting environment. But, with an athletic build and the ambition to make best use of it, Perry was more than just a suave English playboy basking in the seductive glow of a glamorous environment. He was a revolutionary, a working man of energy and ambition. His was also the hard face of a coming time, an athlete who had turned away from a refined and stifled past. Ostracised after winning the last of his three Wimbledon titles in 1936, Perry, the son of a radical Labour MP from Stockport, was always disposed towards sticking his face against the establishment's window-pane. He backhanded his snooty persecutors without ceremony or regret to earn some money for his talent and, in a blizzard of exhibitions across the USA and the UK, he played his near rival and friend Ellsworth Vines an astonishing 172 times in two summers, the American finishing ahead by ten matches. Jack Kramer, himself a terrific player and a pioneer of professionalism, once said of his countryman: 'On his best days, Vines played the best tennis ever. Hell, when Elly was on, you'd be lucky to get your racquet on the ball once you served it.' In these chrysalis days of professional tennis, winning and losing, as central as they were to the integrity of the contest, did not appear to carry the baggage they do now. Sportsmanship and spectacle generally overrode chauvinism. No wonder they smiled so much. But change was coming, and Perry was at the forefront of it.

Vines and Perry would also joust with the peerless Budge, the Californian-raised son of an Oaklands truck driver (and former Glasgow Rangers reserve team footballer). They and their colleagues sailed down to South America as well, lounging there in the hospitality of tin-pot dictators from central casting, mixing with itinerant adventurers and ogling the fruit-filled hats of Carmen Miranda, no doubt. Such an embrace of paid fun in faraway exotic locations would seal Perry's status as an outcast in his homeland, even though he had long abandoned not only the amateur ethos but any affection for an institution and its out-of-touch custodians, who resented his uncompromising northern presence. He became, in every sense, an American.

Perry's revelatory moment had come to him long before this, however. It arrived when he was still an amateur, the best in the world at the time, on the grass of the West Side Tennis Club in Forest Hills in 1932, during the fourth round of the US championships, as they were then known. Sidney Wood, a Connecticut prodigy who played at Wimbledon when aged fifteen and who won the title at nineteen, in 1931 (by default, it ought to be noted), trailed Perry by two sets but had more to give. Against the odds and all expectations, young Wood pegged Perry back to win one of the most physical matches of the Englishman's career. Unafraid of hard self-analysis, Perry acknowledged a trend of fading in big moments; he had lost that year to Jack Crawford in the quarter-finals at Wimbledon and to Roderick Menzel at Roland Garros. Each time, his fitness had let him down.

As ruthless with himself as with his opponents, on his return from losing to Wood in New York, Perry contacted Arsenal's trainer, Tom Whittaker, to fix his fault. He knew that these footballers – who had won the 1930 FA Cup and would go on to win three league titles in a row – were the fittest in the game, and he wanted to tap into their methodology. Running alongside them, he undertook the most gruelling schedule available at the time, lapping Highbury 'hundreds of thousands of times', he reckoned. Never again would his legs fail him.

Perry observed at the time: 'Tennis has always been a bit of an intellectual exercise, but I wanted to make it a physical test too.' (This sentence that would resonate for the next great British player, several decades later.) Although he lost to the South African Norman Farquharson in the early rounds at Wimbledon in 1933 (his last loss at the All England Club), he went on to win three singles titles there on the spin and reached the final of ten of the last twelve Grand Slam tournaments of his career. The loss to Wood in New York changed Perry's life. There is a case to be made, a sound one, that it changed tennis. Nobody had worked so hard away from the game before. Many would do so afterwards.

While he enjoyed the life – marrying four times, squiring a collection of Hollywood starlets and going on to make a fortune with his famous shirts – Perry was one of the first players to bring hard work to a game of touch and beauty. He was the first proper professional, in the wider sense of the word. He made tennis an examination of the will and sinew as much as of the desire to paint a pretty picture on an oblong court. His was a game of paying for your mistakes as much as cashing in on your best strokes, because winning mattered mightily to him, more so after he decided to make tennis pay for his lifestyle. He learned that lesson not on the lovely grass of Wimbledon, where he became mythologised, reluctantly, but in New York, a city of pragmatic values that embraced him from the start.

Not everyone bought into the Perry creed. After the war, most players still kept to the old pace, restricting their off-court running to late sprints for trains or boats or nightclubs. It was unheard of for any player of the post-war era to employ a coach, let alone a physio or a strength and conditioning trainer, as is the norm among players in the top fifty today. Ken Rosewall, the 5-foot-7-inch 10-stone Australian they called Muscles, won his eight Slam titles before the open era and rode the cusp of the revolution. In a radio interview in 2013, he was asked about the modern game and observed that he had never had a coach, apart from Harry Hopman while on Davis Cup duty. He would not even consult his wife, who had been a good club player. It was an age of self-reliance, when blame or celebration were contained on the head of a player's racquet.

Before packing my bags for New York that last Sunday evening in Mason, I had plenty to muse about as I gathered my thoughts for this book. At its conception, the project had been to celebrate the golden age of tennis. That seemed a straightforward brief, and an agreeable one. There was much to applaud. But, in the flick of a few forehands and the click of a few vertebrae, everything changed. The Big Four was beginning to crumble like a slipped disc. Nothing could be taken for granted now. Before Nadal beat Isner, Murray had lost to Tomáš Berdych and took a jet eastwards to get ready for the first defence of his title. Federer followed him, reinvigorated. Djokovic, who lost to Isner, also departed early. He was in decent form, but not so menacing; Murray had ripped his heart out at Wimbledon, and the Serb was still hurting. Even so, most bookmakers made him favourite to win at Flushing Meadows. Perceptions are powerful in tennis, and not always correct. Once again, we lived in uncertain times and it added a frisson that had been missing for too long.

We'd all been wrong before, and we'd all be wrong again. I had covered tennis, more from a distance than near the heat of battle, for more than thirty years. Now, as the sport's correspondent for the *Guardian* and our Sunday sister, the *Observer*, I was required to be adamant rather than discursive. For as long as I could remember, I had similarly been asked to be just as certain about boxing. Confident opinions were fine as long as a prime Muhammad Ali was throwing leather at Cleveland 'Big Cat' Williams, but were more problematic years later when the punches were coming in the other direction from Joe Frazier. There is usually no better way to judge a performance than on the cards or by looking at the drained heap on the canvas, but experience told me that was not always so. Sometimes decline is invisible. In tennis, it is harder to see than in the ring.

To my mind, the two sports had a symbiosis that was not immediately obvious. There was the much quoted one-on-one factor, the exchange of heavy shots, the angles and the chess-like manoeuvring. The other similarity that had become a disturbing talking point, however, was the extent to which participants in each discipline were prepared to push themselves in their preparation as much as on the court, and the spectre of drugs grew alarmingly. Čilić and Victor Troicki fell foul of the testers in 2013, each protesting his innocence, and the veteran Spanish doubles player, Nuria Llagostera Vives, was banned for two years, accused of using a banned stimulant. Yet tennis was accused, still, of being soft on drugs. Djokovic defended his Serbian friend Troicki, who had, at first, declined to take a test in Monte Carlo, then tested negative the following day. The world number 2 railed against the authorities – and was, in turn, chastised by Murray and Federer, who regarded the accused as 'unprofessional'. Regardless of guilt, what was whispered on the circuit was that more players were being tempted to use prohibited substances just to keep up. Federer showed little patience for any of this, and was admirably Swiss about it, neutral and fair. If anyone could deliver a measured judgment on the morality of drugs, it would be Federer. He was always a man apart.

Since Federer won his first Slam title in 2003, he'd been the story, wherever he went, whatever he did, whatever he said. He still was the story now. But not for the reasons that once applied. Now, awkwardly, feet shuffling, we wanted to know: When would he quit? Could he win another Slam? Was the greatest player in the history of tennis washed up? These were not questions he liked to hear but he answered them – or variations of them – with his usual courtesy, knowing they would not go away.

The extent of Federer's dilemma is graphically observed through the eyes of one of his most ardent admirers, the tennis blogger Jonathan Moss, whose hugely impressive website peRFect.tennis.co.uk is full of statistics, videos, blogs, eulogies – and, until recently, few doubts. However, after Federer had scraped into the 2013 ATP World Tour Finals, he was looking determined but weary in the final event of the year. When Nadal beat Federer in two sets, in the setting Federer favoured above all others, indoors on a medium-paced hard court, and where he had always felt most comfortable, Moss declared: 'Isn't it about time Roger sat down in a quiet corner and asked himself a question, "When will this misery end? What do I have to do to turn things around? If I cannot find an answer, is it time to call it a day?"'

Moss's solution was very Federesque. He quoted Theodore Roosevelt:

> It is not the critic who counts; not the man who points out how the strong man stumbles, or where the doer of deeds could have done them better. The credit belongs to the man who is actually in the arena, whose face is marred by dust and sweat and blood; who strives valiantly; who errs, who comes short again and again, because there is no effort without error and shortcoming; but who does actually strive to do the deeds; who

knows great enthusiasms, the great devotions; who spends himself in a worthy cause; who at the best knows in the end the triumph of high achievement, and who at the worst, if he fails, at least fails while daring greatly, so that his place shall never be with those cold and timid souls who neither know victory nor defeat.

I entered the speculation tentatively, and with less certainty than the 26th President of the United States. Like Moss, there was nobody I would rather watch play tennis than Federer, and he still showed in bursts that his best was better than anyone else's best. The problems were frequency and consistency. He was sublime in Australia until he was stopped by Murray. He shone in Dubai and briefly in Indian Wells. But a player rarely troubled by his body now started to creak. He took seven weeks out after Indian Wells and, when he returned, there were magic moments in Monte Carlo, Roland Garros, Halle, Basel and the final Masters 1000 in Paris, but there was much missing. Like victories. The reality was that Federer's best could still win him points, games, sets, gasps of wonder and, until the end of most tournaments, matches – against just about anyone. But what he could not do was win big titles. He had become a compiler of cameos. Neither tinkering with his racquet nor sacking his coach worked. Moss was right to be worried.

It had been some years – probably reaching back to his win over Murray in the final of the Australian Open in 2010 – since he had started an unchallenged favourite in any of the Slams. Pride and self-belief inspired him to declare as recently as November 2013, nonetheless, that winning or losing in a Major against anyone but Nadal at Roland Garros was, 'on my own racquets'. He might not have meant it arrogantly by inferring it was up to him who won, not the others, but not everyone interpreted it so kindly. There were knowing nods in the press seats, and it left a vapour trail of disgruntlement in the locker-room. Players do not like to be regarded as hitting partners, even (or maybe, especially) by a legend. They still respected Federer, but they did not tremble in his presence any more. That was the Stakhovsky factor. Once the fear went, so did the inhibition. Federer felt insulted, it seemed, especially when he perceived – wrongly, in my opinion – that his past deeds were being ignored and that respect that had once been automatic was now ebbing. I think it contributed significantly to his occasional snappiness. Mostly, he was a walking charm school but, stirred to indignation, he found the containment of his frustration difficult. It was odd to see a player who, on the face of it, oozed confidence but, after examining the unvarnished evidence of the scoreboard, let old insecurities return. The joy he brought others was not always evident in his game or his post-match demeanour, and that invited speculation that a player who clearly had revelled in so many great moments might soon tire of mediocrity. Maybe it was inevitable that a discordant note had intruded on the game's symphony. For all that we would love tennis to be full of smiley moments, the reality of high-powered sporting combat is that feelings get hurt as often as bones and muscles.

Federer knew all this. He was a tougher adversary than he looked. He had, lest we forget, been a wild, racquet-bashing youth and only found his cool once he had worked out a career path. That was the Federer tennis people loved; the elegant, confident champion who hit the ball on behalf of a million romantics. Whatever the fading of his talent, you had to admire his faith in himself, even when others doubted him, which now meant nearly every time he was up against the other three. It was not a chore for him, even on days and nights of struggle. He just kept swinging. And, as he approached his thirty-third birthday in 2014, there could be no denying that he strove, still, to go to the place that Albert Murray knew. The place 'where just doing it gives pleasure of itself'.

13

'You can only go as far as
your body will take you'

New York, 28 August 2013

James Blake wins the first two sets of his first-round match against the funniest and perhaps tallest man on the Tour, Ivo Karlovic, the man from Yonkers drops the next two sets, loses the fifth in another tie-breaker – and packs his bags. 'It's not ideal,' he says of his last ever match, his 38th at his home tournament since he first came here in 1999. 'I'm trying to think that it is just one match, that it won't be the defining moment of my career. I've had some pretty good wins. Hopefully this won't be my lasting memory.' Defeat in his farewell appearance earns him $32,000, to bring his career purses over fifteen years to $7,981,786, averaging out at more than half a million dollars a year. It is a pretty good return for a player who once reached No. 4 in the world, and not bad for a kid who had a curved spine as a teenager and had to wear a back brace eighteen hours a day. Blake, one of the most popular players in tennis, is thirty-four – older than Federer, younger than Federer's mate Tommy Haas – and he can give no more.

~

Most of the soldiers were still standing by the time the caravan pulled into New York again at the end of August. Roddick would not be here, sadly, to enliven proceedings, but his rants echoed, and the ball-kids rejoiced. But, more or less, the field was in place, bruised and still punching. Murray, having survived his collapse in Rome, took a bit of a physical hit after winning Wimbledon and there were those who feared he might not be in the best shape to defend his title. They were right. Odds-makers had pretty much written off Federer on the evidence of a poor year, and Djokovic appealed to most as the favourite. Nadal, though, was still stamping his feet at the entrance to the bullring. He had plenty of fight left in him.

Yet, whatever the varying uncertainties about the Big Three Plus One, the rest of the field were still distant contenders. There just wasn't any enthusiasm for anyone outside the obvious choices. Janowicz had scared Murray at Wimbledon, and del Potro had given Djokovic his toughest fight since Wawrinka in Melbourne, but that did not exactly add up to an insurrection. It is a verity of American sport that doubt sells. It is why the draft system works: the best footballers and baseball players from their college system are directed towards the weakest teams in their major leagues specifically to manufacture – or create the impression of – equality. For years, we have put up with the domination of the Premier League by a handful of clubs; the Americans cannot understand that. But there is nothing they can do to tamper with tennis. In a one-on-one sport, the strongest rule. That is why the US Open resembled Wimbledon, oddly: in a setting that so yelled America, New York, they hosted a tournament they could not win. Except now that Murray had conquered Wimbledon, Flushing Meadows was on a par with Roland Garros and Melbourne, the other two Slam venues where home players had not a prayer. The game had shifted eastwards some time ago, but none of those warriors had yet joined Djokovic in the front line. Perhaps they were getting close, but there was no clear sign of them yet.

An American I always felt sympathy for was Brian Baker. He had missed nearly six years of his career through a hospital roll-call of injuries, but is still hitting at twenty-eight and was ranked 358 in the world, having tumbled from a career-high of 52 in 2012. Even though he is unlikely to ever visit again the levels he reached in his early twenties as one of the most promising players on the Tour, he plays on because he loves it, and because there are no better alternatives. Expecting a journeyman tennis player to retire is like asking a carpenter to switch jobs mid-career. He would probably only do so if he had forgotten how to mitre a corner. Nobody appreciates that more than Baker's fellow American, Michael Russell, who at thirty-five won a tournament on the Challenger circuit in 2013, travelling 8,628 miles to Ecuador to pick up $5,000 and 80 ranking points. As he told *Forbes* magazine that summer, he hardly broke even. Although he made $210,000 over the season, with sponsorship and exhibitions bringing in another $60,000, he spent $35,000 on air fares and another $40,000 just living. Stringing his racquets cost him $9,000, he estimated. As Russell observed: 'The top four players not only have a coach, but also a physio, a doctor, a hitting partner with them. Four, five, six people on their payroll.' Russell travelled a good deal lighter than that. Most of them do. And that is why tennis is really not an homogeneous sport. It is split into two distinct levels: inside the top fifty, and the rest. To get to the top, to earn big money inside the top fifty, players have to invest in their talent, or accept their lot, like Baker and Russell, who have to earn at least $2,000 a week just to make it worth their while. While the top ten reach for big titles, the infantry have another bar at which to aim: at year end, if they are ranked inside 125 five times, they qualify for an ATP pension.

Baker was still outside that comfort zone when we chatted over coffee at Flushing Meadows. He'd just gone out in the first round after four entertaining sets against the former US Open champion Lleyton Hewitt, another player who'd fought and won against injury and who, at age thirty-one, would not let the dream go. But Hewitt had been a champion. Baker, fine player though he remains, was not. What, in short, kept him playing tennis?

It's not hard to stay interested. Maybe it's hard to stay positive and be able to handle the ups and downs that you encounter, just because the game is really physical and you only really can go as far as your body will take you. My body was not operating properly for a long time and, you know, it will probably never co-operate with me as some of the other guys experience. I'll never be able to train as much as I like to. But, if I train the smart way and stay injury-free for an extended period of time, for a couple of years maybe, I still have full belief that I'll put up some good results and have a pretty good ranking.

It struck me as a very un-American ambition, to 'put up some good results'. But, as Mats Wilander explains elsewhere, victory comes in many forms in tennis. It is only possible to do your best, which might sound trite but is nonetheless convincing. In fact, it is when you see players in better shape than Baker fall short of that effort that you realise what Wilander is talking about. To not go somewhere near the maximum as often as possible is the real failure, not losing the match. The match, in a way, takes care of itself if both players give all they have. I never got the impression Baker dodged that commitment.

The game still puts an emphasis on talent and ball-striking, but you can't get away not being close to one hundred per cent physically or being a good athlete just because the courts are a little bit slower than average, the ball is a little bit slow and everyone else is so physical. They can turn it into a physical match against a guy that's a good ball striker . . . so, yes, you have to be a good ball-striker to be really high in the rankings but, even if you are one, you might still not do that well if your body doesn't co-operate a little bit.

I wondered what his match with Hewitt had been like, physically – given the Australian has had probably as many operations as Baker over the years.

For me it was a trial of strength, yeah. I haven't been able to train very hard coming back. I've had a little bit of a back issue, then I was coming back from a knee problem. You know, I wanted to play and I was fit enough to play last night, but for sure the last hour of the match I would have liked to have felt stronger on the court, or maybe not have had to play quite as aggressively as I was. I think I was finding the smart way to deal with how I was feeling. But I felt in Australia, for instance, I was good physically. Before I hurt myself there I won a five-set match against a guy [the Russian Alex Bogomolov junior] who can go all day and then tomorrow. The points weren't short, believe me. [The five-setter lasted 3 hours and 42 minutes, and Baker was going away in the fifth, 6–2.] I can get there, it just takes me a little bit of time, because I can train quite as hard as some of the guys on Tour. I'd rather be ten or fifteen per cent less fit and be healthy than hurt myself in the gym doing stuff that maybe somebody can do, but somebody like me would have to start at a lower level to build up.

You have to toe the red line. You have to trust the people who are in your team around you, your trainer, your coach. It all goes into the equation: how much you train on court, how much you train off the court, how much impact it has. My body is different to a lot of people's; I think it's pretty well documented what I've gone through. Some things feel pretty good now, some things I'm always going to be careful with, to consider how to manage. But I'm very confident that my body can be good, just as long as I catch some right breaks and don't have another six-month-out surgery, because that's what takes you back a year, physically. Hitting the ball, sure it might take me a couple of weeks to get back in the swing of things. I'm still not match-tough the way I'd like to be in the middle of the season – playing fifteen, twenty tournaments; playing three is a little bit different. It's tough, but, if I catch some breaks, I'll be OK.

Catching some breaks seems a Baker mantra, because he's had precious few in his career, an experience that would have broken many players. He is the son of a lawyer and a music teacher from Nashville, and somebody could easily have written one of those country-and-western odes about his travails. A high-school star, he was courted by all the big tennis colleges and was featured as *Sports Illustrated*'s Amateur Athlete of the Month. When he was handed a wildcard for Roland Garros in 2012 (he'd lost the boy's final there to Wawrinka in 2003), there was a collective cheer among those who knew what he'd been through over the previous few years: five operations, including his left hip in 2005 after beating 9th-ranked Gaston Gaudio in the first round of the US Open (his last full season), a sports hernia in 2006, more surgery on his left hip, then the right hip, followed by elbow surgery in 2008.

Did all this detract from his enjoyment of a game he was introduced to as a two-year-old baby?

I do enjoy the tennis, still, yes. Occasionally it's a grind if you're travelling all the time but I'm mentally really fresh. Most of these guys have been playing all year, whereas I haven't been. Sure, the injury part's no fun, but I've had to deal with that. It's nice to be home for a little bit but, after the first couple of months, you're like, OK, I'm ready to go do my job, ready to go play. Because it is not a sport like golf, where you can play for ever. It is frustrating to think that I've had a lot of good years go by where I haven't been able to show anything for it. But I can't really worry about that. I've just got to take what hits me and do the best I can.

Do players talk about this in the locker-room, I wondered.

Sure, I think so. It might not be the number one topic of conversation but the guys do – especially a lot of the American guys. We realise how physical everyone else is. We know if you're not as fit as they are, it doesn't matter how talented you are, how good you are, especially if you're in a five-set match, you're not going to play your best every match and you're going to have to win some matches on your legs and not just on your skills. I think people do understand the importance of it. That's why everyone's seen the game change in the last ten years. It's just getting that much more physical. I think before there were guys 30 in the world that maybe were suspect physically, but now I don't think you can go through anybody that you could say, 'Hey, keep 'em out there, you're fine.' The rankings go pretty deep. I think a lot of the guys put just as much emphasis on the physical part as they do on hitting balls. Everybody at this level can hit balls pretty well. You might work on some things here and there to improve your game, but the physicality part, that's probably number one now. They probably put their training on the court around their training off the court . . . at least I bet a lot of guys do.

I sort of knew that stark fact, but to hear it from a player of acknowledged talent whose body had let him down and who was still trying to hang in there as a competitor, it was depressing. Tennis today for the likes of Baker – well, everyone, for that matter – really was a test of strength and fitness, and not any more just a game, a sport, a competition for points, a battle of wits, an opportunity to be clever and artful, aesthetically pleasing, even. Except for one man. Roger Federer. Listening to Baker crystallised the Federer conundrum for me. He was the only player in the top twenty who had never quit during a match. He was blessed. But he was also committed to the purity of the sport. He played with his talent, not just his legs.

'But I still love it,' says Baker. 'I wouldn't be back playing if I didn't enjoy it. Of course there are times that everyone goes through – some of the two-a-days, the gym work, but it's not like you're super pumped-up to do it every day – but it's winning matches in Grand Slams, getting deep in ATP draws that make it all worth it. I still think that I can see the light at the end of the tunnel. I don't know how many more blows

I can take, but, for the time being I am still very dedicated to trying to make it.'

I wondered if the end of his career occupied Baker's thinking. He was considered in the answer to this question. 'Not really. I think it did more when I was out for all those years. It's not that I ever gave up hope but I think I understood that it was pretty realistic that I might not play again. Probably thinking back to 2009, I would have probably given it a thirty-five to forty per cent chance of coming back.'

What would he have done had he not come back, I asked. Again, his answer is pragmatic.

'I've got one more year of school. I've done two years in business and finance. I don't know, though . . . I don't know if I would have gone on to be an analyst and try to get on the financial whirl. I would like to use business in tennis. I want to stay in tennis in some way, just because . . . that's what I've done for my whole life. And I'm pretty good at it.'

And he is. But not quite good enough to beat Hewitt, who was still good enough to beat del Potro in the next round (the shock of the tournament) and get past the young Russian Evgeny Donskoy before running out of gas against Youzhny in the fourth round. It was a brave run by the Australian. Hewitt never quits, even if that is the sensible option. There are not many players like him.

The rest of the draw settled down without surprises. Djokovic, Nadal, Federer and Berdych cruised into the fourth round without the loss of a set. Nadal had reached the third round with the loss of only three games. Romantics began to wonder if someone could win the title with a perfect score. The last player to do so was the Australian Neale Fraser in 1960. It was a tough ask, and, as it transpired, nobody delivered. But the old guys were still there, five of them aged over thirty.

Murray, meanwhile, was progressing quietly. He won his eleventh match in a row to get past Denis Istomin from

Uzbekistan in straight sets and there were no hints of trouble. Then he ran into Wawrinka. The Swiss was inspired, just as he had been against the Scot in Monte Carlo, and he won with surprising ease in three sets, leaving the defending champion nonplussed but gracious. 'He played great,' Murray conceded afterwards; 'served well, hit a lot of lines, went for big shots, played too well.' That pretty much summed it up. Murray packed his bags and headed for Umag, to help Great Britain in the Davis Cup. It was the right thing to do, of course, but it proved to be one commitment too many and Murray was soon on the surgeon's table back in London, having his back fixed. Nobody could accuse him of not caring.

Wawrinka, meanwhile, lifted himself again. His losing effort over five sets in the semi-final to Djokovic was a classic, every bit as good as their fourth-round battle in the Australian Open. But for a return of the groin strain that had cut him down in Rome, Stan might have been the man. But the Serb made a phenomenal fight-back.

Wawrinka got it about right later when he said: 'I think that was a completely different match to the one we played in Melbourne. In the Australian Open I had to play my best game to stay with him. Today I had the feeling when I was still fit, when I was still healthy, I had the match in control. I think I was playing better than him. I was doing much more things than him. But he's not number 1 for nothing. He was staying with me all the match, and at the end he pushed me, pushed me far, far, far back. I had to find everything I had in my body today to stay with him, and he won.'

Baker must have watched that semi-final and agreed with everything Wawrinka said.

So, Djokovic again had been served up to an opponent in the final of a Slam having been battered in a semi-final of the highest quality, recovering from a slow start and another dip in the middle stretch (as against Nadal in Paris) to win 2–6, 7–6(4),

3–6, 6–3, 6–4. Could he do to Nadal in New York what he failed to do to Murray at Wimbledon? He desperately wanted to prove that he could, because this was the sort of test he always had reckoned he was made for, the sort of attritional war Baker spoke about. Again it did not go his way. He met an inspired Nadal, a player who, not for the first time in New York, had reinvented himself. When he broke through for his first US Open title in 2010, the clay-court king beefed up his serve and dedicated himself to changing his strategy at the back of the court, where previously he had been vulnerable on hard courts, because of his over-reliance on his forehand. That time, he worked hard on his backhand returns and stifled efforts to expose him across the baseline. This time, he went back to his serve – but not just for power. This time, Nadal was looking for precision.

In 2010 he was blasting serves past opponents at up to 135 miles an hour. In 2013, three years older and still just a little mindful of his suspect knee, he powered down and got his radar working. His fastest serve going into the final was 124 mph, and it was working. Sometimes, his first serve dipped as low as 108 mph, his second serve getting down to 87. Leo Levin, the IBM stats guru for the tournament, ran some numbers on Nadal and came up with this assessment: 'Nadal is now doing it with placement as opposed to raw speed. He's also figured out that his high-kicking second serve creates more issues for his opponents than if he goes for more speed and less spin.'

With his strategy and his mindset in place, Nadal had the look of a winner about him in that final. He fairly breathed antagonism and energy, and at the end he was winning points at will. The scoreboard could hardly have told it better: 6–2, 3–6, 6–4, 6–1 – four quick sets with one hiccup. Djokovic, however, was hugely philosophical in defeat. It was a part of his development that reflected a new maturity. He knew what Wilander and Baker and all the rest knew: you just cannot win all the time.

'I have to be satisfied with reaching the final, even though I would have loved to win tonight,' he said. 'He played better tennis, and that's why he deserved to win. I congratulate him, and I move on.' Here was a show-stopper, if ever there was one and however correct he was. The next time they met, however, Djokovic would make certain he was not merely 'satisfied' with reaching the final. He would be vengeful.

14

'You don't necessarily lose'

New York, 24 August 2013

The day after Novak Djokovic, Roger Federer and Rafael Nadal had shared laughter and mutual admiration in a New York hotel with the other available legends of the game to mark forty years of the ATP world rankings, they are afforded a more intimate stage at Flushing Meadows, on the eve of the US Open. Djokovic, as sharp as anyone on Tour, notices that the sign in front of him in the main interview room is wrong. 'I had a very good record in US Open in last five, six years that I have been coming back here,' he says, 'so I really look forward to it. Anyway, this says US Open 2012 here. You got to change it.' By the time Roger Federer is brought in, the sign has changed. And times have moved on. Djokovic will again reach the final, but he will be disappointed for the second year in a row.

~

Anniversaries come and go, as some half-wit once said. But the one on 23 August 2013 mattered a lot to tennis. It also did to the twenty-five players who had reached number 1 in the world over the previous forty years. Twenty of them gathered that night for a dinner in the grand ballroom of the Waldorf Astoria, New York, to celebrate their own and each other's achievements. In an era when membership of the game's elite has been reduced to four players – as opposed to the more liquid flow of champions in previous times – it was interesting to hear what former champions thought about the state of their sport.

The occasion, organised by the ATP, also provided a platform across social media and the wine bars around Flushing Meadows and other parts of Manhattan later that night to discuss who was the best of them. The pecking order did not seem to matter to the former champions, though, whatever the strength of particular rivalries. Their fighting had long finished on court, and they were content to shake hands, slap backs and tell old stories, most of them true. This was a night for raising spirits, not crushing them. As competitive as they all were, it was clear that to be brought together gave each player a fresh thrill. Only sixteen of the twenty-five had been ranked number 1 at the end of the year, which has come to represent the sport's world heavyweight championship. Maybe not obsessed . . . but pretty pleased nonetheless. Some enjoyed the hospitality more than others; nobody minded. This was their night of nights, from the first to hold the honour in 1973, Ilie Năstase, to the incumbent that night, Novak Djokovic. Anecdotes flowed like forehands, and each man had their own take on the significance of their achievements.

'It's always important to look back,' Pete Sampras said. John Newcombe said that 'the defining moment of world tennis' had arrived a year earlier (1972) at the US Open, when the ATP was formed. 'You look at the names,' said Jim Courier, 'and I marvel that I'm one of them. I got there . . . and nobody can take that away from me.'

One champion's story intrigued me more than most. 'There's not much to compare to the feeling that you're the best tennis player in the world,' Mats Wilander said in the same uncluttered manner he brought to his television commentary and occasional newspaper columns. It was the simplest and easiest to understand evocation of why they were there. Since only a few will know that feeling of specialness, I imagined their sense of worth would be permanent. But sport is not a movie. It does not always remain fixed in a setting sun, with violin accompaniment. Often, when the applause fades, the ordinariness that went before returns like a sledge-hammer. The effort it took to reach the top is so immense, it leaves some players drained. Not everyone can sustain the excitement or even the sense of wonder. Wilander could not; and that made him more interesting than the others. His was a view not dressed up in sentiment.

Wilander had his golden year in 1988, winning three Slam titles at just twenty-four. He won seven in all. And then he crashed. There were times when he wondered why he was even playing, and, although he carried on until 1996, it was a fitful denouement. He was banned for three months when he tested positive for cocaine at the 1995 French Open. He denied it vehemently, and fought through the courts as the drama fizzled out with a low-key, forgettable ending to a distinguished career. He lost the energy to be much bothered, and withdrew to the snow-covered hills of Idaho, with his wife, Sonya, and five children – Emma, Karl, Erik, Oskar and Travis – playing his guitar, still, then slowly returning to the game that had defined him. Tennis was always his drug of choice.

Coming after his compatriot Björn Borg, Wilander cut an edgier, slightly louder profile. Both were unconventional, a little mysterious – tennis raiders from the north, with their longer hair, their cerebral approach to the game and slightly removed attitude. They followed in the Scandinavian tradition of Torben Ulrich, whose love of jazz and mysticism sat comfortably alongside his life-long commitment to tennis and all its puzzles. When he was forty-nine, he played his 110th Davis Cup match for Denmark – the oldest player in the history of the competition. At the time of writing, Ulrich was eighty-five and living in Tiburon on the southern side of San Francisco Bay.

Whatever the reality, we imagined Borg and Wilander were

cooler than everybody else. Borg was characterised as an ice man, with not a lot to say and an on-court presence that could chill a good bottle of champagne. Wilander was different. As he says now, he talks more than most Swedes – 'maybe that's the American side of me' – and, because he has plenty to say, there sometimes is a risk not all of it will add up. A lot does, though. Wilander understands tennis with a depth many players miss. He sees beyond the scores and the win–loss column. He views tennis with affection and not a little suspicion, because he knows it has the power to do damage. Before his twenty-week reign as world number 1, he'd lost to Ivan Lendl three times in one season. He knew he was doing something wrong, so he stopped killing himself on the running track and started to play more tennis. Simple. At Flushing Meadows in 1988, he and Lendl fought for 4 hours and 54 minutes, and the Swede was gloriously content in victory.

'The goal was to beat Lendl,' he told me, matter-of-factly, 'to become so strong that you feel invincible. He was the target and he happened to be number 1 at the time and hard courts were the one place I couldn't beat him. I became number 1 and I was more than a tennis player in my mind. I lost track of what my goals really were because it happened so quickly.'

Lendl took the mantle back the following January and after that Wilander struggled to put tennis in a context that was in any way relevant to his results. It was not as grim as that sounds, but he admits the drive slowly deserted him. He had put so much into getting to the top of the mountain that the slide downwards was almost a relief. Not every player reacts that way, but it was Wilander's way. He played tennis for a living for fifteen years and, he told me, that was plenty.

Today we are speaking in the media canteen at Flushing Meadows. It's a couple of weeks after the gala dinner, and we are watching the Pennetta–Azarenka semi-final.

'God, nearly dropped off there,' he says as the match gets

underway, oh, so slowly. He is between broadcasting gigs, but he usually sits in here anyway, rather than in the players' lounge. He has made the transition from player to commentator without compromising his integrity. His words are never cheap.

I wondered where he thought his sport was going.

I think the game can go towards a little more aggression, more of an all-court game. I don't think that it's a fluke that we have so many guys over thirty suddenly doing well. They talk about the twenty, twenty-one-year-olds, and how it's a power game and that's why they can't break through . . . Well, that's obviously not the case. How would Tommy Haas and Jarkko Nieminen and Mikhail Youzhny . . . how do they stay alive? They're not power players. They're the opposite. They're 'feel' players. Having said that, they can survive, with their one-handed backhands and slice and defence. With that, though, comes knowing what to do when the moment presents itself. I think that the best players are going to have to say, gotta go to the net, finish the point. I think it's in transition. It obviously hurts. It's a style of tennis that Wimbledon doesn't do anymore.

Did he remember a point in the game when it started to become noticeably more physical than it used to be; with Lendl maybe? Was there a shift in thinking around about that time?

'I don't know,' he says. 'I never got tired, to begin with – so I'm not sure.' You could never doubt his stamina. Playing John McEnroe on the carpet of St Louis in the quarter-finals of the 1982 Davis Cup, Wilander lost over five sets in 6 hours and 32 minutes, which makes the encounter still the longest match in the tournament's history.

Borg never got tired, either. I think with Lendl, he actually talked about what he had done. He made it public what he was doing. At the time, we thought it was prodigious. But I'm not sure what's going to happen after this. I don't know where it's going for the next ten years. We don't have a young player that's arrived and is going to break into the top four. I don't think so. That's the problem. Hopefully Janowicz hitting drop-shots . . . that might prevent him winning a Major, while showcasing his game, that it's OK to hit drop-shots. Hopefully nobody comes up and plays the way that we all think they should play to win a Major: 6 foot 4 inches, beats the shit out of the ball on both sides . . . Janowicz knows how to move forward – but Sam Querrey, for instance, doesn't know how to move forward – big serve, big backhand, doesn't have to have anything else – except know how to move forward.

Random observations such as these sprinkle our conversation, as if Wilander is pulling me this way and that across the court in a match. Did he think, then, that the cleverness, the artfulness maybe, had gone out of the game?

Yes, exactly. Well it's not being taught. It's clear that there's room for it, because that is the only reason the over twenty-five guys are still in contention on the Tour: because they're clever. They know how to play the game properly. Anyone born '85 and onwards has in general grown up in the game without actually being taught how to play tennis. They've been taught how to hit balls. And, believe me, they hit a lot of balls. I don't believe in that.

I ask if he is saying that in the old days, if you had a talent for tennis and the skills that made it good to watch, you would come to the fore. 'Sure,' he replies. 'Players in Rod Laver's era, for instance. I think they certainly worked more hours on the court than they do today. The actual tennis was more sophisticated – easily so. And it's all down to the equipment. That is the reason, of course.'

Wilander was not afraid to experiment as a player. He not only took up one of the early fibre-glass racquets (a Rossignol F-200) when he went on the Tour as a teenager of exciting precocity, but in 1987 he also dramatically changed the core of his game.

He beefed up his serve and unveiled a lethal one-handed sliced backhand. The results were not immediately apparent in the Slams; Lendl beat him in Paris and New York, and Cash stopped him again at Wimbledon. Within months, however, he won his third Australian title.

The first thing when I switched, I got more spin. Don't know why. Maybe because it was bigger. It was carbon graphite then. It seemed like it just came naturally to me, to hit this loopy thing, and it made all the difference because, suddenly, you could not just hit it high, but the spin didn't go away. And it was easier to place the ball. There's nothing like the feel you get with a wooden racquet, no way, but I loved my racquet – that Rossignol, with an inverted bridge; the eight strings in the middle of the racquet were the same length. Wonderful sweet spot.

I remember that when Borg came back and tried to play with a wooden racquet, it clearly didn't work. Did he resist playing with the new equipment because he was trying to hang on to the purity tennis, I wondered. Wilander pauses and looks at me for maybe five seconds. 'Borg?' he says. A longer gap follows. I decline to fill it – a rally should run its natural course – as I sense I have said something idiotic. Finally there's a response. 'I think he was attracted to come back for something to do. As when he stopped playing, because he was bored, now he wanted to play again, just to play. So he didn't want a new racquet. I don't think he came back to play to win . . . He just came back to play tennis – something to do . . . and something that he loved to do. Not everybody loves winning. Winning is not special at all for some people.'

Wawrinka had told me something similar: not that you get used to losing, but that you get used to accommodating defeat. Wilander's response: 'Yeah.' He said it was uncomfortable some-times, when you haven't won anything for a while. Wilander: 'Yeah.' But you look at him now, and he seems to be more of a tennis beast (Wawrinka had just beaten Murray to reach the semi-finals). 'Unreal.'

I press on. Most Tour players must get used to losing, surely? They play so often . . .

No, I don't think so. I don't think it's like that. You don't necessarily lose [even if you don't win the match]. I never thought of myself as losing a match . . . Very, very rarely do you actually lose a match. Let me explain. Most of the time, if it's a big match, you actually don't lose. You sort of win, even if the score says the other person won. In a big match, you figure out a way to give yourself the best chance to win. And, if you've done that, it doesn't feel like a loss . . . You're just out of the tournament.

It was a beguiling philosophy, but one at odds with everything I had gleaned from watching and listening to the Big Four. Were we not, after all, in the age of super-tennis? Had we not been led to believe that these four athletes were different to all the others; that their commitment and sacrifice was total, not because they would be content with the fact they had figured out their best 'chance to win'?

Maybe that is what made them special? Perhaps it was no mystery at all that they so completely dominated their opponents and found parity only against each other. In the past, there had been a single champion (or sometimes two or three) who stood out from the rest. But these four were on another level. Wilander again . . .

I learned something. Take Federer the other day [going out of the US Open in an unusually tepid performance against Tommy Robredo, the Spaniard who a year earlier was not sure if he would ever play again]. That clearly was just a loss, because he wasn't really trying to do anything different. When you get older, winning tennis matches, winning points in a tennis match, is not the most important thing in your life. So if things are not going your way, you're not necessarily ready to critique [your performance], to dig around to find the right way to play. It doesn't mean he's going to quit. It means that his worst game is going to be worse and worse . . . and more inconsistent. But, when he shows up and he's playing well, he's still dangerous. And he's going to keep playing until he says to himself, 'My best game cannot win me a Grand Slam.' Now, he must be a couple of years away from that, I would think . . . I would think so.

Wilander did not always have such a high opinion of Federer. In 2006 he famously offended half of Planet Tennis when Federer lost to Nadal at the French Open after taking the first set 6–1 and then camping out on the baseline. Wilander took the view that to play Nadal from deep on his favourite surface, where he gets such enormous purchase on his high-bouncing, topspun forehand, was an act of surrender. 'Rafael has the one thing that Roger doesn't,' Wilander said. 'Balls. I don't even think Rafael has two; I think he has three. He [Federer] might have them, but against Nadal they shrink to a very small size, and it's not once, it's every time.' This did not go down well in the Federer household, and Wilander later apologised. Yet there were people who whispered that maybe he had a point. Federer rarely gave the impression he would die on court. He might very well take a lot of cuts and bruises, and give plenty back, but his body language did not match that of Nadal or Djokovic or, once he had seen off Djokovic at Flushing Meadows, Murray. Federer's victories were born of grace and elegance, his racquet a rapier, not an atomic bomb. He had more scalps and more wins than anyone except Connors (who finished his career with 1,253 opponents spent and thrashed on the other side of the net), Lendl (1,071) and Guillermo Vilas (929), whom he trailed by just six in the closing stages of the 2013 season.

Now, in Federer's worst year in a decade, Wilander was prepared to recognise the flashes of good as well as the dispiriting bad. As he saw it, after all, you could not lose if you put yourself in the best possible position to win.

We discussed Federer's loss to Nadal in Cincinnati when, for an hour, he was the master from the past. I suggest that Federer was irresistible at that point. 'Yeah' is the response. This is liking winning odd points in a match, but now Wilander opens up and the candour has not gone away.

'The genius is still inside him. Absolutely. But you can't just flick a switch. Tennis doesn't work like that. No . . . You just lose the everyday hunger. It's not there. You can't find a solution for every little problem that's out there in front of you on the court. You lose the hunger . . . it's not that important today. I don't know for whatever reason . . .'

I ask if he remembers it happening to him – a specific moment, when it didn't matter, when the hunger had gone? He does, but not in sharp detail.

'Yeah. It happened in '89, one time I lost.'

Was it a release?

'No . . . It was an awful feeling. What happened to me at 3–1 and 15–30 in the second set? I can't remember. I won the first set 6–3, or 6–2. I was up 3–1 and 15–30 and I got the guy . . . hit a second serve and I hit it in the middle of the court, he came in, won the point, 30–all. But I could have won the match right there. I think it went three sets. After that . . .'

He falls silent for a few seconds and then returns to what seems to be the uncomfortable recollections of a dark time.

You gotta know that every shot needs to mean something to you, like a painter or a musician, right? You don't just push down because you do it, right? Because this is what it means, right? In tennis, you're 40–love down: this is the shot I need to hit right now. Every shot needs to be hit with purpose – whether you're trying to win the point, or trying to lose the point . . . it doesn't really matter. That's irrelevant. Some points you're not even trying to win. You're just trying to hit it. You've gotta

know what you're trying to do. If you don't know that? That's
when it's time to quit.

It is an intuitive reading of the art and craft of tennis. I did
not want to interrupt, even though he lost me once or twice,
because it was coming from somewhere deep. It didn't matter
that all the words and thoughts were not immediately joined
up because, in the end, they were. The circularity of his thinking
was like watching a tennis player solve a puzzle in a match,
searching for openings and 'pushing down' when he thought it
appropriate. And, as he said, whether the purpose was to win
the point or 'just hit it', it perfectly described a sporting discipline in which once the action has begun with the serve, both
players are locked in. There is no escape. And, if you did not
care any more about the end result, if it ceased to matter and
you were doing it only because you always had – and always
had to – it was, probably, 'time to quit'.

We talked boxing for a while and drew some analogies.
Wilander had once worn sixteen-ounce gloves, I learnt, and in
June 1988 he and John McEnroe had boxed three two-minute
rounds for charity in Dublin. By all accounts, although no blood
was drawn, it was a willing affair, neither giving much ground,
each calling on that spirit of doing it 'because it matters'. But,
as with boxers, if tennis players are just doing it from memory,
'that's when you get your butt kicked', as Wilander puts it.

He reflects on his finest moments, not from choice, but good
manners. They are from his golden year, 1988, when he was
just twenty-four. Within a year, he was spent. He could not
find a convincing reason to struggle any more. Perhaps it was
booking a seat – then cancelling at the last minute – on the
ill-fated Pan-Am Flight 103 from London bound for New York
via Lockerbie four days before Christmas that gave him perspective. He says not. But escaping death, when all 243 passengers
and sixteen crew on board that plane did not, surely made this

intense thinker wonder a little about the overall integrity of his 'purpose', of his role as a mere athlete. He once said: 'I don't know about anything in the world except tennis.' After half an hour in his company, I find this hard to believe. Wilander knows a lot about human nature – much of it learnt on the tennis court.

And he knows this: 'Even the best players in the world are definitely not close to perfect.' It is a judgment he is entitled to make and one that comes from looking inside oneself and taking a tough call, going against the perception of others, who are mystified by the seemingly sudden fall and the apparent disinterest in the process or the consequences. He didn't lose interest; he lost passion, for a while. When he got it back, he didn't translate it into performances on court, because his time had gone. Instead, travelling around America in his Winnebago RV teaching tennis with a random sense of on-the-road freedom, he takes pleasure in transmitting his rediscovered love of the game to others. And he shares the knowledge that all players have: perfection does not exist. Nadal speaks about this regularly, although maybe it gets lost in the post-match analysis because there is no time to stop and think about what is essentially a very simple philosophical point of view.

That's why I find Wilander more interesting than most other players, or ex-players. He has experienced the highs and lows of international sporting celebrity and has come through the self-indulgence of his partying years, basking in the glory of victory; he has learnt to live in the shadows of decline, then found that need and purpose to get involved in tennis again, through teaching.

Did he find the golden age interesting? Pat Cash didn't, necessarily. Others were undecided. The media certainly did.

I find that it's gotten more exciting because of the likes of Murray. He's physical, he plays with power when he wants to, he plays with feeling when he wants to. Murray against himself would be an interesting match. Novak against Novak probably would not be so interesting, because he's fairly one-dimensional. Given what he does, his game is kind of the modern way of playing tennis. I kind of hope we don't have ten more Novaks in the top ten for the next ten years. That would be weird. I don't mind ten Andy Murrays, because you don't know which Andy Murray will show up.

I laugh. Wilander doesn't. 'No, because it's true. He's very interesting as a player. And Novak is very interesting as a person, but not a very interesting tennis player, although a great one – one of the best ever, when he plays well, but there is not that unknown factor with him. You know what's coming. Rafa has an extra dimension to his tennis too – full on, yeah.'

And how did Nadal do what he did in 2013, I wondered, which, allowing for hyperbole, was something of a minor sporting miracle.

It's his passion for the game. I would think, in a way, those problems were helping him to come back. They helped him stay focused, to want it again – and not changing coaches, like some players do. It's, like, he has that safe place to go back to, his home town – and maybe because there's pretty much nothing there, he concentrates on his tennis again. Otherwise he's walking the beach, right? Ha! It's an escape from all this.

That's a shrewd take on Nadal. When he leaves a tournament, he does not head for his tax haven. He goes home to his island, to his small town, the place where he grew up, surrounded by the same supportive faces that have been there all his life, who demand nothing of him and upon whom he leans heavily when things are going not so well. They travel as a tight-knit group, almost like a football team permanently on tour. And, although he appears self-contained on court, he feeds on their presence. In professional sport, those moments of trial can arrive from nowhere. When it is over, Nadal has probably the most reliable safety valve in tennis, a Mediterranean hideaway with a tennis court and a coach, as much sunshine as anyone would want, and, perhaps most importantly, no prying eyes, no inquisitors. Murray has had to invent his sanctuary. Djokovic and Federer, also, flit from one base to another. Nadal always goes home.

'I agree,' Wilander says when I put this to him. And he further observes that the grind of the Tour, with the mundane demands of travel and acclimatisation, jet lag and hotel rooms, disruption and discord all build up. Some players are not bothered by it; others find it tiresome and an irritation. 'It's kind of an art form, doing all that,' he says. 'You have to create time for yourself. You might want to play guitar, say.'

There is a YouTube clip of Wilander sitting in with the Trey Clark Band at the Galleria Tennis and Athletic Club in Houston, Texas, after playing an exhibition in June 2012. He's knocking out a pretty soulful version of 'Knocking on Heaven's Door'. There is, somewhere, a five-song CD he and a friend called Seldon put down in Sweden more than twenty years ago, called *Ghost of Margareth*. In an interview with the *Guardian* in 2007, he revealed: 'Margareth was a vocal coach who died in the house we recorded the album in and her spirit lives on there – at least, that's what the engineers told us. But of course, I'm not sure what they were on! Let's just say we were closer to the Stones than Dylan.'

In wilder times, Wilander was occasionally closer to drunk than sober – Smithwicks dark ale was a favoured tipple – although when he fell down the stairs during the Australian Open in 2012, hurting himself badly enough to miss a commentary gig, it was just a clumsy tumble. It was made clear through third parties that he had not been drinking.

In another impromptu set with Trey Clark in April of 2012, Wilander does a passable version of 'Honky Tonk Woman'. The chords are few, but they are struck with conviction, not unlike his tennis. Back at Flushing Meadows, the Pennetta–Azarenka semi-final is crawling to a conclusion, and Wilander is distractedly crunching his way through a second packet of crisps.

He reflects on the Tour, which was good to him as a player and, briefly, a coach, and still is, as an astute commentator. 'You've got to make it fun,' he says of an occupation that can often be a grind. 'You have to enjoy all parts of the experience, otherwise it's impossible.'

Wilander subsequently found a way to fill in the hours in a rather innovative way.

I was stuck in an airport for four, five days in Denver, I think it was, on the way to doing a few clinics in Vermont. We got snowed in. Couldn't get to Vermont. We were sitting in the bar, having a few beers, so I said to my friend, 'Why don't I just throw my shit in my Winnebago and go to your place, and we'll play tennis for the weekend?' I love to go camping in the Red Rocks in Nevada. He said, 'Great. Do that.' So I met Cameron, my business partner, we set it all up and it just took off. Good fun. We go anywhere. We go on any tennis court, wherever we get the interest from. Sometimes the whole town sponsors the event, sometimes a company, sometimes players pay themselves. Sometimes they give us the money in cash. Sometimes a director of tennis will write a cheque for whatever it costs to have three clinics, eight people in each. It's all so different. I love it.

Wilander says he has seen no players on his travels who would make it on the Tour, but that is not the point. He's not talent-spotting. He's not an agent or a coach looking for the next Federer. He's just an ex-pro on the road, having a great time and spreading the word.

I just want each player to reach his or her potential. They might be seventy-five years old. The object is to help people to learn how to practise. Most people hit a tennis ball and they never get any better. Or they hit one serve and they stop playing.

They say to me, 'Mister, can I have another one?' I tell them it doesn't work like that. That's where we try to help them, to learn, to practise. But more important is to just have a bit of fun with people. I've been doing it for four years. I've been to maybe half the states in the country, and into Canada.

He finishes with a simple explanation of his philosophy, of tennis and life: 'We don't have any goals. I've never had any goals – at anything. The goal is to do this for as long as I physically can . . . It's good for your mind.'

I like to think Torben Ulrich would agree with all of that.

15

J'accuse

Jo-Wilfried Tsonga is one of the game's contented souls, albeit a player who has suffered more injuries than most. Currently, his knees are giving up on him. There is a fast-growing trend in the game, embracing the fad that Novak Djokovic is promoting so enthusiastically: the gluten-free diet. It is said to solve most physical woes. Jo thinks not. 'No, no diet anymore!' he insists in French. 'A lot of constraints and I didn't see any specific results.' As keen as athletes are for anything that gives them an edge, they are equally as drawn to those things that give them comfort. For Jo-Wilfried Tsonga, food is near the top of his list.

~

This is the true story of a man doubly innocent: guileless yet also not guilty of the crime of which he was accused. Like Albert Dreyfus, he was convicted and, after a protracted farce, pardoned. Unlike Dreyfus, whose deprivations on Devil's Island a century earlier dwarf the trivialities of sport and took years to rectify, Marin Čilić merely plays tennis for a living. Nonetheless, if the gifted Croatian could be cited for anything in the drugs-bust that sort of wasn't, it would be Dreyfusian naivety. Whether that is a credible defence in a quick-click world of instant information is for the player and his advisers to discuss over a cup of WADA-approved tea, perhaps. But what is indisputable is that what happened to him does not reflect well on tennis . . . or that well on Čilić himself.

On 29 October, in the 12th arrondissement of Paris – just across the Seine from Dreyfus's resting place in le cimètiere du Montparnasse – the penultimate tournament of the 2013 ATP World Tour witnessed something that transcended the sport. Čilić, who had agreed to a provisional suspension at Wimbledon, pending the results of tests for banned substances, returned that day after four months away from the game that had been the centre of his life since he was seven years old. In that time he could not earn a living and his world ranking had fallen from twelve to thirty-seven, putting him outside the relative comfort zone of the top sixteen. For a handful of elite players, the ninth Masters 1000 tournament of the season was a last chance to qualify for the World Tour Finals in London the following week; for twenty-five-year-old Čilić, who briefly was in the top ten himself in 2010, it represented something more fundamental: redemption.

'Being with all the players here in Paris is my gift of the year,' he said, his soft, dark eyes darting among the gathered hacks in search of a friendly face after he'd sweated out a win against the Dutch qualifier Igor Sijsling. There was sympathy, but they wanted to know more. They needed convincing. The hard-wired gulf between player and inquisitor perhaps strengthened Čilić's view of himself as an outsider. He was widely liked on the circuit, but he was damaged goods; those who neither knew him well nor were immersed in the nuances of his case would stand aloof a little longer. You could not blame him for feeling ostracised . . . or the journalists for continuing to wonder. He had, effectively, been out on bail. On appeal, the Court of Arbitration for Sport had reviewed his case and, just before Bercy, the International Tennis Federation announced that Čilić would be allowed to resume his career.

In a statement as palpably lawyered as it was stripped of explanation, the ITF said:

The International Tennis Federation announced that the Court of Arbitration for Sport ('CAS') has partially upheld the appeal by Marin Čilić against the decision of the independent tribunal dated 23 September 2013. The independent tribunal had determined that Mr Čilić should be suspended from participation for a period of 9 months, commencing from 1 May 2013 (the date on which the sample containing the prohibited substance was collected) and so ending at midnight on 31 January 2014 for the commission of an Anti-Doping Rule Violation under Article C.1 of the Tennis Anti-Doping Programme (presence of a Prohibited Substance in player's sample). The CAS panel decided that the independent tribunal's decision be set aside, and replaced with a period of ineligibility of four months, with the start back-dated to 26 June 2013, the date on which Mr Čilić accepted a voluntary provisional suspension. He thus will be eligible to participate on 26 October 2013. Mr Čilić's results from the BMW Open remain disqualified, including forfeiture of the prize money and ranking points won at that event. Mr Čilić's results subsequent to the BMW Open will not be disqualified and he is permitted to retain the ranking points and prize money that he won at those events. The full decision, with reasons, will follow in due course.

Were he a student of Balzac (and there is no reason to suppose he would not be), Čilić might have reflected on the French writer's observation that 'Laws are spider webs through which the big flies pass and the little ones get caught.' He might have felt that there were offenders out there escaping the guillotine while he had been pilloried in the stocks for reasons that had little to do with natural justice; that this was human comedy in a minor key.

It was also sports administration at its most ham-fisted. The ITF's concept of twenty-first-century justice, giving Čilić a reprieve with a caveat but no reason, typified the way many sports bodies treated athletes. His appeal was 'partially upheld' the statement said, but which part and by what margin? And, more to the point, why? So, into this vacuum of information stepped the relieved but frustrated player to put his case after being allowed to return from an unwanted sabbatical that sapped his self-confidence but not, it seemed, his love of the game.

Čilić, who had ticked over nicely in practice and in the gym, was in decent shape for an 'ex-con'. There was no denying, either, that he looked more relaxed with a racquet in his hand than the last time most of us had seen him, in front of a microphone at Wimbledon on 26 June. He was not so accomplished that day. He said he was withdrawing from the tournament after beating Marcos Baghdatis in the first round because he had a knee injury. Čilić and several others knew why he was leaving Wimbledon: it was not primarily for any real or imagined physical ailment – even if that were a factor – but because he had been busted for taking a banned substance. What he could also not say at the time was that, if he declined to agree to a suspension before his case was heard, he risked losing any ranking points or money earned at Wimbledon. Although this was the protocol, it also smacked of a deal.

Even after his reprieve and comeback, Čilić continued to protest that he had been injured at Wimbledon; what was not disputed, however, was the fact that there was no mention of the drugs ban that first Wednesday of Wimbledon. So the readers of our supposedly informed accounts of the farrago at the time were none the wiser. We told them Čilić was injured, because that was what Čilić told us, and the guardians of the game's morals and values were happy for that impression to be left lying in the public domain like a dying tree that would have to be chopped down eventually. The ITF would no doubt argue that no crime had been proven, that due process had to run its course and that they did not want to hang the player before he'd even stepped up to the gallows. Perhaps so. But, given the subterfuge, it is reasonable to ask if the ITF would subsequently have made it public had Čilić been cleared instead of convicted at his first 'trial', or would they have let it slip quietly into the 'too hard' basket? It was a busy time for the drugs testers and the ITF's Independent Anti-Doping Tribunal, Viktor Troicki having been charged with missing a blood test at Monte Carlo in April, the very tournament where Čilić's fall had its genesis. Troicki would later receive an eighteen-month ban, reduced to a year on appeal to the Court of Arbitration for Sport. But in some ways the Serb's case was more straightforward. It was his word against that of the drugs tester, who testified that he had declined to take the test because he said he was ill. If the inference was that he had something in his system and it somehow disappeared overnight, well that's a very thin rope by which to hang someone. Avoiding a drugs test, rightly, is a serious matter and other players have found themselves in similar difficulties. But Troicki's punishment did not seem to fit the crime, as his compatriot Novak Djokovic and Rafael Nadal said later. Nadal wanted to know, for instance, why, if Troicki was dodging a bullet, he was able to take the test the following day. It was a point, persuasively put, that addressed justice and logic rather than the letter of the law. Čilić's case was different. His was a story of bone-headedness, of failing to observe the simplest of precautions and then paying the price.

If it did not constitute a conspiracy of silence, then the handling of the Čilić bust at Wimbledon was at the very least a clumsy, on-the-hoof call by the ITF, and was accepted by anyone at the All England Club aware of it, as well as Čilić, his team and his legal advisers. Nobody won. Dreyfus, no doubt, would have spun wildly in his Montparnasse grave. In the interests of the sport and a quiet time, we had all been subtly hoodwinked.

Four months later in Paris, Čilić maintained he was no cheat and no liar; he had been injured, he said, and was a victim of the system. Well, that system had also put a shield around him for their mutual interests and had stuck a dagger in his gizzards that now, to his palpable contentment, was quietly being pulled out. It left a minor scar that all concerned hoped would heal and, eventually, disappear. While Čilić emerged from his ordeal more sainted than besmirched, he half-wittedly contributed to the most cock-eyed public relations shambles any of us could remember; one that put everyone concerned in a poor light. Possibly we in the media were guilty, too, of not pursuing the obvious. But the first draft of the script was written by others.

This is how it unfolded. The tale is more Poirot than Hans Christian Andersen, and it is a salutary one.

Around the time Čilić hit the high point of his career, in February 2010, when he was rated the ninth best player in the world, his conditioner, Slaven Hrvoj, expressed concerns that Marin was 'not eating enough'. He looked around the tennis jungle and saw nothing but beasts, strong players who seemed to have inexhaustible supplies of energy, especially in Grand Slam tournaments, where it really mattered. Curiously, it was Čilić's best showing under such pressure that led Hrvoj to urge a change in his regime. In the first big test of the season, the Australian Open in Melbourne, Čilić pushed his body to the extremities to win three five-setters on his way to the semi-finals. This, many good judges said at the time, was the flowering of a wonderful new talent on the circuit. His opening trial was against Australia's own teenage enigma, Bernard Tomic, and Čilić won 6–7(6), 6–3, 4–6, 6–2, 6–4 in 3 hours and 48 minutes; next, he dismissed Stanislas Wawrinka in four sets, before coming through his second five-set examination, over 4 hours and 38 minutes of exquisite torture against del Potro, then number 5 in the world and the reigning US Open champion. Surely, he could not do it again, critics said, as he stepped up in the quarter-finals against world number 7 Andy Roddick, a player of renowned grit and attitude. He did, and, in just under four hours, he came through a mid-match crisis to beat the American 7–6(4), 6–3, 3–6, 2–6, 6–3. Having gone to the well three times in a week, was there anything left, Hvroj wondered? In the semi-final Čilić met Andy Murray, a player for whom pain in the gym and on the training track not only underpinned God-given gifts but made opponents weep. Čilić took the first set to excite speculation that he could upset the world number 4. He could not, having to save eleven break points just to stay with the Scot. Murray dug deeper for longer and won 6–3, 4–6, 4–6, 2–6.

Čilić left Melbourne on a high. All the hard work with his coach Bob Brett looked to be paying off. 'He's a very good teacher,' Čilić said. 'I'm with him already several years, and he knows how I breathe, how I stand on the court, what things he could give me, which advices in which moment. He helped me a lot in this Grand Slam level. Without him, the achievement would be very tough to get to.'

As for Brett, he was pleased as well. 'All I've done is work with a great talent,' he said. 'I just work with someone and point them in the right direction. At the end of the day when it's 30–40, they've got to put it over the net. I've been lucky to have had good players, people who have drive.'

It had been a mighty team effort, and there should have been much more to come, but Hvroj, a perfectionist like Brett, was not satisfied. He would have to look again at his player's nutritional needs to make sure he could play as many five-setters as it would take to win a Slam. Nobody could argue with such a philosophy in the age of sacrifice. Unless you dreamed of a more beautiful time, one in which Čilić might well have profited more.

One of the Tour's willowy protagonists, Čilić stands 6 foot 6 inches and rarely has weighed more than 180 pounds. By an inch, he falls into the category the 6-foot-2-inch German veteran Tommy Haas jokingly reckons should be 'banned from tennis'. As his victims in Melbourne that year learned, he has a game that shorter players dread, constructed behind a serve that leaves

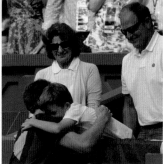

Members of the tennis tribe cling fast to their
heroes, none more movingly than young Essex
schoolboy Henry Caplan who rushed through
the crowd to embrace Murray after he won the
Olympic gold medal at Wimbledon in 2012.
Seven months later, fans mobbed Murray in
Melbourne after he beat Gilles Simon to reach
the quarter-finals of the Australian Open

Usain Bolt, the fastest man on the planet,
stopped in Paris long enough to
present Nadal with the Coupe des
Mousquetaires after his three-set win
over David Ferrer in the final

It was Federer's turn to offer
congratulations, however, when the
Ukrainian serve-volley underdog
Sergiy Stakhovsky rushed him out
of Wimbledon in the second round, one
of the great shocks of 2013

For the loser, Djokovic, the 2013 Wimbledon final ended in slumped shoulders and water to drench his weary body. For the winner, Murray, there was only sunshine and smiles as he raised his racquet to acknowledge the support of the Centre Court crowd on an unforgettable afternoon

After delivering the nation a Wimbledon men's singles title for the first time in seventy-seven years and burying the ghost of Fred Perry for ever, Murray went back to the scene of his triumph the following day – after minimal sleep – to face the media

Federer rode the rollercoaster of emotions throughout the year and, following his Wimbledon disappointment, defeat by 114th ranked Federico Delbonis in the semi-finals at Hamburg was obviously tough to take. How he would love to emulate Pete Sampras, one of his favourite players, who retired after winning the US Open title – his final match – against Andre Agassi in 2002

Surprises came in many forms for Federer in 2013, such as this gift of
a cow during the opening ceremony of the Swiss Open, where
he lost to Juan Martín del Potro in a competitive final

When the Tour rumbled into New York in late August, the players still competing in the US Open were joined by several great players from the past at a gala dinner at the Waldorf Astoria to celebrate forty years of the ATP rankings. Putting their racquets aside for one evening, Djokovic, Nadal and Federer were able to relax before resuming battle

There was a rare chance for tennis fans to acclaim three of the greatest players in the history of the game when Rod Laver joined Nadal and Djokovic at the net before the final, in which the Spaniard avenged his 2011 loss to the Serb

Djokovic probably has the most elastic body in tennis, and his kick-boxing leap against the backdrop of a South American sunset illustrates this vividly

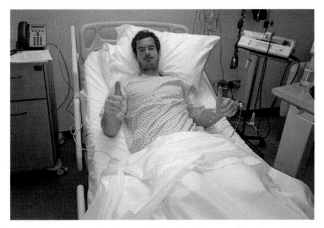

Murray's movement was seriously curtailed when he went into hospital in September for an operation to cure the back problem that had dogged him since late 2011, cut him down in Rome in 2013 and forced his withdrawal from the French Open. It is remarkable that he was able to win Wimbledon before going under the knife

The Scot missed the ATP World Tour Finals in London, but Federer was there and in sublime form again, adored as ever by his fans. He dipped a little in the semi-finals, however, where he lost to Nadal in straight sets

The 2013 season was not short of incident – away from the activities of the Big Four. Juan Martín del Potro met his fellow Argentinian, the new Pope Francis, and was thrilled to have his rosary beads blessed by the pontiff. A few months later he was devastated when a thief stole them, along with his passport, at Gare du Nord on his way to the ATP World Tour Finals

A meeting with the former world number 1 Mats Wilander at Flushing Meadows provided the sort of enlightenment a free spirit such as the Swede has been spreading at all levels for many years. Here he is atop his Winnebago looking out on the Pacific Ocean, as he tours the United States giving clinics in towns big and small

The gifted and infuriatingly inconsistent Ernests Gulbis finds his freedom elsewhere, such as smashing his racquet during a match against the similarly gifted and turbulent Pole Jerzy Janowicz at the Stockholm Open in October

Janowicz promised more than he delivered in 2013, but he gave Murray a major scare by taking a set during their Wimbledon semi-final. He is a player to watch

If the headlines belonged to Nadal in 2013, Federer flickered still. This striking image of him moving out of the shadows and into the sunlight again in Madrid in 2009 is one to which he would love to give substance as he approaches his thirty-third birthday

Murray could reflect on his year with considerably more satisfaction, despite a back injury that put him out of the game for four months. A moment he will cherish is his visit to Buckingham Palace to receive the MBE, joined by his mother Judy, his girlfriend (now fiancée) Kim Sears and his father Willie

Whatever their differences and rivalries, these four wonderful players can still get on (for commercial purposes, at least), as Nadal and Djokovic did in this spectacular setting for a mocked-up match on the deck of the Glacier Perito Moreno near El Calafate, Argentina, in November. Two weeks earlier they had slugged it out for real, in the final of the ATP World Tour Finals at the O2 Arena on the southern shores of the Thames his racquet from close to ten foot. He then relies on his long levers to deliver delicate placement as well as occasional rasping, killer ground-strokes. But generally, his is the antithesis of super-tennis. Čilić is not one of the beasts. He has always been a delight to watch, and, when he hits a peak, there are not many players on the Tour, whatever their ranking, who relish being on the other side of the net. That is his real strength: his superlative game.

Sometimes, though, his stamina, spirit and focus collapsed simultaneously. At too many points in his career, he had folded without explanation towards the end of matches. In the quarter-finals of the 2012 US Open, he was a set and 5–1 up against eventual champion Murray before crumbling like an autumn leaf in a hurricane. Murray had also outlasted him at Wimbledon that year, in the fourth round, and Čilić had failed to cope with the power tennis of del Potro in the third round at Roland Garros. It would appear, then, that Hvroj, who had developed his skills at the National Tennis Centre in Zagreb, knew what he was talking about two years earlier when he urged Čilić to add muscle to his smarts. To that end, Hvroj said, what Čilić needed was a mix of electrolytes, protein and glucose. For years, Čilić had taken dietary advice from Croatia's National Olympic Committee, who provided 'safe to take' supplements free of charge. To these, on the advice of Hvroj, the player added glucose, buying it mainly in powder form from a chain in Croatia called DM, under the trade name Traubenzucker, a German word meaning 'grape sugar'. For a sweetener, it would leave a very bad taste indeed.

Here the script grows tentacles. Traubenzucker's product contained 'nikotinamid' (as the Croatian word had it), which Čilić knew from an internet trawl early in 2011 to be 'harmless'. Drugs tests he had taken after using it always proved negative. He had, he properly assumed, no reason to worry. But international sports nutrition is a minefield littered with misunderstandings. So, to help players monitor what they put in their bodies, the ITF provides a UBS stick and a wallet card (in English, which Čilić understood pretty well, French, ditto, and Spanish, less so), which lists banned substances and the number of a helpline available twenty-four hours a day. Help was a phone call away, the ITF contended, for Čilić and the many hundreds of players on the Tour. Somebody, surely, read their advice. Brett, who had seen most things in the game, was sceptical. He reckoned players treated these pamphlets like phone bills, stuffing them in a drawer . . . which, of course, is exactly what Čilić did.

Anyone looking at this from the outside, however, would have to say that a player would have to be at the very least indolent to ignore such expert back-up in an era of high-profile drugs busts across the whole of sport. There were daily stories or rumours about some dumb schmuck getting it wrong and then claiming he/she knew not what he/she did. Impatience with some of the more outlandish excuses proffered by the accused curdled over time into indifference; there was a growing public perception that 'they were all on it'. Many athletes, too, greeted improved performances by their rivals with a knowing shrug. Some asked questions. A few gambled. And chemists continued to outfox the drugs testers and seduce those players who were willing to have a punt on not getting caught. Tennis, the first sport to introduce drugs testing, in 1985, hoped it could stay ahead of the curve by giving players all the help they could. Not all the players responded as they should have done.

Čilić did not keep the stick or the wallet with him. Instead, as Brett feared, he put them 'in a drawer'. And, as the Anti-Doping Tribunal would reveal, 'He believed that, as long as he did not take anything different from what he was taking, he would be safe.' While this sounded like a reasonable assumption on the face of it, a similarly naive view of life would bring Čilić to grief the day when his mother went shopping for him in Monte Carlo. Had he not left that gadget and the card of sin out of reach when he most needed it, had he been more alive to the dangers that the vast range of prohibited substances posed to his legitimacy as a legal athlete, he might have avoided the most damaging episode of his career.

Despite the best efforts of Hvroj, Čilić did not grow into a tennis monster. He was the last player anyone would suspect of using a banned substance. If anything, he sometimes looked as if he would benefit from a shot of strong coffee in the middle of a match. By 2012 his form had dipped alarmingly and, not long before Christmas, the player, his parents and his nutritionist fell out with Brett.

The nature of the growing rift with the canny Australian – described once as his country's best tennis coach since Harry Hopman – has never been properly explained. Čilić was fifteen when the pair were introduced by Goran Ivanišević, who profited greatly in his own career from Brett's shrewd tennis brain. It seemed a perfect fit. But, in the inevitable low periods, it is clear that the player's parents were not happy with the way their son's career was going and they urged him to reconsider his options. Now, in the spring of 2012, the team had gathered in San Remo, the training base half an hour's drive from Čilić's apartment in Monte Carlo – the place where several players from all over Europe choose to live . . . for the tax breaks as much as the mild climate and the lovely coastline. The tensions that had already seeped into Čilić's relationship with his coach intensified. On Hvroj's recommendation, he had begun taking creatine, a permitted energy booster popular among boxers, and, to dilute the gravelly taste, he added glucose, which he knew from experience to be legal. Hvroj told him the glucose also helped the body absorb the creatine, which he kept taking, on and off. He could hardly have anticipated the storm to come. (Well, he could have . . . had he read the ITF's crime sheet more closely.)

He and Brett were now in a strained relationship, but he continued to drive to San Remo each day, with his father and brother, to prepare for the Monte Carlo Open. This was the acknowledged kingdom of Rafael Nadal, who had been crowned at the champagne-heavy country club overlooking the Mediterranean eight years in a row; this time he would lose to Novak Djokovic, but the real drama was occurring away from the court. On the eve of the tournament, Čilić's determination seemed renewed. It was then that his mother, Koviljka, entered the narrative. Čilić, who had moved out of his apartment and into a hotel the night before his first match so he could focus more clearly on the job ahead, was running low on the glucose powder on which he had come to depend as an important part of his dietary regime. He asked his mother to replenish his supply. There was none at the supermarket closest to his apartment, so he told her to go to a nearby pharmacy where she might be able to buy it. Before she could make the purchase, however, on 18 April Čilić had crashed out in the first round to Richard Gasquet. He was in low spirits. As the investigation in London would hear, 'It was obvious to him that his parents and his coach were not getting on well and this was a source of stress for him, made worse by his defeat on the court that day.'

When his mother, who speaks no French, went to the pharmacy for his glucose, the story took its first unfortunate twist. She told the pharmacist twice in English that it was for her son, 'a tennis professional', but the staff did not understand. A stranger who spoke French then intervened on her behalf, and the pharmacist sold her a product called 'Coramine', which had the word 'glucose' printed on the packet. She took this to indicate safety for Marin; after all, she had told the pharmacist about her son's line of work and had tried to convey to him the importance of the glucose being legal. Surely they would know that a 'tennis professional' needed extra stewarding? On the side of the packet was printed 'nicethamide', and the dosage level, 0.125 grams, as well as 'glucose monohydrate 1,500 g'. The notes (in French) said the product was an 'antiasthenique' to treat tiredness, especially at high altitude. Mrs Čilić, probably unaware of any of this, thanked the pharmacist, went back to her son's apartment and left the Coramine in the kitchen, giving the packet not another thought.

However, the product carried a warning . . . in French: the tablets could cause a positive test in dope control. As the tribunal later remarked, 'Anyone reading the side of the packet or the leaflet, even with only a very limited knowledge of French, would easily have identified the danger for an athlete with anti-doping responsibilities.' As for Čilić, he knew that the product would enhance performance for 'a short time', it was argued; he also should have known that these were not merely glucose tablets. On such niceties would his later appeal hinge.

Čilić's row with Brett did not ease. After losing to Gasquet, he talked to Ivanišević, who was working as a commentator. 'If you want to be top five,' Ivanišević told him during a lively car journey, 'you have to be ruthless.' Čilić spoke to his parents about it at his apartment that night – and noticed the glucose tablets for the first time. He saw they were in tablet form, not the powder he usually took. He read the outside of the packet and took the word 'nicethamide' to be French for the Croatian 'nikotinamid', which he knew was harmless, rather than 'nikethamide', which was not.

Čilić would later argue he did not know that the French word 'nicethamide' indicated the banned 'nikethamide' and consequently he did not recognise it as a prohibited substance. Whatever his mother's ignorance of French, or his own, for Čilić to confuse a word familiar to him as a drugs asterisk because of a single consonant, a *c* for a *k*, represented staggering linguistic confusion. Čilić was a well-travelled internationalist. Perhaps he was not so commanding in languages as was the five-tongued Roger Federer, but he lived in Monte Carlo. He knew a lot of French tennis players, and, surely, had a smattering of the language. His Monégasque neighbours included top-tenners Djokovic and Tomáš Berdych, as well as a slew of former players working as coaches, and some players from the women's Tour, including Caroline Wozniacki. That he could imagine 'nicethamide' did not equate to 'nikethamide' appeared naive or complacent. Čilić was, after all, a cosmopolitan professional athlete, aided by a well-paid team who had toured the world for eight years.

Whatever the internal logic or otherwise of his argument, Čilić, unable to consult his ITF drugs list, photographed the front of the packet and texted it to Hrvoj. He wondered if the tiny level of glucose, in tablet form, would work. His doubts were about the efficacy of the glucose rather than its legality. Hrvoj replied that he had never heard of Coramine. Nor, it seems, did he know that the stimulants in the product were banned. He gave Čilić the okay to go ahead. Between 22 and 26 April, Čilić took eleven of the tablets.

In Munich, Hrvoj brought Čilić's usual glucose powder to the tournament, and they thought no more about the tablets. Čilić was still training with Brett, but neither party was particularly happy. Čilić's first match was on 1 May: Mayday in more ways than one. After losing to his fellow Croatian Ivan Dodig in the second round, he was selected at random for testing. He declared he had taken aspirin and 'some vitamin supplements', but not Creatine, although that had been a regular part of his regime and he had always declared its use before when tested. Nevertheless, he was not concerned. Up to that point in his career, he estimated he had been tested 'more than fifty times' stretching back to 2005. He had always passed. What was there to worry about?

From Munich, Čilić went to Madrid, where he fell at the first hurdle to the Spaniard Pablo Andújar, ranked 118 in the world, and Rome, where Kevin Anderson, from South Africa, put him out in the second round. This was poor preparation for the upcoming French Open and he had another meeting with his parents in Zagreb on 18 May about Brett, who apparently had twice refused to shake Mrs Čilić's hand. The following day, Čilić sacked Brett. Five days after that, on 24 May, the doping control laboratory of Le Centre INRS–Institut Armand-Frappier in Montreal advised International Doping Tests and Management in Lindigo, Sweden, that Čilić's A sample from Munich contained nikethamide 'in a concentration of approximately 66 ng/ml'. That was enough to nail him. However, the player was blissfully unaware of his fate as he headed for Roland Garros. There, he would go out in the third round, losing a tight three-setter to Troicki, of all people (both were operating on borrowed time but did not yet know it). News of Čilić's failed test broke first in the Croatian media – at the end of July, three months after the test in Germany and nearly two months after he had pulled out of Wimbledon – in both *Slobodna Dalmacija* and *Utarnji List*. The latter newspaper quoted his manager Vincent Stavaux as saying: 'There are no comments until we will be able to comment' – which ought to go into a top ten of pointless answers.

Once the story was out, Brett broke cover. 'He said he had tested positive,' he told the *Guardian* of a conversation he had had with Čilić. 'The one thing I found out was that he tested positive for high glucose and Marin had co-operated with [the ITF] about the product and the pharmacy. One of the people in his team bought it in a pharmacy – basically what you've been reading in the papers. Some people will say he made a mistake. But it was carelessness. All through the years I've always explained the importance of not buying products over the counter because of the risk of contaminated products. They believe that everything is going to be OK. In a sense they are naive to the risk. The player hopes it's OK and it's not. They are then tarnished, sponsors are reluctant to sign them to contracts and promote their products.'

Čilić by now knew all of this. He had been charged about

three weeks earlier, on 10 June, and the following day in his London apartment – after the start of the Queen's tournament in London in which he would play his best tennis of the year – he received the chilling news by letter and email. He was, according to the tribunal, 'shocked and horrified'. He composed himself sufficiently well to beat Dodig, Feliciano Lopez, world number 6 Berdych and former world number 1 Lleyton Hewitt that week to reach the final, where he would meet his nemesis Murray. There were no outward signs of anguish, though; not a hint that he was either physically or mentally traumatised. Čilić was in sparkling form and played without any obvious hindrance. He kept the favourite on court for more than two and a half hours in a high-quality conclusion. But for six double faults and failure to convert six of eight break points, he might have made it even closer, or even won. Immediately afterwards, he sounded in splendid spirits.

> I will say [there was a] great, great level of tennis, and [I am] just really excited that I had great week, played a lot of tough matches, a few three-setters, and just happy that I did real well this week and prepared for Wimbledon in a good way. My form is on a very good level, on the level where I want it to be. I'm going to have now also a couple matches in Stoke Park [at the Boodles tournament] playing a few exhibition matches. I came here already ten days ago and had enough play on grass, so definitely going to be feeling very well and just hoping that I'm going to keep my form and still in a positive spirit. I feel like I'm playing very well. I had different opponents during the week, played servers, played Lleyton who is great defender, played Andy today, also, who is extremely [good] all-around player, and Berdych who is great hitter. I played most of the types of the game and felt pretty good on the court, pretty good with my own game what I did well, and just gonna take bit of rest and of course to be very positive for preparation and to start Wimbledon hopefully in a good way.

What could possibly go wrong? Čilić was worried, though. He knew he was a marked man. Having being informed of the details of the allegations six days earlier, he had contacted Hrvoj, who was still in Zagreb. The trainer went to his computer and, after ten minutes of cursory investigation, discovered that the former world champion American sprinter Torri Edwards had also tested positive for nikethamide after taking glucose tablets in 2004. Čilić rang his mother. She sent him a photo on his Blackberry of the Coramine packet she had bought from the pharmacist in Monte Carlo in April.

If he was in turmoil, it did not show. In fact, he displayed impressive sangfroid. Before going on court at Wimbledon and winning his first match against the experienced and dangerous Marcos Baghdatis in straight sets, he rang lawyers in Brussels. Again, he seemed able to separate off-court worries from the day job. It would be his last victory of any kind for a little while.

No less a judge than the American Bud Collins, whose expertise stretched back several decades, said of the Croatian in the *Independent*,

> This is a guy who is going places – and he is a potential threat to Andy Murray down the line in these championships. Whatever the Croat does over the next week, or two, he is a Slam winner-in-waiting if he gets it right. I have watched him go up and down over the last few years. He's been on the roller-coaster, man. He was top ten back in [2010] . . . but slipped down the rankings over the next couple of years. This time last year he was mid-twenties but now he is back to the top dozen and, by my reckoning, ready to go higher again. We're talking top ten and counting. This is a guy whose time is coming: the right guy in the right place at the right time. Looking at all the players across the game and those coming up, the next big things, I believe that Cilic has the ammunition to be a top contender, to beat anybody in the world and to have a chance to win slams.

After he beat Baghdatis with another encouraging performance, events moved rather more quickly for Čilić than even Collins might have imagined – but in the wrong direction. The player's legal advisers agreed that he should accept a provisional suspension, waiving his right to analyse his B sample. The ITF's independent Anti-Doping Tribunal received a letter in which the player admitted 'the presence of the substance in his body and, consequently, the commission of a doping offence'. Within hours, he sat in a press conference and announced he was withdrawing from the tournament rather than going into the second round against the Frenchman Kenny de Scheppers . . . because of a knee injury.

The difficulty he had with his English in explaining his withdrawal must have been as nothing to the problem he surely had trying to reconcile the competing strands of his argument.

'Yeah, well, I started to have difficulties with my knees also during Queen's, but even before, a couple months back, it sort of started to come back because I had a major injury with that a year and a half ago,' he told us. We scratched our heads collectively; nobody could remember mention of an injury at Queen's. That was because there was none. Never mind, we thought.

News of Čilić's exit was swamped by the bigger stories on what came to be known as Wild Wednesday. Roger Federer lost in the second round, and followed first-round loser Rafael Nadal on the plane out of London, along with the Spaniard's conqueror, Steve Darcis, who had injured his shoulder; Maria Sharapova lost in straight sets to Portugal's number 131 and champion screacher, Michelle Larcher de Brito, in what was the tournament's unwanted screamfest; and four other players withdrew with injury, among them the number 2 seed Victoria Azarenka. The slippery grass of the All England Club was now painted with knee-jerk alacrity the *villain du jour*. In this maelstrom of noise, pain and disappointment, Čilić's story inevitably got a little lost.

'Then also during the last week,' he continued, 'I was during practice feeling it already. Then on Sunday before my first-round match, felt it really bad in my serve when I would, you know, go down in the motion. It was just big pain. But sort of for the match, I was also feeling a little bit, but play through it. Obviously little bit with playing the match and then three sets, and yesterday, I think I felt it much, much worse. It was difficult for me to put weight on my left leg, which is where the pain is. So today I had basically no choice to. I can also risk something bigger to play.'

He was unsure over whether the problem had been with him a 'couple weeks' or 'a couple months ago', or if it was rooted in an injury he had 'before two years ago'. This is understandable. Players carry niggles all the time. One can merge into another. Some are serious, others less, most of them manageable. But Čilić was struggling to establish both the nature and the timescale of his injuries.

Had he ever had to 'stop because of problems, injury', he was asked. 'Hmm, I can't exactly remember,' he said. 'I don't think I did, no.' In fact, he had handed a walk-over to Murray in the quarter-finals at Queen's two years earlier, and again there in the final in 2012 he had retired against David Nalbandian when a set down and 4–3 up in the second. Čilić might have been confused, and sometimes a little flakey in matches, but he was not known as a quitter.

Adding to the confusion, however, he went on to discuss his schedule, even though he knew then that it was going to be shredded for reasons that had little to do with his health. 'I have to discuss a little bit with my team what I'm going to do, basically either to take a bit longer period to take care of it or to see, because there are some therapies that are a little bit quicker, some are a little bit longer, just to pick what would be better. Concerning tournament schedule, my next tournament was supposed to be Umag in end of July.'

Rumours swirled, as rumours do. Then the ITF let it be known they thought Čilić had cited injury, 'to avoid adverse publicity'. The unanswered question was, adverse for whom?

Umag would go by the board. So would all the others, right up to Paris in October. Yet, after losing to del Potro there in the second round, perhaps irritated by continued speculation about the veracity of his Wimbledon injury, Čilić issued a statement in clear and specific English.

I had already developed a significant knee injury before Wimbledon and aggravated it during my first-round match. The tournament doctors at Wimbledon examined my knee before and after my first-round match. The medical documentation that I was given records that my knee was already then in a bad state and that any further matches could risk a more serious injury. I was nonetheless very keen to continue playing at Wimbledon, because the tournament means so much to me. At that point it no longer made any sense for me to risk causing my knee a more serious injury and to deprive someone else the opportunity of playing deeper into the tournament. I therefore took the painful decision to pull out of Wimbledon and to accept a voluntary suspension, pending the determination of my case. I don't know what else I could have done. I subsequently flew to Monte Carlo to receive treatment on my knee. I was unable to put any weight on my knee for several days after my treatment.

So, instead of admitting that the overriding reason he pulled out at Wimbledon was because he had been told he would forfeit his points and his purse if he lost his case, he cited injuries which were not serious enough to prevent him stretching Murray at Queen's and then inspiring the venerable Bud Collins to name him as a player who could 'beat anyone in the world'.

None of this drama concerned Čilić when he became a working professional again, at the Paris Masters that October Monday in the Palais Omnisports de Paris-Bercy. This is a building whose external symmetry of integrated grass and concrete gives the impression it is a bomb shelter . . . which, metaphorically, it becomes, as players dodge heavy artillery in order to reach the safety of the O2 Arena for the last big show of the season. The brutal modernism is of a piece with the early winter chill that closes in on Paris. It needs a big heavy overcoat . . . or a hug.

I remembered the chill from long ago. One of the first events held in the venue when it opened, in 1984, was a rolling jazz masterclass by the supremely cool Miles Davis, augmented by Gil Evans and Bobby McFerrin. I recall Davis, age fifty-eight but looking older, with seven tough years left to live and sickly thin as he stood side-on cloaked in black leather, playing like the prince he still was, blowing some exquisite heat through the joint with his aching trumpet. For the man who gave life to *Birth of the Cool*, this was a fridge-like place in which to perform. It was a difficult place, also, in which to play free-flowing tennis. Andy Murray complained years ago about the cold. But Čilić, a lovely shot-maker when relaxed, did his best, which was too good for Sijsling but not quite good enough for del Potro in the second round. He gave him a credible argument before going out after a second-set tie-break. The tall, kind-faced Argentinian hugged the Serb affectionately at the net. Čilić had banged down nineteen aces past him, although he gifted seven double faults and could not convert any of four break points. Nevertheless, it was a fine comeback. Bud Collins would be proud. Hvroj, too. Even Brett, perhaps. No matter now. Čilić had been taken back into the fold. Goodwill flowed. He was not going to London. Nor was he going to hell.

Paris was not all about Čilić. Parked towards the end of the longest calendar in sport, the tournament had as its primary function the filleting of the stragglers trying to squeeze into the final eight places reserved for the game's best a week later in London. The atmosphere was tense in nearly every match, as fringe contenders and favourites stepped up for one final round of heavy hitting.

Federer had been living on the edge for months. As he drifted away from the top of the mountain, he searched for a lifeline, but, with a week left, he was still not sure of his place in London. He had never been in this position before. Nor had his fans. He might have wrapped it up in Basel, if he'd beaten Djokovic in the final, but, coming to Bercy, if he lost in the first round, he was out: simple as that. So, the relief on his face when Kevin Anderson's last slap of the match drifted long at precisely 9.45 p.m. on Wednesday night, 30 October, said it all. Nearly five months after Nadal had qualified, the Spaniard was joined by his oldest rival. Federer was safe, free at last from the grip of anxiety. What happened thereafter was gravy. Djokovic beat him in the semi-final, which he never enjoys, but he packed his bags and headed out of town for the final shoot-out. He had plenty left to prove.

16

Finally . . .

Paris, Saturday, 3 November 2013

Juan Martín del Potro, famous and 6ft 6in, is hard to miss in a crowd. Despite his imposing physical presence, he is far from intimidating. Few players on the Tour are as accommodating, with the media and with fans. As he queues at Gare du Nord for the Eurostar to London, where he will compete with the seven best players in the game at the ATP World Tour Finals, he is approached for his autograph. He puts down his briefcase which contains not only his passport but also the rosary beads that his fellow Argentinian, Pope Francis, had blessed for him when they met in Rome earlier in the year. He hands back the signed paper and the pen, turns to pick up his briefcase and is mortified to discover it has been stolen – all in the space of twenty seconds, at most. After helping Parisian police with their enquiries, he is supplied with a replacement passport and heads for London. He will not see the rosary beads again.

~

The following day, the leaves of London had agreed to start falling more like autumn leaves should do. The players who travelled from Paris were not so ready to surrender their oxygen. They had another week's tennis in them – and they had each other. This was the championship of champions, the ultimate last-man-standing fight after all the other arguments had been had. They arrived in varying degrees of fitness, and focus. Del Potro, already light one passport and a set of rosary beads, also arrived with just one racquet, but that was not unusual. The big man travelled light; he would make do, he said – and he would say a prayer to St Christopher that night for the return of his rosary beads.

Paris, as it happened, was getting a bad rap with other tennis players. After Nadal won his seventh French title in 2012, he returned late to his hotel in the 8th arrondissement, took off a limited edition E300,000 RM027 Tourbillon watch which had been lent to him by his watchmaker friend, Richard Mille, and went to sleep. When he woke up, it was gone, lifted during the night by a thirty-nine-year-old hotel barman, who was latter apprehended and charged after the timepiece was found near a railway track in the Parisian suburb of Evry. During the Rogers Cup in Toronto in 2010, incidentally, someone broke into Rafa's locker and stole another of M Mille's exclusive watches. Rotten luck – but quite a deal of publicity for the watchmakers. Time is money, as they say.

Murray (who has had his own wristwatch moments – remember the US Open?) was the notable absentee in London. He was recovering still from what we understood to be a 'minor surgical procedure', but he looked perky enough on his non-playing return to Wimbledon, a fitting backdrop for interviews to plug his new book, before heading for the Christmas sunshine and more training-track pain in Miami. Federer said his own back trouble had eased, and he was fit to try for his seventh title at one of his most lucrative hunting grounds, an event in which he had collected nearly $12 million in eleven visits on the spin. Who wouldn't come back? There was nothing visibly wrong with Djokovic, except that he declared himself 'exhausted' and he seemed rightly nervous about Serbia's Davis Cup final against the Czech Republic a few days after the final. The ATP drugs tsars, after all, had taken away his deputy and friend, Viktor

Troicki, even banning him from entering the arena in Belgrade. Novak was not happy.

Wawrinka was in a much better frame of mind, a welcome finalist, beaming still after his most encouraging season. Few players on the Tour engendered as much goodwill as did the quietly spoken Swiss – except maybe Tsonga, who was also missing. Ferrer was as strong as a bull; no change there. Gasquet had found new enthusiasm and was some people's choice as a surprise winner. Berdych? Well, you never knew with Tomas. He could blow them all away, or fold like origami paper. It had the makings of an interesting finale.

There is always a party atmosphere at this year-end shindig, especially in the five years it has been camped in the tentlike O2 Arena in Greenwich, on the southern shores of the Thames. At the risk of giving up too much information about our rugged lifestyle, journalists covering this even have the use of a dimly lit and luxurious cave of a room in which to relax between sweating blood on deadlines. It was not designed for us, naturally, but we are happy to fill in for the rock stars and entertainers who are its regular customers for the rest of the year in this massive entertainment complex. Some players enjoyed it more than others. Federer, the most amenable of players, spent several hours chatting with Chris Kermode, who fought tigerishly to bring the event to London, ignoring all naysayers, and who towards the end of 2013 was given perhaps the most influential job in tennis, executive chairman of the Association of Tennis Professionals. Even if his camaraderie with the players helped him get the job, there was no one more deserving. Few tournament organisers on the circuit have such a good rapport with the people who make it possible in the first place. His challenge in 2014 is to cement that relationship and sort out a few minor bugbears, such as the schedule and drugs testing. Some players, though, do not fraternise much. Djokovic, for instance, was hardly seen except in the walk from the locker-room to the court, then to the media centre, and then back to his hotel. He always has a large entourage and perhaps there was more socialising to be done with them. For whatever reason, the Serb was very much strictly business at the O2. And it would pay a handsome dividend.

As with nearly all the finalists, Novak admitted the season had again been tiring, although it has to be said that he husbanded his resources better than most. And he was kind to Federer after beating him in three sets at the start of the week. 'It was probably the toughest start I could get,' he said, 'considering the scheduling that I had – playing two days ago in Paris Bercy finals – then playing Federer here, where he has such a terrific record. It was always going to be a tough match for both of us.' It looked a deal tougher for Federer than for Djokovic, though, and there was no doubt who would go further.

In the players' lounge on the third floor one evening, Pat Cash was in sociable mood – and expansive in his theories about the game. The Australian always has something fascinating to say, and he is never afraid to say it. Three years previously in an interview in Sydney, the former Wimbledon champion instantly made himself thousands of enemies when he pretty much said Federer was finished as a force at the top level.

'In a nutshell, the string technology is the key thing in this debate,' he says, as we keep half an eye on the tennis below. 'These guys are imparting too much spin. Roger's not a strong guy. His timing is exquisite; we know that. He can hit the ball hard, but where he's been struggling is with his single-handed backhand. I've seen him over the years, pushing more and more and harder and harder, trying to do something against these guys who sit at the back of the court.'

He goes on:

It's really unfortunate that tennis has got to the stage where a good sliced backhand, which Federer's got, is not any good against these guys. They are able to get on top of it and smash it away because of the technology. What that means is that you've got a more limited range of effective tennis shots. You can almost take the volley out of it, you can take some of the slice shots out of it, too – not completely, but sliced shots being used as a variation as opposed to an effective type of shot. It's now a change-up shot, not an effective shot.

In my day, a sliced backhand to get into the net was an attacking, effective shot, or there was a defensive sliced backhand that keeps low over the net and puts the other guy in trouble. With the ball skidding off the court, you actually were able to get yourself back in the point. Federer does that, and there's nothing. It's really unfortunate. Federer is really an old-school player, playing in modern times and with modern technology. The court conditions and the ball conditions have just made it really tough to be effective with that sort of game, against players who can run all day and grind, grind, grind. I don't necessarily see it as a healthy situation in tennis. I'm starting to think that it's not a great thing for tennis in general to have a great all-round player like Roger Federer not be able to be effective. If he can't do it, who can?

Was there anyone who could, I wondered? There had been a bit of a buzz, for instance, about Jerzy Janowicz since he took Murray to four sets in the Wimbledon semi-finals in the summer.

He [Janowicz] can't volley. If he learned to volley, he could be very good. He's got a good all-round game, he's effective. If he learned to volley even thirty per cent better, he'd be really, really effective. The volley is a great weapon. Watching Stakhovsky beat Federer at Wimbledon as an out-and-out volleyer was one of the most surprising matches. For me it was not about the result, necessarily, because I don't really care who wins and loses – I really don't. People don't believe me, but I just love watching the game. But I was amazed that Stakhovsky could keep it up. It showed that you can serve and volley at Wimbledon.

This is a pet subject of a man whose entire career was built around his ability at the net. He thinks that any young player who learns to serve and volley well might just have a chance of breaking the stranglehold the physical baseline players have on the game right now. And he thinks they could have a hero: the man he said was all but done three years ago.

Before Federer finishes, I would just love to see him come out there and serve–volley. He knows his game better than I do, of course, but an attacking game is still effective at Wimbledon. And he can do that. Stakhovsky showed him it can be done. You can't maybe do it all the time, but you can use it, you can. I've said this before and people criticise me about it, but I doubt that anybody who knows about technique will disagree with me: Roger's volley technique is not what it used to be. And he has really bad days on his volley, so he hasn't quite got that confidence. In many ways, he could go back and improve his volley. If he can improve that shot ten per cent, then it's just a couple of minor technical things, I think he really could come out there and serve–volley. He's the only one who can do it, really.

Cash suggests all of this is unlikely, however, because players are risk-averse. Their eyes are eternally on the scoreboard, and they are not willing to take risks that could cost them even a point.

We could actually win a point doing it in my day, that was the difference. Players aren't stupid. They'll do what works. They're not going to care about the aesthetics of the game. In our day, the court was quick enough. Although clay was really slow, the grass courts were really fast. You never really saw anyone who could go from the French to Wimbledon, not even close. Boris was about as close as anybody got. Clay was really slow, grass was really fast. It made it interesting, because anything could happen at Wimbledon.

Players now will do what it takes to win – but also they don't learn it growing up. You've got to understand that the kids today, the twelve-, thirteen-, fourteen-year-olds, a lot of them are quite big, they've got the same strings and the same racquet technology as Rafa Nadal. They get the same thing out of their racquets, so they can whip lobs over an opponent. So what twelve-year-old kid's going to go out there and learn to volley? He's never going to win a match. What's the fun in that? So they don't learn the skill of volleying.

My coach said, 'You're on a grass court, you serve and volley, first and second serve.' I could not volley at all as a kid. I remember looking at him, and saying, 'Second serve?' He said, 'Yes, both serves. I don't care, and, if I see you staying back, I'm going to get out there and kick your arse.' He was serious. And that's how I learned to serve and volley, and I thought, wow, this is fun. I could actually win matches as a junior, and that's the bottom line. My coach was clever: he said, 'Look, you're going to beat this guy anyway, just learn to serve–volley.'

And that's what Federer should be doing. He should have done it a few years ago. That's what Djokovic should be doing, and that's what del Potro should be doing. It's so bloody tough out there, you've got to make some sacrifices. You've got to say, OK, I'm going to lose a few matches, but I'm going to be a better volleyer at the end. Djokovic has been able to get away with it because he's a machine, but the last two Grand Slams he's nearly got caught out. He got caught by del Potro in a monster semi-final at Wimbledon and again in the semi-final in the US against Wawrinka. Basically, he came in just a little flat. We saw him recover against Wawrinka in the Australian Open, which was just phenomenal. But you can't do that all the time. You've got to find a way to finish points off. I know Novak has been trying to do it in practice, but you've got to do it in matches, and you've got to do it against first-round opponents. Sometimes you're going to lose.

They're very focussed on their number 1 ranking and stuff like that. I was never focussed on my ranking. In my day, they weren't focussed on the rankings. They were focussed on winning Grand Slams and being better players. Sometimes you've got to ask yourself what matters. The most important thing is to become a better player. Everything else will come with it.

But don't players play to their strengths?

It depends who you are. You need to be a better player. The one person who has continued to become better and better is Rafa. He had a terrible second serve; he improved that. He didn't have a great backhand, although it was a good backhand; he improved that. He had a terrible volley; he improved that – to the point where he's probably one of the best volleyers on the Tour. He was a bit too defensive, once; now he's more attacking. Every time, every year he comes back to the Tour, he's worked on something. He got to the stage where he jumped above Roger as a player. Basically, he's a better tennis player than Federer. It's clear. Look at the records. It's unreal. Murray's done that a little bit, too, since he's been with Lendl, become a little more attacking. And while Novak is unbelievable in what he does, he gets himself caught out sometimes.

Sometimes. But not this time. Djokovic looked over at Nadal at the beginning of the final of the last Tour match of 2013 and he was not going to try anything fancy. He knew if he kept it deep and put pressure on Nadal, he would have his moments. In the end, the finish was as flat as house paint, 6–3, 6–4 to Djokovic. As I watched it dwindle to a rather meek conclusion, I thought about Cash's words. He was right: if only someone would gamble, they might find the new way, a method to resurrect the invention that is at the heart of tennis's appeal, a way to kill the robotic physicality that is in danger of strangling the game. And he was right, too, to say that players will not even give such a notion a passing thought. They are here to win. Djokovic won, and deservedly so, but we left with hardly a memory worth saving.

Nadal, meanwhile, managed to get through the week without anyone breaking into his hotel room and stealing his watch. 'When I don't wear the watch,' he said, 'I feel like something is not working.' There was no blaming the watch this time. Djokovic was just too good.

17

Who's Next?

The questions that faced Roger Federer at the beginning of 2013 – how far to take his quest for an 18th Grand Slam title, and when to retire – had not eased by the end of the year. He would contend it was not a quandary of his own making, but was an obsession for the media. He was not far wrong, but that did not quell the debate. If by the time you read this, Roger Federer has decided he has nothing left to add to the game he has graced with dignity and style for so long, garlanded by many good judges as the greatest player of them all, 2013 will be remembered with a mixture of amazement and sadness. If, on the other hand, Federer is still playing in 2014 – and winning significant titles again – we should be grateful, as well as amazed. If there is one quality he has in as much abundance as his talent for tennis, it is his love for tennis. In the autumnal days, after fifteen years on the Tour, he still takes unalloyed delight in hitting a fluffy ball. Not everyone is so doubly blessed. Many have found the game a burden, weighed down by expectation and disappointment, yet could not let go, because to do so was to create a void into which they feared plunging without purpose. Others had no hang-ups at all. Jimmy Connors, ten years after he had been world number 1, was still making a classy nuisance of himself at Flushing Meadows in his late thirties. Tommy Haas, who reached number 2 in the world a decade ago, is playing as well at thirty-five – three years older than Federer – as he has done in a long while, and came desperately close to qualifying for the ATP World Tour Finals. It is no coincidence that Haas and Federer are good friends.

The perfect time for Federer to retire, if there is such a moment, probably has already passed. When he beat Andy Murray in the 2012 Wimbledon final, he simultaneously regained his world number 1 ranking, the sun shone on his sainted head and his favourite audience rose to acclaim him. To leave then, at the height of the British summer on the court where he announced his arrival ten years earlier, would have been so pleasingly symmetrical it is hard to imagine he resisted the temptation. Except Federer is not driven by such considerations. As much as he sometimes reveals an embarrassing lack of self-awareness, he also knows he has nothing to prove – except, perhaps, to himself. While the perceptions of others are important to him, he values his own judgment highly. He justifiably reckons he has earned the right to go when he wants, not when others might want him to. The more people ask him about it, the more he ignores the question. Nevertheless, he will not be able to do so indefinitely. If he has one more Slam title in him, maybe then he will reassess the situation. If, on the other hand, he slips outside the top sixteen, he will be condemned to a late career of high-risk matches in the first rounds of the Majors, where once he was the one to be feared. He squeaked into the end-of-season top-eight tournament in London and you could sense rare urgency in his tennis there, as he jostled for a seat at the top table of his sport. Each time he goes through that experience, he is being shown a glimpse of the future. Selfishly, we do not want to remember him losing. We want to put him in aspic, forever swivelling in the shot, like Nijinsky.

Federer is one of those few athletes – such as Pele, Muhammad Ali or Tiger Woods – of whom it can be said we were privileged to be breathing the same air. So gifted is he that the weapons he uses to win confound the experts. I doubt it will happen again, although wiser voices than mine see it differently. The game has changed, the old order has changed, and it will continue to change. Shortly after Chris Kermode was appointed executive chairman of the ATP, we chatted over lunch near Queen's, the tournament he has run since 2007 and where he has enjoyed the confidence and friendship of the game's leading players. From running that tournament and the World Tour Finals in November, he knows them all as well as anyone on the circuit, and he sees the current regime lasting just a little longer.

How much longer would Federer play, I wondered.

'Maybe a couple of years,' he says. 'As long as he wants to. I don't see any signs that he doesn't want to keep playing. I spent several hours with him at the O2 talking tennis. It was fascinating. He's a remarkable man. He will always be very much in love with tennis.'

Nevertheless, it is no longer the Big Four, and throughout 2013 it was the Big Three. Nadal is still there, so too are Djokovic and Murray, waiting to extend their own rivalry while hounding Nadal all the way to the final weekend of the four Majors. Behind the new Big Three, there are the increasingly loud footsteps of Raonic and Janowicz, the familiar grunts and growls of Ferrer, del Potro, Berdych and Switzerland's newly crowned number 1, Wawrinka. All of them, and some lesser players yet to make significant noise, had come to regard Federer as a venerable rather than threatening presence. He is still respected, but no longer feared.

While there cannot be a genuine fan of tennis who is looking forward to Federer quitting the game – bar those with whom he competes week in, week out, perhaps (and even that is doubtful) – it has to happen at some point. He wants to leave on his own terms, preferably after winning another Major, and with his pride intact. He deserves a dignified departure, but sport is not like that; it's cruel and was designed to be so, because there has to be a loser. Any of the hundreds of players who have felt the weight of Federer's hurtful ground-strokes in 932 wins will testify to this. By the end of 2013, he had lost only 215 times, just forty-one times in Majors, seventeen of those against top-ten opponents, and eleven of those before he had won his first Slam. That is an extraordinary return.

Tellingly, however, in seven matches against the Big Three in 2013, Federer did not win once. Djokovic went 6–1 against the others, Murray finished with a win and a loss against Djokovic, a win over Federer, and did not play Nadal, who won and lost three against Djokovic and beat Federer in their four matches. Those are numbers it is tough to ignore. So is his age, thirty-two. When Agassi won the last of his eight Slam titles, in Melbourne in 2003, he was thirty-two – but he did not have to play a single top-ten player, or even anyone who had won a Major. When Federer looks at the draw for a Slam, he knows he might have to play one of the other three earlier than he would have liked. How long can he stand that pressure?

Nadal could not have had a season more different, however. Even when Djokovic dismissed him in the last match of the season, at the ATP World Tour Finals, the Spaniard could look back proudly on recovering from the very depths of his career, much as Agassi had. Like Agassi, he was grateful for a second chance. But, curiously for a man who had looked spent in the fading weeks of 2013 and admitted there were moments when the campaign started in which he wondered if he could continue, this was not the last tennis of his year. The miracle man said he would go to Necker Island to play in a charity event with Richard Branson. Then he would play 'a few exhibitions in South America'. After that he would go home to Mallorca to check on the state of his knee, do some rehab and leave himself fifteen days in December before flying to Abu Dhabi and Doha, his tune-up tournaments ahead of the Australian Open in January. But he was not alone in this puzzling choice after a season of such physical and mental stress. Djokovic, after raising his game one last time to beat Nadal in London, had found enough energy to win two matches in Serbia's losing Davis Cup final against the Czech Republic the following weekend, despite declaring himself 'exhausted' before and afterwards. Surely he would retire to his home in Monte Carlo or spend some downtime with his friends in Belgrade? No. 'As soon as I play the Davis Cup final,' he said, 'I go for a week of exhibition events in South America, first in Chile with Rafa, then in Buenos Aires, in Argentina, another two matches. One of them for sure again is with Rafa. We'll be seeing each other quite often. I see him more than my mum actually.'

The humorous aside could not disguise the anomaly. Here were two players who had revved their engines to the point of explosion for eleven months, complaining there was little left in the tank, yet now they were hooking up to collect some easy money in South America. 'After that I'm going to allow myself to have a few weeks off,' Djokovic added. 'I deserve that time. I'm going to speak with my team, see if I'm able to rest.'

It was the second funniest line of the season, after his mum joke. And it struck at the heart of the relationship between the players and their sport. It is their job. Would they play for nothing? Of course – but why? While they are all immensely wealthy, they become locked into a cycle, maximising their worth while they can. Very few players have climbed off the gravy train while it was hurtling along at top speed. Most of them just keep buying a ticket.

At the end of 2013, Jesse Huta Galung, a twenty-eight-year-old Dutch right-hander in his ninth season as a pro, was the 100th best player in tennis. A pleasing single-handed backhand could not save him from twelve first-round defeats in twenty-eight matches, although he beat enough opponents to earn $154,567, a reasonable return for a professional athlete of some worth, but not life-changing money. At number 50 was a player more familiar to fans, the thirty-one-year-old French marathon man, Nicolas Mahut, whose seventeen wins against seven losses earned him $596,751 and the first two titles of his thirteen-year career. If you look at the fringes of the big-time, the power-serving South African Kevin Anderson, also twenty-seven, was ranked 20 and had accumulated $3,142,441 over ten years. So the mega-money remained elusive for these players and it is likely their ambition has been fashioned accordingly; they go to work with hope in their heart rather than expectation, especially if they happen to get a lousy draw in a big tournament. They have not been excluded from earnings a good deal beyond the reach of most people, but neither have they entered the stratosphere of serious wealth. That kicks in a little further up the food chain.

Richard Gasquet, in or around the top ten for much of his career and regarded as a teenager as almost certain to go on and win at least a couple of Slams, has yet to make the big break-through at twenty-seven, although he has won $10,021,913 prize money in eleven years. While that sort of money can breed contentment, Gasquet looked hungrier towards the end of 2013 than he had done for a while; perhaps he was inspired by the world number 8 Stanislas Wawrinka, whose improved results had taken his earnings to $8,008,944. Tomáš Berdych, one place higher than the Swiss at number 7, had earned $15,372,223, a considerable jump and nearly two million dollars more than the first Slam winner on our trawl upwards, Juan Martín del Potro, at number 5. Murray, at number 4 and with two Slams and a huge profile after his Wimbledon triumph, had listed career earnings of $30,271,843, about ten million dollars more than David Ferrer, who was at number 3 but had not won a Slam and was unlikely to. Six-Slam Djokovic had pocketed $54,240,895 in prize money, and Rafael Nadal, back on top of the mountain, had earned $60,941,937.

Federer, meanwhile – although uncomfortably off the pace at number 6 – who had taken $79,218,415 in purses, more than anyone in the history of the sport, and whose net worth is boosted by endorsements of $65 million a year, is the second biggest earner in the world of sport behind Tiger Woods.

Men's tennis, however, is at the cusp of change, and Federer is looking vulnerable. Jim Courier agrees.

> Eventually, Federer is going to retire. Nadal as well, and there are going to be opportunities, and these younger guys are going to win some of the big ones. It's hard to say who or when, but they are starting to see some daylight, because physically we've seen some cracks in the top four. Federer is playing less, Murray [was] clearly suffering from a substantial back issue, and Rafa's knees kept him off the Tour for quite a while last year.

In a game that makes more body-wrecking demands on its participants than ever before – especially on the players who consistently go deepest in the big tournaments and are engaged in the most drawn-out finals – something, sometime, has to crack. Even the players do not know how long they can hold the next wave at bay. That they have established this hegemony at a time when the game has become so unrelentingly attritional, with hardly a rest, makes their achievements all the more remarkable. And there is no immediate sign of relief. Indeed, the tempo and the level of physicality are likely to hit new levels before anybody finds 'another way'. It is a scary prospect, and one that does not altogether find favour with those in the game who hanker after more beauty, less muscle. As Murray pointed out at Wimbledon, 'Ten or fifteen years ago, you would get more upsets. Not so much now. It just doesn't happen very often at all, and you have to say that has been the case since Rafa and Roger came along. They are that good.'

This is a vision of hopelessness, then . . . but with a dash of hope. Those excellent contenders who have been inside the top ten in recent years suspect their chances of winning a Slam are negligible as long as the current generation of generals refuse to lose in the big battles. No matter the quality of their game, or how many other titles they might win, or how many occasional successes they might have against any one of the Big Four, it was difficult to envisage the *ancien régime* abdicating in the Majors. But there is one acknowledged point of weakness in the wall, a weakness that has been the strongest for longest.

So feverish has speculation about Federer's career plans become that a prankster thought it timely to set up a spoof report about his impending retirement on the eve of the 2013 French Open. Driving some of the game's major players to Roland Garros, he filmed their reactions as they read the 'news' on a screen in the back of his hospitality limousine. All of them, at first, believed it. All of them were saddened, even his rivals. 'No way,' said Dimitrov, the twenty-two-year-old Bulgarian already being groomed as the 'New Federer', because of his one-handed backhand, marketability and obvious potential. 'When did he say that he was retiring? Really? How can you describe a person into history, man? It's . . . I never had the chance to play him. I'm sad already . . . if that's true.' It wasn't . . . either true or that funny. And he would get his chance soon to play Federer.

'It's flattering sometimes to hear that,' Dimitrov told the driver/ joker when reminded he was known as BabyFed. 'Here and there, there's some similarities and stuff, but I want to build up my own reputation, my own personality. Tennis is a job, but it takes more than work, more than dedication to understand the game. When you find that fine line between being mature on and off the court, then you can say, yeah, I achieved something.'

In Basel in October, Dimitrov was still searching for that fine line. This was where Federer once had been a ball-boy and where he subsequently was five-times champion. And his first match against Dimitrov, in the gloaming of his days, would be more significant than many of the others he had played in the city where he spent his youth. It is unreasonable to ask Federer to fly for ever, but journalists are not always reasonable. As his disappointing year rolled on, he gave a press conference on the eve of the tournament. Inevitably, he was asked about the one topic over which he has least control: the future. 'As long as my body and mind are ready to go to travel, [and] I'm happy to be doing what I'm doing,' he said, 'I'm successful. I'll be playing for some time and that hasn't changed due to a tough six months right now.'

A couple of hours later on that opening Sunday, Dimitrov was winning the first Tour title of his young career, in Stockholm. Five days on, the Bulgarian was in Basel and playing the man to whom he had been ludicrously compared, in the quarter-final of Federer's home-town event. The Swiss took advantage of Dimitrov's nerves to win the first set and had to fight back from 3–5 down in the second before easing through the tie-break to earn a place in the semi-finals. It was not a classic. Federer lost in the final to del Potro, showing glimmers rather than swathes of his best tennis, and the debate rumbled on.

The evidence had been mounting for a while – probably from around the time of Pat Cash's *Sunday Telegraph* interview shortly before the 2010 Australian Open – that Federer might be a spent force at the summit, a blasphemy that even as I write is probably still generating derision. He has, after all, a congregation numbered in the millions, high-end sponsors who still pay him in those numbers, and a game that, when it clicks, is capable of illuminating any tennis court with its understated brilliance. Nevertheless, even he can do nothing about turning thirty-three in August 2014, by which time he will have either made a nonsense of the previous couple of sentences or given them substance. There are other numbers of which he will be aware. Among his record seventeen Majors, only one has arrived since Melbourne 2010, and his prospects of adding to the collection have not been improved by the pain that started to spread in his back in 2013. For the first time in eleven years, he did not reach the final of a Slam. These are the uncomfortable facts.

The night before Federer lost to del Potro in Basel, another sports phenomenon was chiselling out a late-career victory. In a promotional video before his world title fight against Karo Murat, Bernard Hopkins, an ex-con from Philadelphia, said: 'I've shown for twenty-plus years, with a legacy that will be talked about way after I'm gone, that I am different.' Once he was known as the Executioner. Now he called himself the Alien, trading a balaclava for a green mask. Hopkins that night boxed with his trademark awkwardness over twelve rounds to confound Murat, an Iraqi-born challenger of limited skill, and retained the International Boxing Federation light-heavyweight belt he had won the previous March. Whether or not Federer watched the fight, I do not know. If he did, he might have gasped in admiration or shaken his head. Bernard Hopkins, unbelievably, was forty-eight years old, eighteen years older than his mesmerised challenger, and he now laid claim to the distinction of being the oldest champion in the history of boxing. He was different, all right. As was Federer. And Roger had his own fights to fight.

As much as he said things his sponsors and fans wanted to hear, Federer was always searingly honest with a racquet in his hand. It is probable he has never hit a shot that did not carry total conviction. He has always played with scant regard for the scoreboard. He is so sure he will prevail, he is happy to trust his ability, knowing that eight times out of ten such self-belief will earn him the point and, ultimately, the victory. It is a rare gift, but it has a shelf life . . .

Such blind faith has resulted in a few scattered and unexpected defeats throughout his career. For instance, in 2003 he did not drop a set winning his first Slam title, at Wimbledon, yet only a few weeks earlier at Roland Garros, working behind a dangerous but unreliable serve, he went out in straight sets in the first round to the Peruvian doubles specialist Luis Horna, who was ranked 88 in the world. David Nalbandian, who had Federer's measure in the fourth round of the Australian Open that year, also stopped him at that stage at Flushing Meadows, but the Swiss had arrived. He won seven titles, finishing his season by beating Agassi (twice),

Nalbandian, Juan Carlos Ferrero and Andy Roddick in a week to take the Masters Cup. In 2004 he won three Slams – the first player to do so since Wilander sixteen years earlier – but also lost in the first round in Cincinnati, to the Slovak Dominik Hrbatý, who hit a career-high ranking of 12 that year, then slid down the scale with as much grace as he could muster, and still plays occasionally. These Federer losses, though, were blips. It was in the big matches where he would be judged.

In 2005 he was sublime, losing just four out of eighty-five matches. Only the ridiculously talented but temperamental Russian Marat Safin in Melbourne and Nadal on the clay of Roland Garros stopped him doing the Slam. The following year nobody disturbed his reign bar Nadal in the French, and their rivalry was now firmly established. In 2007 the Argentinian Guillermo Cañas, lurking in the fifties of the world rankings, pulled off a rare double, beating Federer twice in a fortnight, and the 53rd-ranked Filippo Volandri thrilled his Roman fans when he won in the third round in straight sets. Nalbandian, probably near his best, struck twice also, in Madrid and Paris, but nobody could stop Federer adding the Australian, Wimbledon and US Open titles to his collection. These were the years in which he established his legend. What followed was not a decline; it was a levelling out, and it wasn't really until 2010 that the flow of victories slowed noticeably.

By 2013, however, he was in crisis. He reached and won just one title on the Tour, coming from a set down to beat the mercurial Russian Mikhail Youzhny, seventeen days his junior, on the grass of Halle, when warming up for Wimbledon. Elsewhere, Federer lost to seven players outside the top ten and two outside the top 100. In the Slams, he lost to Murray in the semis in Melbourne, Tsonga in the quarters at Roland Garros, Stakhovsky (116) in the second round at Wimbledon, and Robredo (22) in the fourth round of the US Open. He changed his racquet and he sacked his coach. This was not a blip.

Paradoxically, it is Federer's vulnerability more than the appearance of any new stand-out prospect that has reinvigorated tennis, however depressing a concept this is for fans who have enjoyed his head-to-head rivalry with Nadal since the two first met on a tennis court in Miami in 2004 (Nadal won in two sets), because we now have what we have not had for a decade: uncertainty. Federer is no longer the undisputed world heavyweight champion of his sport, although he is still swinging, and that lends pathos as well as anxiety to his quest for one more shot at the big time.

But now Nadal was moving up on his shoulder, winning two Slams to get to a total of thirteen, just four behind (the same gap as on the lower slopes between Djokovic and Murray). Becker reckons Nadal will catch and pass Federer.

He's always going to be the big favourite for the French. He's healthy. I think he's believing in himself. If he goes by the rate he has this year, in two-and-a-half years he's there. He's only twenty-eight. He's not thirty-two and on his last lap, hoping to win another one. He's in the prime of his life. The only worry he has physically is how long – and then how good is the competition? How good is Djokovic? How well is Murray coming back? Del Potro. Those players. But I think he can.

And how would Federer take that? 'He would not like that,' Becker says. 'I think the Swiss gentleman would not like that.' It is one of the givens of the game that Federer is a nice guy. But there is always an undertone, a suspicion that the teenage brat, who by his own admission took stock and radically adjusted his attitude to create Brand Federer, was bubbling just below the satin-smooth surface. What, I wondered, was the real dynamic between the Big Four? I was hardly alone in suspecting it was not what it appeared to be. That summer, Murray had described his relationship with Djokovic – whom he was about to thrash in three sets to win the Wimbledon title – as one between 'professional friends'.

Becker smiles, pauses and nods. We had been talking about boxing, and the quite wonderful skills of Floyd Mayweather junior, who remained unbeaten after forty-six fights. Becker also reckoned the sports were comparable.

> I think tennis is similar in many ways to boxing. It's men against men. We have a net in between. We don't have gloves, but we have racquets. In boxing it's all part of the show as well. But I think it's very much real. They don't like each other. And I would say in most cases in tennis, players as well. It's more of a family friendly sport, sure, a lot of microphones on the court, and these young players are ambassadors, they endorse great companies, so they cannot be completely honest and true to their feelings. But I think deep down none of these top guys are friends. It would be lying. There's respect and admiration, maybe – but I don't think they're going to be friends.

Nadal, of course, is no more immune from the demands of his taxing sport than is Federer, even though as Becker looks back on the season, the Spaniard is sustaining his awe-inspiring comeback from injury. His was an outrageous and wholly unforeseen show of brilliance. In Federer's worst year, Nadal had come back to have his best season, of many great seasons. But could he sustain it? His knees were fine now, but they would always be his great liability. Were there other gremlins lurking in his highly tuned frame?

As for Djokovic and Murray, they too have faltered. Although universally regarded nowadays as freakish in his elasticity and probably the best defender in the history of the game, Djokovic once was what the gambling fraternity would regard as an unreliable conveyance, and, although he reached the final of three Slams in 2013 – beating Murray in Melbourne, losing to him at Wimbledon, and losing to Nadal in the semis in Paris and the final in New York – he surrendered his world number 1 ranking to the Spaniard towards the end of the season. In a book in which he outlines his devotion to a gluten-free diet and a Spartan training regime, the Serb reveals that, if everything is not perfect on match day, if his regime has been even slightly disturbed, he is as beatable as any novice. 'Top seeds like Nadal, Federer, Tsonga and Andy Murray are probably stronger, faster and fitter than any tennis players who have ever strode the court before,' he writes. 'We're like precision instruments: if I am even the slightest bit off – if my body is reacting poorly to the foods I've eaten – I simply can't play at the level that it takes to beat these guys.'

Such striving for perfection – and sometimes falling short – not only widens the field of expectation (which does not bother Djokovic, apparently) but increases the chances of failure. Will he not automatically think the likelihood of beating Nadal, say, is diminished if he cannot lay his hands on some gluten-free oats, cashew butter and bananas on the morning of a major match? From Ferrari to jalopy in one disastrous breakfast. When he won the 2013 Australian Open, Djokovic famously celebrated by having just one small piece of chocolate. When Murray won the 2012 US Open, he got drunk on a couple of glasses of champagne on the flight home and brushed his teeth with face cream.

There is a monastic earnestness about the game at the highest level that is diametrically at odds with the values and priorities of the distant past. There is now an unfixable disconnect between the game that people enjoy as a social distraction and that which those same enthusiasts pay to watch in the cathedrals of the sport, performed by professionals so dedicated that Djokovic, for instance, feels comfortable allowing his medical guru, William Davis, MD, to author the following introduction to his book, *Serve To Win*: 'Peak human performance: that is what Novak Djokovic has accomplished in the world of tennis. Only a select few achieve this level in any field, and it takes a culmination of talent, courage and determination – plus the removal of all impediments – to do so.'

I rather suspect Gordon Forbes, who gambolled through the

game so freely in the fifties and sixties, sought out a few impediments in his time, and had a damn fine time doing so. That is not to denigrate Djokovic. He is a superlative practitioner of his own scientifically devised philosophy and one of the wonders of modern sport. Yet sometimes there is a mechanical feel to his genius, with every calorie counted, every muscle stretched, no impediment left unaddressed. Repetition builds perfection, yet players who lived in less programmed times and hit as many balls over as many nets, such as McEnroe and Andre Agassi, were more interesting precisely because they were not prisoners of method. 'Freed from the thoughts of winning, I instantly play better,' Agassi said once. 'I stop thinking, start feeling. My shots become a half-second quicker, my decisions become the product of instinct rather than logic.'

Federer is the keeper of that flame, one that might soon be extinguished, or at least temporarily dimmed until someone is prepared (and talented enough) to play with such exhilarating abandon. He has often said he cares not whether he hits a ball out by an inch or into the stands, as long as he was going for the correct stroke on that point. He nearly always trusts his instincts. How ironic, then, that Federer should chide Djokovic, of all people, for belting two hit-and-hope winners that saved match points against him in the semi-final of the 2012 US Open. Maybe Djokovic has an inner-Federer. Or maybe he might just have been desperate . . .

That said, there is a masochistic pleasure to be had watching Djokovic extricate himself from the most awful messes. While writing this, I watched his idiosyncratic performance in winning the final of the 2013 Shanghai Masters against Juan Martín del Potro, a three-set fight of his own making in which he several times resembled a broken marionette, his core twisting wildly, his knees collapsing and his normally sure feet giving way in the shot. Djokovic is the human equivalent of a sports car that splutters and wheezes if the carburettor is not tuned just so, and this was one of those days when there were more than a few knocks under the bonnet. Maybe he forgot to pack his gluten-free oats. Yet he won. Genuine champions find a way. So, it is perversely encouraging that a player who in 2011 looked as if he was capable of the never-ending 'peak human performance' to which his mentor Mr Davis refers is occasionally returned to the pack to suffer like all the rest. Although Djokovic's capacity for five-hour finals inspires awe in the crowd and trepidation across the net, Murray has outlasted him and Nadal also has taken him to the very limit of his physical and mental resources. Nole, as he is known to his friends, is not always Superman.

Murray's devotion to the gym and the training track is perhaps as fanatical as Djokovic's – although he abandoned an experiment with the gluten-free diet after a few months, complaining that it made him weaker. His strength derives not just from the power of oats and blueberries but sweat left on the floor of his gym in Miami and the muscle-sapping sand of the nearby beach. Over several Decembers at his sun-blessed torture chamber he has reinvented himself, from Clark Kent to man of steel, from the skinny wimp who ran out of gas in his first Wimbledon appearance as a teenager into a mature, rock-hard titan. He is a superb physical specimen, a tribute to modern sporting science and his own dedication to hard work. According to the tired cliché, Scots come in two forms: tee-total ascetics or rabble-rousing drunks. While Murray is no Calvinist, neither is he Rab C. Nesbitt. But I have watched him train and it is exhausting; probably it is no bed of roses for him, either. Still, Murray, like Nadal and Federer (and indeed many high-performance athletes), has inbuilt physical flaws. He was born with a split kneecap, his ankle ligaments require heavy strapping, his left wrist is weak and the central source of his grief is a lower back that required surgery towards the end of 2013. It has collapsed twice on him in recent years, at the French Open in 2012 and in Rome the following summer, after which he decided he could no longer merely manage the pain with painkillers that would stop a horse, but would have to seek a definitive medical solution if he were to carry on. It is a wonder he can get up in the morning. And on some mornings, especially since he went under the knife in September, getting up was a Herculean task. So he declined an invitation to the Boxing Writers Club annual dinner in mid October on the advice of his doctor, who counselled against him even leaving his house in Surrey until the injury had settled, fully three weeks after his operation. (He did manage to drag himself to Buckingham Palace to receive an OBE a few days later, but there probably was no getting out of that one.) Like Nadal a year earlier, Murray had faced the starkest of choices: take a break or think hard about quitting the sport. It was no choice at all, as both of them admitted.

Djokovic conjured up a wonderfully apt phrase during the 2013 edition of Wimbledon to describe the dilemma of athletes whose brilliance consistently puts them into finals against their immediate peers: 'the privilege of pressure'. They have chosen to make the sacrifices and endure the pain because they are consumed by a passion not just for their sport but for winning. Now these four players are pursued by a gathering pack growing in the conviction that their own time, their own era, cannot be far away, that the pressure on the Big Four will tell sooner rather than later. Will it happen in 2014? We might at least see further evidence of its approach.

One or two of the coming generation might land a blow when it matters. Perhaps it will be Raonic. Or it could be the leaner, quicker, sharper Jerzy Janowicz, who gave Murray a scare at Wimbledon with a game of frightening intensity and no little craft. Will the stormy Tomic ever deliver on his obvious potential? It is impossible to say; who can be sure with such a talent, such a temperament? In early December, Tomic took on a new coach, in the absence of his father, John, who had been banned after his conviction in September for assault on Tomic's training partner,

Thomas Drouet, earlier in the year. The Spanish court suspended the eight-month sentence because it was under two years – and the logic of that is as impenetrable as some of his son's crazy press conferences, which, nevertheless, are invariably entertaining.

Tomic junior – number 1 in Australia and ranked 51 in the world – chose the former Croatian Olympic team coach Velimir Zovko as the man to guide yet another phase of his rollercoaster career, and said: 'This guy will be more there on court, spending more hours with me. My dad will sort of be less . . . but obviously my dad knows me best, and if he sees something that's wrong or mistaken then they'll have a talk about it. He's from Croatia, he speaks my language, and it's very important for me to have a good communication, someone that understands me, my background, because it's not easy – I'm a difficult sort of guy.'

You could say that. Perhaps his move from Queensland's Gold Coast, where he found trouble with ridiculous ease, to live and train near the National Tennis Centre in Melbourne will give him a chance to concentrate on the sport that provides him with a pretty good living. Tomic earned $697,132, won his first title (in the first week of the year, finishing with a loss to Illya Marchenko, the world number 163, in the first round of a Challenger in Bratislava) and can be happy with career aggregate earnings of $1,903,116 over five years.

Maybe some of those numbers will encourage Daniel Evans, of Birmingham, to give the game his full attention. He played superbly to beat Tomic at the US Open and gave Robredo a very good argument before heading for the bars of Manhattan to celebrate with his mates. He is determined to do it his way, play his shots and wait for the zing of the faster courts, where he is most effective. He is more dedicated than he was, but it is unlikely he will ever lose his rebelliousness.

There is João Sousa, too, a Portuguese player of immense promise who won his first ATP World Tour tournament towards the end of 2013 – a little late, perhaps, at twenty-four, but so emphatically that as shrewd a judge as Brad Gilbert instantly raised a clamour for him. Sousa is two spots ahead of Tomic in the rankings and, like the Australian, struggles for consistency. He wiped the court with the clever Frenchman Julian Benneteau to win $158,000 in Kuala Lumpur in September and, a week later, lost in the first round of the Kremlin Cup in Moscow to . . . Sergiy Stakhovsky. At least he was in good company.

And what of the 6-foot-6-inch Russian teenager called, improbably, Karen Khachanov, who beat former top-tenner Janko Tipsarević to reach the quarter-finals of that Moscow event, in only his second ATP appearance, just six months after finishing school. The tournament organiser, former world number 1 Yevgeny Kafelnikov, was impressed enough by his seventeen-year-old countryman to declare: 'He will be top twenty by end of 2015. I don't say this a lot about many people, but this kid is the real deal.'

And there is Dimitrov, burdened with those endless comparisons to Federer, and who has several times hinted with the majesty of his single-handed backhand that he could be 'the one'. On balance, he has disappointed. But Federer, too, took a little while to establish his credentials; he did not win his first Slam title until he was the same age as Dimitrov is now.

All these players can soar, but none has yet stayed up long enough to frighten the gods. Their time could be now, or soon, or their wings could melt like those of Icarus. It is no longer enough for young players to trust only the gifts they are born with; they live in a jungle, with jungle rules.

If anything, then, the next few years could be more engrossing than the past few have been. And, although audiences have become used to tennis of immense physicality, there is hope for the romantics who yearn for beauty and invention. While the players are hitting their physical and mental limits, crunching the ball from behind the baseline in rallies that exhaust their stamina as much as the patience of the audience, there are some in the sport – such as McEnroe and Wilander – who think change is coming. They believe that some young player, sooner or later, will bring subtlety to blunt the brutishness. Someone, in short, to succeed Federer. They reason that an evolution of method and tactics is inevitable, because that is what has always happened in the past; otherwise, says McEnroe, players would still be rushing to the net like lunatics.

Whoever makes it, any breakthrough will come down to intangibles: heart, commitment, the ability to control nerves as well as ego, the courage and inclination to grab 'the moment'. These are all qualities shared by the Big Four . . . although, at year's end, there were just three left standing.

After his victory over Djokovic at Wimbledon in the summer of 2013, Andy Murray did not make it to the Tour Finals finish line. He chose to rest because he feared the likelihood of falling behind front-runners Nadal and Djokovic if he did not fix his back, sliding down the rankings in the company of Federer and being overtaken by rising aspirants whose charges at the castle gates were becoming more insistent. He has made the break-through. Without a good pair of wings, and a few prayers, it will not be easy to stay airborne. With Murray, it rarely is.

~

Melbourne, Sunday, 26 January 2014 (Australia Day)

The Swiss with the murderous single-handed backhand triumphs, at last, over his nemesis, Rafael Nadal. But the winner's name is not Roger Federer. It is Stanislas Wawrinka. With one concluding stab of his racquet, a forehand from mid-court, he puts the ball beyond the reach of the wounded Spaniard to win the Australian Open, 6–3, 6–2, 3–6, 6–3, and a packed Rod Laver Arena rises to acclaim the quiet man from nowhere. Wawrinka, twenty-eight, had never even taken a set off Nadal in their twelve previous meetings. Now, against all expectations – not a single commentator predicted he would win – he claims just the sixth tournament victory of his career, and his first Grand Slam title. Nadal is left to rue a rare back spasm that cut him down in the second set before he launched a stirring fightback, but he is quick to acknowledge the legitimacy of his opponent's remarkable achievement. Wawrinka not only jumps from number 8 to number 3 in the ATP rankings, he dramatically disturbs the natural order of supremacy, with Murray sliding to sixth in the world as a consequence, and Federer falling to eighth, nearly 10,000 points behind his old rival Nadal. Rafa is still number 1 and Djokovic sits just behind him, but two of the Big Four are left bruised outside the castle door. The spell, finally, is broken.

Postscript

Life After Lendl

In January 2014, four months after he had gambled on surgery to his lower spine to save his career, Andy Murray flew from Miami to Melbourne for the Australian Open. He had previously said that he would not play unless he thought he had a realistic chance of winning the title; this was caution well placed. The tournament would be the start of a grim struggle for him, the most frustrating of his career to that point. By the time Roger Federer had halted his progress at the quarter-final stage, it was clear Murray's back had not properly healed, and he flew back to America and the hard-court swing still searching for his best tennis. There, he would endure pain of a different kind: an assault on his spirit.

On the very March afternoon that Murray lost to Milos Raonic in desultory fashion in Indian Wells, Ivan Lendl was in Nashville, arguing with drunks in the crowd while playing in a seniors match. This turned out to be more than a disconnection of time and place between player and coach: it was about their priorities. A few evenings later over dinner in Miami, Lendl gave Murray news he did not want to hear. He had never much cared for Indian Wells anyway, Lendl explained, and, while he gritted his teeth for the long-haul flights to Australia and Europe, flitting around America was not his idea of fun, unless by road. He wanted to spend more time with his family and his golf clubs. So, just as Murray was starting to hit the ball with more confidence, and his body was slowly beginning to readjust to the trauma of an increased workload following an operation that was at least a calculated roll of the dice, Lendl walked away from the most successful partnership in tennis at that time. In the acknowledged way of these separations, this one was said to have been reached by mutual agreement, yet it was obvious to all (apart from those who chose not to see it like this) that it was no organic parting of the ways. As far as Murray was concerned, he and Lendl had not been heading towards the rocks: there was no rift, no disagreement over career strategy, no personal animosity. Murray most definitely did not want a divorce – but Lendl did. It has never been definitively established who had initiated the partnership, however there was no doubt who finished it.

It was a blow Murray did not see coming, and someone of his transparent sensitivity was always going to struggle to disguise the hurt. For all that Lendl's excuses sounded reasonable, a business arrangement that was barely two years old and had looked strong all the way up to the previous September was shattered into small pieces in one devastating conversation. There was speculation that if Murray had offered Lendl more money, the coach might have stayed. There was also the possibility that Lendl was leaving because he had lost confidence in Murray, suspecting he would never be the same player after surgery. Lendl, after all, had had to quit playing in 1994 at the age of thirty-four because of a degenerative spinal condition known as facet joint syndrome. It kept him away from the game for eighteen years – until he met Murray.

Early evidence supported the latter theory, the former amounting to little more than rumour. Whatever the truth, Murray could hardly believe what had happened to him. Having played on a different level for two years, he was returned to uncertainty. He would have to rebuild his career on his own – until he found a replacement for Lendl, the man he trusted and respected more than anyone he'd met in tennis, the architect of his greatest achievements, someone who, like himself, knew the frustration of serial disappointment in Grand Slam finals as well as the physical pain of a failing back.

If Murray had ever suspected his arrangement with Lendl would end before he wanted it to, he had not allowed himself the emotional space to deal with the possibility. He was too busy playing tennis. He had invested in a high-profile coach so he could direct his full attention towards improving his game and consistently start winning the big events. And what a wise move it had proved to be: two Slams and an Olympic gold medal in less than two years. Lendl's magic had worked. With previous coaches, Murray had dictated the terms – the time-commitment, the travel and, of course, the money – and he'd brought the deal to a close if he thought it would help his tennis. When Lendl arrived, Murray ceded some control because of the former world number 1's status and listened attentively to everything he said while leaving the day-to-day details of his preparation to his friend Dani Vallverdu, and conferring with them both about tactics, strategy and scheduling. Dani and Ivan eyed each other cautiously at first, but settled into a working relationship with encouraging swiftness, given their contrasting personalities. Vallverdu was quietly spoken but knew his worth; Lendl was a legend with a manner that could be too brusque for some tastes, although he rubbed along just fine with Vallverdu and the rest of the team. It seemed they had all made adjustments to suit the common goal. The bombshell break-up, however, blew a hole in Murray's career strategy, pretty much wrecking his comeback season before it had even begun.

In an earlier era, a coach and a player splitting up would have been a mere blip, but the dependency culture of the modern game has created a bubble around players who can afford a travelling caravan of coaches, trainers, physios and nutritionists. When a player hits a simple forehand wide, the whole team shares the blame. The racquets and strings and bottles of special energy drinks have to be in place, the towels too, as well as the hats, cream and ankle straps. Court times have to be managed precisely. Team members are assigned to make wake-up calls or ensure tournament transport is organised. Food is calibrated to the very calorie. Each extraordinary athlete moves like a small army, raiding one city after another across Planet Tennis, and their war machine needs to be in sound working order to repel the other battalions of elite players as they fight for the major prizes. Once the structure is dismantled or shows signs of distress, anxiety spreads and the ranting starts.

Players cosseted in this way wonder if they can compete without all the advantages for which they have paid so handsomely, especially when their rivals have made similar battle plans. Even thirty years ago, there were no such entourages and hi-tech back-up. When we chatted before Wimbledon in 2014, Rod Laver told me that he travelled without a coach, referring only to the expertise of the legendary Harry Hopman when Australia played in the Davis Cup. 'I trained with the other guys. What better coaching could you get than hitting every day with the likes of Lew Hoad, Ken Rosewall and Roy Emerson?' Their tennis was high-grade but carefree.

Today, only players down the rankings – outside the top fifty in the main – tour without the anxiety that comes with the financial and emotional commitment the most ambitious players choose to make. The very best have to stay sharp, primed to take advantage of any weakness among their peers. They need a team.

Murray was the commander-in-chief of Andy's army, Lendl his cunning general. The Scot and the Czech had become close. They shared the same mildly cruel sense of humour and both were committed to the work ethic essential for success. Lendl curbed his ego to fit in with Murray's long-established team, and success followed. There were accommodations on both sides, but there were no obvious fissures. However, the inscrutable face that Lendl presented to the world from Murray's courtside box was not an illusion: there was a streak of silent toughness in him, borne of his upbringing and life experience. It was not that he did not originally commit totally to the gig, either; indeed, he embraced the surprise appointment with almost uncharacteristic enthusiasm – the best decision Murray had made since opting to train in Spain as a teenager. And they got off to such a dream start, Lendl helping Murray win Olympic Gold in London in 2012 and, for those many happy months that followed, there were no signs that it would end until Murray stopped playing tennis. When Murray said back then that he did not envisage having any other trainer, he meant it, and Lendl did not demur. It transpired, however, that Lendl was only ever going to be there for as long as it suited him, even though Murray had several years of his career ahead of him.

While Murray appears to bear Lendl no ill, it would be no surprise if he gave vent to his anger in private. He has previously split with coaches, and he knew this was business – except he was always the one who left. He had not felt the wound of rejection as an adult. In fact there had been no such psychological bruise on him since his parents divorced when he was a young boy. Having found the perfect coach, he was now bereft. They had had such wonderful times together, touching many highs and only a few lows. He had never contemplated the possibility of separation and the consequent loneliness. It seems Lendl had. It was his right to leave, of course, and his family concerns were legitimate, but what the episode revealed was the achingly human side of Andy Murray.

For months he was rudderless. He put a professional face to the media, said all the predictable things and got on with playing tennis – not badly, either, although without the success he had previously enjoyed. Yet, for all the protestations that he was quickly over Lendl's departure, I wasn't convinced. Nor was I alone. Most of the British tennis writers picked up on his mood;

he couldn't hide it for long. In some matches he played with a disconcerting smile on his lips, a sight few could recall previously. 'Am I not allowed to smile?' he replied when asked about the change in his facial demeanour. However, when a few of us chatted with him after he had lost to the Colombian Santiago Giraldo in the third round of the Madrid Masters in May, he appeared lost and confused. Giraldo is a good player but was then ranked at 46 in the world, and he had allowed Murray only five games in two sets. We wondered what was missing from Murray's game. 'My coach,' he said quietly. With that, the conversation ended. Fully two months after the split, he was still suffering.

Speculation over who would replace the irreplaceable Lendl filled the gaps between football stories on the sports pages of the national newspapers and on TV and radio. Names buzzed on social media. It became a running parlour game with both insiders and the less-informed feeding rumours to tennis writers and bloggers on an almost daily basis.

One afternoon at Roland Garros, I had a conversation with Mark Petchey, Murray's first full-time coach on the Tour. His views were informed and enlightening.

> If Andy doesn't have anybody definite that he has worked with before now, it's almost a poisoned chalice. He might, in the long run, be great, but let's say Andy doesn't have a great Wimbledon, or doesn't defend the title, people are going to go, 'It's the coach.' And I think that puts the relationship under an enormous amount of pressure from week one.
>
> The reality is there are not many people out there who are hitting the credentials that Andy needs. And, if we're being totally honest, Ivan's shoes are impossible to fill, given where they started from to what Andy went on to achieve. He needs a very different kind of coach right now – if he needs a coach at all. It seems as though he does need one, from what he's been saying, especially in Madrid. Personally, I think if his self-motivation is high

enough on its own, there aren't too many people on this planet who know more about tennis than Andy.

That same Paris fortnight, over an agreeable bottle of wine or two in a nearby restaurant, a few of us journalists sat down with the British coach David Felgate, and Stanislas Wawrinka's manager, Lawrence Frankopan, among others, and thrashed out the various computations. Only Mike Dickson of the *Daily Mail* stood by the most outlandish choice mentioned: Amélie Mauresmo. 'I've just got a feeling Andy will do something off the wall,' he said. We laughed, of course, but wondered.

A week or so later, on the afternoon of the French Open final, Murray told us he'd texted Mauresmo in Paris, they'd spoken at length on the phone for the first time, and the French former world number 1 had responded positively but cautiously. Having retired in 2009, ground down by the pressure of being her country's best player, she had slowly turned to other interests. She told Murray she still had a lot on her plate as France's Federation Cup captain, as well as running the GDF Suez Open tournament in Paris. There was her love for wine, a passion she cultivated as a renowned collector. There was much to give up in pursuit of someone else's glory and, in an interview with CNN in March, she had spoken of how she was enjoying her new life in retirement. 'To be lucky enough to have lived one passion – tennis – is great, but to learn many things and meet new people in a completely different area, atmosphere and world, why not? . . . The pressure [when she played] that came out of my shoulders was huge. I was finally able to live a normal life, let's say, to enjoy the things that I could not enjoy before.' Nevertheless, Mauresmo agreed to join Murray on a trial basis at Queen's and Wimbledon. He must have used all his Caledonian charm.

If it worked out, Murray said, they would extend the arrangement to twenty-five weeks per year, an increase from the seventeen weeks Lendl worked. This time there was no doubt who had made the approach. Murray had taken soundings from other people in the game, including the Australian coach Darren Cahill, with whom he'd worked in the past through Adidas. 'Killer', as Cahill is known, is regarded as one of the most astute judges in the sport; if he did not have media commitments and family to rush home to in Las Vegas, he might have been the ideal candidate for the job. He had no doubt that Mauresmo would be good for Murray. Marion Bartoli, who had shared the winners' podium with Murray at Wimbledon in 2013 and who had played under Mauresmo in France's Federation Cup team, would also have been on hand for a quiet word of advice for her friend Andy. But this was all Murray's project. He wasn't hiring a female coach to shock people or please the media; he had simply concluded that she was the sort of person he wanted to work with: knowledgeable, intelligent, pragmatic and, most important of all, perhaps, empathetic.

Mauresmo, in many obvious ways, did not have the physical presence of Lendl, nor his rather forbidding mien. With Lendl, there was always an edge. Murray said once that his early days with Lendl were like teenage times when you're trying to impress a new girlfriend. Their relationship grew into mutual respect, but for a while Murray was clearly in awe of the hard man with opinions as strong as his jawline. He had benefited from their liaison enormously, shedding the indecision that had choked the attacking side of his game. When he looked up to the player's box and saw Lendl staring down, he drew strength from his taciturn, virtually motionless pose. Here, after all, was someone who had done it all (except win Wimbledon, something Murray would always have over him). Here was a strategist and tactician of deep knowledge and intelligence. He oozed certainty. Lendl was a human rock.

At first, the changes under Lendl were subtle but significant. Murray came to the net with increasing assuredness, killing the point rather than extending it. He hit his forehand with conviction, rather than relying so heavily on the attritional force of his metronomic double-fisted backhand, the shot that wore down so many opponents in long rallies. In time, his forehand became his weapon of first resort. At his best, he hit it flat and hard to the corners, most tellingly on the deuce side from mid-court with his opponent stranded behind the baseline. It was unreturnable. But the attacking option had to be done to a pattern. There was no point tearing in on a whim, Lendl reminded him. Murray knew that; what Lendl brought to all their conversations was affirmation rather than some blinding insight. Some matches Murray had won before he even stepped out on court. He knew he was going to win. Old doubts were banished. This was a different Murray, shorn of diffidence, walking now with a strut. There can be no doubt that Lendl was hugely influential in turning Murray into a champion.

Now, after the divorce, he was with a coach who listened just as much as Lendl, was also savvy about strategy and tactics, keen on the work ethic and preparation – but was she 'a soft touch', the very opposite of Lendl? Mauresmo understood Murray in a different way to Lendl. Lendl and Murray bonded because they had both needed four Slam finals to make their breakthrough, and they had male sensibilities: pride, ego, the drive to impose their will, machismo. If Lendl had been able to conquer the game after such an uncertain start to his own career, Murray figured he could also. They talked about the disappointment of Grand Slam defeats often; they understood the language of despair that only such experiences can bring. Murray needed Lendl to reinforce his self-belief, to convince him he could do it one day, that he was as good as the other three. And, when he did so, Murray believed in Lendl implicitly. There were no doubts – and that made the break-up all the more difficult. He had put his complete trust in Lendl, and now Ivan was swinging his clubs in the Florida sunshine.

The relationship with Mauresmo would be more subtle. She,

too, had known disappointment at the highest level and, like Murray, was often accused of lacking the cold eye to complete the task when it mattered. But she had two Slam titles to her name (the Australian Open and Wimbledon), and had made it to world number 1, a feat which had so far been beyond Murray, although interestingly he has always insisted that attaining the top ranking is not as important as winning Slams. Mauresmo did not make unreasonable demands of Murray: she did not challenge his ego or engage him in the sort of psycho-macho war that passes often for male bonding. This would be a gentler regime, one in which Murray imagined he might have a little more space in which to find himself, to bed in with a readjusted game after his operation. While he was cut to the quick by Lendl's departure, he had been handed a fresh opportunity to reinvent himself – just as Federer had done, guided by his hero, Stefan Edberg; as Nadal was doing on an almost annual basis; and as Djokovic was trying to do, with his new coach Boris Becker. It would not be easy, but Murray had made his mind up: this was the woman for him.

With Mauresmo on board for a trial period during the brief grass-court season, he bombed out at Queen's, losing to Radek Štěpánek in two tight sets, and did well enough at Wimbledon before losing limply to Grigor Dimitrov in the quarter-finals. The experiment was in its early stages, of course, but Murray craved a win to prove to himself that his recovery was on track. His tennis was hitting occasional highs, but there were too many dips – alarmingly, coming straight after bursts of his former excellence. What he needed badly was a consistent run of steady form, not the worrying highs and lows that had characterised his tennis before the arrival of Lendl, and to win a tournament again, something he had not done since Wimbledon the previous year.

So, as he approached the last major of the year, Murray's self-belief and contentment was under pressure. In the unusually mild August of 2014, a week before the US Open, we sat on the players' balcony at the Lindner Family Tennis Center in Mason, Ohio, a quiet conurbation twenty miles from Cincinnati. We talked about his past and his future. Murray, along with all of the world's leading players except the injured Nadal, had gathered here, as they do every August, to contest the Southern & Western Open in preparation for the last Grand Slam tournament of the summer.

'When I'm physically stronger,' Murray said, 'I'm mentally stronger.' The right components seemed in place. He had formalised his arrangement with Mauresmo, who had flown to Miami after Wimbledon to join him in an extended training block, and she felt comfortable in committing to a long-term arrangement as his coach. Murray also reckoned he had finally recovered from the trauma of the operation on his back nearly a year earlier. However, connecting the physical and the mental was proving difficult. Since he'd won Wimbledon in July 2013, he had reached nine quarter-finals and two semi-finals but had not contested a single title. His ranking had fallen from number 2 in the world to number 9 (it would dip as low as 12 before recovering), and that was with the continued absence of Juan Martín del Potro. Murray was in danger of missing the end-of-year ATP World Tour Finals in London in November, reserved for the eight players who had gatherered the highest number of points in the calendar year.

While not being a catastrophic descent, it was certainly a worrying one. It also mirrored Roger Federer's 2013 season, during which he took just one title and fell as low as number 7 in the rankings. He came within a couple of defeats of missing out on the London finale, where he had been a constant presence for a dozen years. By January 2014 he had slipped to number 8 but the Swiss had already begun to reinvent himself. He changed his racquet and his coach and, by the time of the US Open in September, he had climbed back to number 3 in the world, behind Djokovic and Nadal. After probably the first real crisis of his career, Federer had returned to where he felt he always belonged and he was playing with certainty and smoothness again. It seemed the old order had been restored, if somewhat shakily.

Yet Murray was no longer part of the Big Four. He was only just part of the Big Ten. 'All that matters is getting wins,' he told me. 'It's just about getting that winning mentality back.' But here was the paradox: a player known for his ruthlessness seemed to have lost his killer instinct. This was a player who, in July 2011, inflicted a rare triple bagel on the hapless part-timer Laurent Bram in a Davis Cup tie in Glasgow. 'You want to win as quickly as you can,' Murray said at the time. 'It was tough for [Bram], he doesn't play that many tournaments any more.' In fact, Bram played six more times and returned to coaching in the suburbs of Luxembourg.

Now, after all his big wins in major tournaments, Murray had begun to lose matches from winning positions, albeit in a different stratosphere to the one in which he devastated poor Bram. In Toronto the week before Mason, he blew a 3-1 lead in the third set against Jo-Wilfried Tsonga. In the opening rounds in Ohio, he played pretty well, beating the talented young Portuguese João Sousa and then defusing the time bomb that was John Isner's booming serve. But he didn't do himself justice against Federer, allowing the Swiss to come back from two breaks down in the second set. Murray was on his way out at the quarter-final stage again. These lapses echoed a slip-up against Nadal in Rome earlier in the summer. Without a coach and with something to prove, Murray produced some of his very best tennis, taking the first set 6-1 and leading 4-2 in the third, only to fade and lose. This was not a loss of form, it was a collapse of confidence and concentration. With victory at hand, he seemed to let the energy and focus drain from his body, as his mind wandered simultaneously towards the exit. As he said, when the physical and mental were synced, he felt good, but he still did not feel that great in Mason.

Better known as the Cincinnati Open, this is a Masters 1000 event parked in the slumbering Midwest and surrounded by rollercoaster rides that rise from the landscape like metal monsters, and provide an eerie metaphorical backdrop for players who are always vulnerable to the up-and-down nature of their calling. The people in Mason are unendingly nice, the food is good and plentiful, the players are nervous. It is a surreal environment in which to disguise anxiety. If a player wins here, he goes to New York on the sort of upward gradient that can bring glory. And that is what Federer did. He made mincemeat of Milos Raonic in the semi-finals and, after a blip in the second set, routed David Ferrer in the final. He believed again that he could win the US Open, a tournament he'd won five times, where he'd lost only ten out of eighty-two matches and where he'd amassed $10 million of his fortune.

When I returned to my hotel, the tallest man in Ohio was checking out. Isner chatted freely with the staff, hoping to see them again next year and, as he climbed into the car to head for the airport, he gave every impression of being happy enough with his effort in the tournament and relaxed about going to Flushing Meadows. But Isner's expectations, while similar to those of Murray and all the other players who would give themselves a chance in a major, were calibrated just a notch lower. Nobody expected Isner to win his home major. If he did, that would be amazing. If he didn't, that would be fine too, as long as he went as far as his talent could take him. It was not like that for Murray. He was an established champion. He needed to maintain – or, rather, regain – that status.

As the caravan headed east to New York, a lot of reliable observers were predicting that Federer could win his sixth title there and his eighteenth Grand Slam final. 'Guys can come back,' Murray remarked. 'That can always happen.' And now Murray was in that position. He needed to come back. Quickly.

He was not the only player suffering a dip in form and fitness before arriving at Flushing Meadows. Nadal, the defending champion, again had succumbed to injury. This time it was his right wrist, the one he used to guide the two-fisted backhand from his converted lefty stance. Gloomier prognoses said his season was over. Nobody was writing off his career, of course, but he had not played since the sassy young Australian Nick Kyrgios had embarrassed him at Wimbledon in July, and this injury came on top of all the others: the ankle, the knees, the back. He was twenty-eight and running out of working bones.

Djokovic, too, was in an uncertain place. He had reached another high by beating Federer in the Wimbledon final, and then was lifted still further both by his marriage to his long-term partner Jelena Ristic and the prospect of their first child arriving before the end of the season. It seemed he was back to the Novak of 2011 and would sweep the field. Yet his tennis fell away after Wimbledon and his demeanour screamed confusion. Was he having trouble adjusting to domestic life? Did he miss the freedom of the road? He spoke at Wimbledon about how he admired Federer's ability to combine family and playing commitments, but doing it himself was a different matter. Jelena was pregnant, for a start, and understandably that might have been a distraction. Heading for the last major of the 2014 tennis battlefield, Djokovic seemed far from the contented player who had just won Wimbledon.

The Serb lost to Tsonga in the Frenchman's terrific run in Toronto (where he also beat Murray, Grigor Dimitrov and then Federer to take the title), and now, a week later, he succumbed in Mason in more worrying fashion to Tommy Robredo in just 105 minutes; at his peak, some of his sets lasted that long. The Spaniard, meanwhile, operated at the same level as Isner: without the pressure of expectation. At thirty-two, he seemed as ageless as Federer who had just turned thirty-three. Robredo, though, could not sustain his run, and lost an up-and-down semi-final against his compatriot and friend Ferrer, also aged thirty-two.

The Mason final was the first in the twenty-four-year history of the Masters series to feature two thirty-somethings – but in fact it was the fourth time it had happened on the 2014 Tour. What was happening to the game? As players repeated whenever asked, tennis at the highest level now required not just mature physicality, but more old-fashioned smarts. A lot of the young players had relied so heavily on gym-bought strength and stamina in their developing years that they had sometimes neglected the art of their sport. Often they lacked the subtlety to deal with players like Robredo when on song. He pre-dated the era and had learnt the art as well as the suffering. Rogue results came along often enough to inject fresh uncertainty into the Tour. Not much was taken for granted any more, either at the start of a tournament or in the concluding stages, especially by the Big Four. Tennis was getting more interesting – and the US Open would be yet another turning point.

We are back in New York and the noise is as crushing as the silence was in Ohio. The place throbs to the rhythm of Wall Street, Broadway, sirens, the ant-like urgency of people rushing from subway to office to sandwich bar to gym to home. A ribbon of manic energy runs through the city and that pulse is reflected in the tennis at Flushing, across the Hudson. There is no quiet at the US Open, no space for rest. Everything is loud. Everything. Conversation in restaurants. Whooping and hollering at the court. Even the media centre can be like Grand Central Station, full of bustle and barked instructions about press confer-ences. But that is a minor irritant compared to the challenge facing the players. Murray badly needs to do well here. If he can reach the final, he will save crucial ranking points. If he can win it, his immediate troubles will be over and his medium-term future will be considerably brighter. He cannot afford to let his mind wander beyond the challenge at hand, however.

On the face of it, Murray appeared as calm as I had ever seen him before a big tournament. On the Friday before the first Monday, he drove twenty-five miles across the State line into New Jersey to watch Rory McIlroy struggle in vain to stay in The Barclays golf tournament at the Ridgewood Country Club, then he returned to Manhattan with the Irish golfer to watch the United States and Puerto Rico in a basketball match at Madison Square Garden. Murray also fitted in a workout and some yoga to relax ahead of the demanding schedule that lay in front of him. He looked primed.

However, there was a rumbling subplot: Lendl. Murray bumped into his former mentor briefly on the Saturday before play began and they had a pleasant exchange. There plainly was no lingering animosity, but there was surely a little melancholy. Murray seeing Lendl at the place where they were once a team, the place he made his Grand Slam breakthrough, could either lift him or leave him confused.

The following day, Lendl spoke to a few British reporters and expanded on why he had left Murray. There was nothing startlingly new in the revelations, but distance lends perspective and it was interesting to hear what he had to say about one of the most sudden ruptures in the modern game: a farewell delivered over dinner.

It was lots of little things combined, like playing more on the vets tour, and one of my daughters returned home. The youngest one is sixteen and she had been away at horse-riding school, but now she has come back to live with us. My mum is now seventy-nine and lives in Prague. I need to go more to the Czech Republic than I used to. The planes are a pain in the arse. The places, the hotels – England was good, Australia was good, here it was all right. It was the smaller trips I didn't like. All these things combined. And, you know, with Andy, after his surgery and after winning Wimbledon and all that, I felt that if anything he needed more time rather than less time.

Lendl also conceded that it would be hard to hit the heights that they had both enjoyed. 'Yeah, and that too. Everyone is different, and when you win a big tournament like Wimbledon, it's not easy sometimes. Some people find it more difficult than others, and I'm glad Andy found Amélie, who can give him the time he needs.'

Much of this we knew. What we didn't know was how Lendl regarded Murray's long-time training assistant, Dani Vallverdu, a quiet but intelligent man who privately resented being regarded as his hitting partner. He was considerably more than that, as Lendl acknowledged.

You guys don't understand how much I relied on Dani, and I hope Amélie relies on Dani as well. Many times he would come to me and say: 'Hey, you need to stop the practice.' And I would say: 'What? Andy looks fine to me.' And Dani would say: 'No, he's done.' And two or three minutes later, he was done. So you get that two or three times and you start listening much better.

With that, he was gone: a mysterious, intelligent man who might never have known – or much cared – why people regard him as enigmatic.

When the tournament got underway on the Monday, expectations for Murray were tempered by his recent ordinary form and the fact it had been nearly a year and a half since he'd won a tournament. These sorts of facts can add up to a heavy burden if allowed to multiply, and Murray nearly justified the pessimism by collapsing after establishing a two-set lead against the Dutchman Robin Haase, before coming back from 2-4 down in the fourth to save the match. It was desperately close and, perversely, one of his finest wins given the struggle he had to endure. The level of his tennis, however, was worryingly low until he woke up and, as he conceded, it was 'not pretty'. Even allowing for the lactic acid that had swept through his body in the third set, handing it to Haase on a plate and letting him establish threatening momentum, Murray's serve was all over the place – nine double faults cancelling out eight aces – and he seemed in two minds about how to finish a point. But he got the win, as he invariably does. That night he went to bed a worried man, probably suspecting that the debilitating cramp was not the only reason a player ranked 70 in the world had nearly eliminated him from the first round of the tournament.

After three encouraging sets against Matthias Bachinger, the world number 235, there were four more troublesome sets to get past the 96th ranked Russian Andrey Kuznetsov. Then some light: victory in three impressive sets over Jo-Wilfried Tsonga, Murray's first success against a top ten opponent since winning Wimbledon – he was in the quarter-finals. At last, he was back in familiar territory, the back-end of a Slam. And he was playing well enough to beat Djokovic before fading again and losing in four sets. It was not a wholesale disaster, because Murray played some excellent tennis, with his wicked forehand making the Serb suffer, but again it was patchy. His game was not yet reliable. He was vulnerable under pressure.

So, Murray left behind him in New York what at first glance looked like a familiar scenario: Djokovic and Federer heading for a showdown in a Grand Slam final. Victory for the world number 1 would confirm his return to something like the form with which he had shocked the game in 2011; if the Swiss won, he would own eighteen majors, a resounding answer to those who had been writing him off since his last Slam title – against Murray at Wimbledon in 2012. But none of this was to be. Kei Nishikori, one of the most physically suspect players at the top of tennis, came through his semi-final against Djokovic on the back of two five-setters against top ten opponents, Raonic and

Wawrinka. Federer, meanwhile, had no answers for the power and sublime invention of Marin Čilić, and we had a US Open final not a single commentator had predicted at the start of the fortnight.

For the first time in thirty-eight Grand Slams, neither Djokovic, nor Federer nor Nadal would feature in the final. It was the most unexpected decider since Marat Safin beat Lleyton Hewitt at the 2005 Australian Open. And you have to go back to the 1997 final in New York, when Pat Rafter beat Greg Rusedski, for a concluding match between two players outside the top ten. As Simon Briggs observed in the *Daily Telegraph*: 'That was a different era, when the top players were not as phenomenally well prepared or consistent as they are now.'

In 2012, Čilić defeated Nishikori in the third round, having lost to him in 2010; in 2013, Nishikori went out in the first round in straight sets to Britain's unpredictable Dan Evans, and here was Nishikori in the 2014 final, on a roll after an astonishing recovery from injury, bidding to be the first Japanese player to win a Slam – he'd had a cyst removed from his right foot in early August and just a week before the tournament, had had to do his hitting up while sitting down. The man across the net was similarly gifted, and bearing baggage of a different kind: in 2013 he was subject to a ban of four months for using a prohibited substance. Čilić, beaten in the Australian Open semi-final in 2010, had not 'trained on', as they say in horse racing, yet he was now on the brink of making Croatia immensely proud of him, even though there was not a single representative of his country's media on hand to witness his historic appearance in a final. Čilić, ranked 16 in the world, had beaten Tomáš Berdych and Federer in straight sets. He remained focused and played splendidly again to beat Nishikori (11) in a final over three one-sided sets, a match that hit no great heights as a contest. The final also left the tournament and the game with a sense of shock and wonder. Was this the end of the Big Four

– or at least the beginning of the end? Čilić thought not. 'They are great champions, and it's going to take so much to break them and to break the finals of a Grand Slam or to be able to win it,' he said later. 'And I would say I was also a little bit lucky here. There was no Rafa. And I had a good draw. I didn't play Novak or Andy or those guys.'

All true. But he got there. And he prevailed. He was a Slam champion in an era when nearly everyone was saying that was never going to happen until the incumbent rulers had moved on. Well, they were being moved on against their will. It was not just 'on their racquet' any more. Victory at last could go to those who believed rather than merely hoped. If Čilić could shake off his diffidence – something Wawrinka found difficult after beating Nadal to win the Australian Open earlier in the year – if he could win another Slam, even, or get to a final, maybe then the tremor would build to an earthquake.

For the Big Four, the picture was varied. Djokovic was still world number 1, a good way ahead of Nadal who had yet to return to the Tour; Federer was buoyant again, at number 3, and rising – he could once more entertain thoughts of overtaking Nadal; and Murray was marooned outside the top ten for the first time since June 2006, stuck in some quality traffic behind Tsonga, Dimitrov, Čilić and Nishikori.

Elsewhere in the tennis jungle, Kyrgios, who had announced his arrival by beating Nadal at Wimbledon with the most exhilarating free-form tennis any of us had seen for a long time while improving his world ranking from 182 to 51 in the space of just nine months, declared he had nothing left to give in 2014. After winning a couple of Davis Cup matches for Australia against Uzbekistan in September, he announced: 'I'm emotionally spent, I'm a bit gone and burnt out. This [the Malaysia Open] is my last tournament of the year, so I'm going to just go out and give everything I can. Physically I've probably only got enough left for one more tournament, and mentally I'm a bit worn out.

So I am looking forward to the break.' Kyrgios was aged nine-teen, a year older than Murray when he too complained of tiredness after an impressive debut at Wimbledon. As Murray said in Mason, the mind and the body depend so much on each other to reach a perfect pitch.

By the time we left New York, we were reasonably sure that the old order had been disturbed. In 2003, the titles went to Andre Agassi in Australia, Juan Carlos Ferrero (French), Federer (Wimbledon) and Andy Roddick (US); the spoils would not be so democratically shared again for nine years when, in 2012, the winners were Djokovic, Nadal, Federer and Murray. Now the Slam season finished with four different champions again: Wawrinka, Nadal, Djokovic and Čilić. And then, unexpectedly, came a late burst from the master himself. After winning the Shanghai Masters and moving to within striking distance of Djokovic at the summit of the rankings by beating him hand-somely in the final, Federer spoke candidly about his rejuvenation at thirty-three years old. Asked how he had stayed at, or near, the upper reaches of his sport for so long, he said,

I feel like I've worked hard and gotten really fit. You need to be able to back yourself. Doesn't matter how long the match goes on, how tough the game is . . . three sets, two sets, five sets. Doesn't matter. You got to be ready. You know you're going to be fine. Haven't had a cramp since 1999. That was my only time, in Davis Cup, when I was panicky. I was young. I'm very proud of that. Never pulled out. Never had cramps. Never lost very much because of fitness, especially later on in my career where I knew, okay, I've put in the hard work, I've done that.

Then my game followed because it allowed me to get to balls faster. It improved my defence. I became . . . quicker and more nimble on the court. That's when my potential all of a sudden went into this league that I never thought possible. I've been very fortunate and clever as well, I guess, to understand how I need to work, when I need to work. I'm very happy to have stayed injury-free for so long. Hope I can still maintain a few good years on the Tour.

The man who had appeared in all ten finals between the 2005 Wimbledon and the 2007 US Open, had broken his drought in 2014 by reaching the Wimbledon final for the first time since 2012. Although he lost to Djokovic, he won back his believers. In China, he was scaring his peers again.

On the afternoon of Sunday, 19 October, Murray beat Ferrer in three sets of the Vienna final – only his third victory over a top-tenner since winning Wimbledon in 2013 – to bring crisp drama to the concluding stages of the 2014 season. It was one of three Tour wins in six weeks of playing back to back to reach the ATP World Tour Finals in London. He got there, but was spent. So too was Federer, to everyone's amazement, when he pulled out of the final on 16 November, just hours before he was expected to step on court against Djokovic. It was only the third time in his sixteen years on the Tour that he'd quit. A back injury had flared, he explained, and he had to keep in mind that Switzerland were playing France in the Davis Cup final in Lille the following weekend. And what a climax to the season that proved to be: Federer and Wawrinka carried the day, bringing their little country their first Davis Cup in eighty-five attempts.

Still, 2014 had been a season of growing uncertainty. The feeling that we were on the cusp of change was undeniable. There never had been any complacency among the Big Four. But where once there had been utter conviction, now there was doubt at the very essence of the sport.

～

There were a couple of unexpected casualties towards the end of the season, not on the court, but not that far away. Andy Murray had surprised everyone – including those closest to him – when he appointed Amélie Mauresmo to replace Ivan Lendl. Now he trumped even that shock by terminating the contracts of his friend and training partner, Dani Vallverdu, and also of Jez Green, the conditioner who put him through hell every December in Miami. Like Lendl, he acted without sentiment. Perhaps he learnt that from him, too. This was business. Just as Lendl had delivered the knife to Murray's ribs, so the player made the hard call himself. Why did he do it? Again, it was not simple.

Murray had almost certainly heard the whispers about his choice of Mauresmo as coach that she was not pro-active enough and that she could not properly understand the physicality of the men's game, yet he remained loyal to her. However, there were other concerns in the camp about Mauresmo emanating from Vallverdu and Green, who made no secret of their disgruntlement when Murray announced her appointment without consulting them. Green had been with Murray for nearly eight years, Vallverdu for five – although they had known each other since they were teenagers sharing accommodation at the Sanchez-Casal Academy in Barcelona.

It could be argued that Green – excellent conditioner though he is – was presuming too much in considering that he should be part of the discussion about Lendl's successor, but Vallverdu had a case. As Lendl pointed out, he was invaluable to the understanding of Murray's performance in training, and he was more familiar with his game than anyone else. Vallverdu, though, was probably miffed that he was not even considered for the main job. He rarely spoke to the media but, as already mentioned, it was known he did not like being referred to as a mere hitting partner. He had legitimate ambitions of his own and it did not look as though they would be fulfilled with Murray.

The murmurings during Wimbledon did not help their cause. The three men had cleared the air but tensions lingered, as did Murray's physical problems. Despite being one of the fittest and strongest players in the game, he was concerned that, post-surgery, the brutal training regime Green put him through might not be the best strategy as his body strained at the extremities. He wanted to tone it down, and Jez had to go. As for Vallverdu, his exit was more problematic. It would seem he was not prepared to play second fiddle to Mauresmo and, in what was said to be a polite discussion just a few days after Murray proposed to his long-time girlfriend Kim Sears, they all agreed to move on. Vallverdu would eventually be replaced and, for now, Mauresmo was in control. As he headed for Melbourne again, Murray took with him a slimmed-down team and recalibrated ambitions. In the toughest era in the history of his sport, he was still standing.

Acknowledgements and Sources

Thanks for all the books I've read. Thanks for all the things they've said. Thanks for all the shots they've played. And thanks for those mistakes they made.

Writing this book has been enlightening in many ways. Proximity to the best players in tennis – among the best athletes in sport – has reinforced my understanding that striving for perfection is a doomed but noble ambition. The dedication these players show in pursuit of the impossible is every bit as impressive as what they actually achieve, which is considerable. So thank you to them for trying. And don't stay too long in that ice bath . . .

Another lesson learned (or reaffirmed) was that what was said in January did not necessarily apply in December. Trying to understand the relationships between Murray, Nadal, Djokovic and Federer is as challenging a task as constructing a perfect point, made more difficult by their understandable reluctance to bring the tensions of the locker-room into the public domain. So thank you to Ernests Gulbis for your candour, and to Novak's father too. And hello to Serena Williams and Maria Sharapova, to Annabel Croft and Charlie Sale, all of whom enlivened 2013 away from the court and lived to blush again.

Without one man, however, this would be a blank page. The rise of Andy Murray has not only saved British tennis from mediocrity, but has changed the dynamic of the game. His arrival, shortly after that of Djokovic (a little long in coming, perhaps, but he got there), put Nadal and Federer on notice, and ensured that this four-cornered rivalry would never be dull. Each tournament is a delight of possibilities, each match between them sporting theatre of the highest calibre. We are privileged to have them.

So we rumbled through a succession of ups and downs, Andy, the guys and girls and me. Sometimes it felt as if we were all sharing a giant psychiatrist's couch, mumbling incoherently about where it all went wrong. We all wanted him to do it, partly because we might have committed the cardinal sin of sports-writing: we had become close to him – not in a totally best-friend way, but with an undeniable degree of admiration and affection. There was nothing to dislike about him, which is why the murmurings among little Englanders were irksome. They had made no such demands of Tim Henman, he of the impeccable, and very English, tennis pedigree. Timbo had a hill named after him at Wimbledon, even though he had reached just one final there (as well as four semi-finals, it must be said). That was just another mountain for Murray to climb. Well, he's done that. My main thanks, then, go to the very interesting young man from Dunblane, now at least partly Anglicised in Oxshott, Surrey . . . except during World Cups.

Murray himself, of course, contributed much in the post-match press conferences and sit-down chats with the small band of writers that trails him from Wimbledon to Melbourne and back. As did his mother, Judy, who is not only a fine coach – and captain of Great Britain's Federation Cup team – but as knowledgeable a judge of the game as I have met. And how clever of her to give birth to left- and right-handed sons; maybe they should play doubles more often. Murray's press agent, Matt Gentry, was always on hand to nudge us in the right direction. And coach Ivan Lendl and conditioner Jez Green also gave his story a broader brush-stroke.

Greg Sharko, the ATP's statistician who seems to know more about the players than they know about themselves, has been invaluable in tracking the host of milestones and records that appear in this book.

It was a joy to trawl Jon Henderson's wonderful biography, *The Last Champion: The Life of Fred Perry*, for unique historical perspective, and I know my former *Observer* colleague (and kind godfather of the paper's itinerant cricket team) was as glad as the rest of us when Andy Murray made the first part of that book title redundant.

There were a good few books I found worthwhile reading, among them that of my colleague from *The Times*, Neil Harman, whose *Court Confidential* is packed with juicy whispers from various corridors. Marshall Jon Fisher's forensic *A Terrible Splendour: Three Extraordinary Men, a World Poised for War, and the Greatest Tennis Match Ever Played* and Gordon Forbes' hilarious *A Handful of Summers* described times when tennis was less frenetic, perhaps, but no less drama-filled and maybe more beautiful. Peter Bodo's *The Courts of Babylon: Dispatches From the Golden Age of Tennis* hinted at much of what was to follow. Andre Agassi's *Open* confirmed it, as did Jimmy Connors in *The Outsider*.

But it was in conversations and interviews that this story unfolded most clearly. The most fascinating hour I spent all year was in the company of Mats Wilander, a truly original thinker. Who else would come up with the notion, 'You don't necessarily lose', and make it sound plausible? Pat Cash was as forthright as in his newspaper columns, and was unequivocal in his judgment that Rafael Nadal is a better tennis player than Roger Federer. Stanislas Wawrinka, as personable and self-effacing as anyone on the circuit, provided insight on what it is like to be the second most famous Swiss tennis player. Brian Baker, an American whose fortitude seems bottomless, reflected on his injured past and hopeful future. John McEnroe, Boris Becker and Greg Rusedski, all of whose expertise I mined, cover a lot of the waterfront, and the new executive chairman of the ATP, Chris Kermode, was not only a generous host but an insightful observer of all things tennis, from the grassroots to the top.

If there is anyone alive with a more intimate and wide-ranging knowledge of Wimbledon than John Barrett, he or she did not appear on my radar. Barrett was not only generous with his time but, in reminiscing about everything from his playing days to his work as a writer and broadcaster, endlessly fascinating. Eric Babolat, whose firm makes the racquets a lot of famous players swing, was informative about the advance of technology and not always in sync with the opinions of romantics who think the game has suffered because of weapons that increasingly resemble bazookas.

A host of players and their connections provided insights, one way or another, that, I hope, enlightened the text, among them Dan Evans, Dustin Brown, Ernests Gulbis and, one sweltering night in New York, Bernard Tomic's father, John. Ion Ţiriac, who annually entertains the British media in Paris, is never dull, and if half his ideas ever came to fruition, tennis might be just a little livelier (his failed experiment with blue clay in Madrid notwithstanding). He still flies a plane and grows a moustache, and is one of the game's enduring oddities.

Thank you, also, to Roland Philipps for commissioning this book in the first place, and to my agent, Eugenie Furniss, for doing all that stuff with contracts that are a mystery to me.

Finally, a grateful nod towards the people I regard as friends and rivals as we roam the world together, namely my fellow hacks. Thanks for the laughs and the good times, for the help on deadline, for the anecdotes, true and stretched, and just for sharing a wild journey. And, for the privilege of a good seat from which to witness all of this, thanks to the *Guardian* and the *Observer*, and to all the tournaments for foolishly letting me in.

Picture Credits

Index

Index